Rorty and the Religious

Rorty and the Religious

Christian Engagements with a Secular Philosopher

EDITED BY
JACOB L. GOODSON
AND
BRAD ELLIOTT STONE

Foreword by Stanley Hauerwas
Afterword by Charles Marsh

CASCADE *Books* · Eugene, Oregon

RORTY AND THE RELIGIOUS
Christian Engagements with a Secular Philosopher

Copyright © 2012 Wipf and Stock Publishers. All rights reserved. Except for brief quotations in critical publications or reviews, no part of this book may be reproduced in any manner without prior written permission from the publisher. Write: Permissions, Wipf and Stock Publishers, 199 W. 8th Ave., Suite 3, Eugene, OR 97401.

Cascade Books
An Imprint of Wipf and Stock Publishers
199 W. 8th Ave., Suite 3
Eugene, OR 97401

www.wipfandstock.com

ISBN 13: 978-1-61097-428-8

Cataloging-in-Publication data:

Rorty and the religious : Christian engagements with a secular philosopher / edited by Jacob L. Goodson and Brad Elliott Stone ; foreword by Stanley Hauerwas.

xxiv + 224 p. ; 23 cm. —Includes bibliographical references and index(es).

ISBN 13: 978-1-61097-428-8

1. Rorty, Richard. 2. Philosophy and religion. 3. Pragmatism. I. Goodson, Jacob L. II. Stone, Brad Elliott. III. Hauerwas, Stanley, 1940– IV. Marsh, Charles, 1958– V. Title.

B945.R524 R679 2012

Manufactured in the U.S.A.

For Angela, Donald, Maggie, and Roger

In memory of Richard Rorty

Contents

Foreword   ix
Stanley Hauerwas

Acknowledgments   xi

List of Contributors   xiii

Introduction   xvii
Jacob L. Goodson and Brad Elliott Stone

Part I: Reflections in Rorty's Mirrors

CHAPTER ONE   The Priority of Democracy: The Public, the Private, and the Primitive   3
Donald G. Wester (with Jacob L. Goodson)

CHAPTER TWO   Therapy to Apocalypse: Encountering the Abyss of Epistemology in James and Rorty   14
Roger Ward

CHAPTER THREE   Can (Analytic) Philosophers Tell Theologians the Truth? Richard Rorty and Methodological Nominalism   23
D. Stephen Long

CHAPTER FOUR   For and Against Richard Rorty: Christian Convictions, Liberal Democracy, and the *Christenfrage*   46
Barry Harvey

Part II: Moral Dispositions and Religious Belief

CHAPTER FIVE — What the Apostles Will Let Us Get Away with Saying: Plantinga and Rorty on the Social Establishment of Religious Belief   71
Keith Starkenburg

CHAPTER SIX — Pragmatic Charity: A Synthesis of Rorty and Milbank   91
Eric Hall

CHAPTER SEVEN — Contingency, Irony, and Vulnerability: Richard Rorty and Scriptural Reasoning   119
Jacob Goodson

Part III: The Philosophy and Theology of Social Hope

CHAPTER EIGHT — Rorty's Religion   141
David L. O'Hara

CHAPTER NINE — Can There Be Hope without Prophecy? Richard Rorty as Prophetic Pragmatist   153
Brad Elliott Stone

CHAPTER TEN — The Difficulty of Imagining Other Persons, Reimagined: Rorty on Moral Imagination and the Transformation of Conflict   173
Jason A. Springs

Afterword   197
Charles Marsh

Bibliography   211
Subject Index   221
Name Index   223

Foreword

STANLEY HAUERWAS

Richard Rorty was a delightful human being. He loved life because he found life delightful. That he did so does not mean he lacked seriousness. The way he did philosophy was at once delightful and serious. The combination, however, of seriousness and delight is not easily reproduced, depending as it must on a profound humanity. So I am grateful and happy to report that this is at once a delightful and serious book that theologically engages Richard Rorty's thought.

For any serious attempt at thought, and in particular theological thought, the choice of conversation partners is crucial. Rorty does not seem to be a natural conversation partner for theologians. After all, for some time Rorty thought that theology was a "conversation-stopper." Because of Jeff Stout, he revised—I think rather begrudgingly—his views in that regard. Yet, when all is said and done, he remained disinclined to take theological claims seriously. At least that was the impression I had at the famous event at the American Academy of Religion held in response to Stout's *Democracy and Tradition*.[1]

These essays, however, would have convinced Rorty that theologians might have something interesting to say. Rorty assumed that Christianity named the "establishment." In contrast, these contributors represent a Christianity that would have intrigued Rorty. I cannot help thinking that he would have found their appreciative but critical engagement with his work interesting. I am sure, moreover, he would have taken it seriously.

---

1. See the transcript from that meeting: Hauerwas et al., "Pragmatism and Democracy."

Rorty may not have sought out theologians as conversation partners, but as these essays demonstrate, we certainly need to be in conversation with him. Rorty wrote honestly from a secular position. To be in conversation with Rorty is to be in conversation with the best account available for the way we now live. His work, therefore, matters for those of us who think God matters. Richard Rorty was the voice of philosophical modesty in defense of a humane secularity. One of the crucial questions that his work raises is whether the secular on its own terms can sustain his humanity.

One aspect of Rorty's work particularly important for theology is his use of literature that is often ignored by philosophers. He read widely and, just as importantly, he thought what he read to be philosophically important. He did so because he refused the professionalization of contemporary philosophy. One of the reasons it is so important for theologians to engage Rorty is because we should read not only what Rorty wrote but also what he read if we are to understand the world in which we find ourselves.

Lastly, Rorty was a philosopher of hope. He thought it necessary to deny God in the hope that justice might be a deeper reality than injustice. As several of the essays in this book suggest, Rorty could not articulate an account for the hope that sustained his passion for justice. Rorty's disarming modesty, his sheer humanity, never tempted him to say more than he could say. That is why the conversation this book begins with this delightful philosopher is at once overdue and extremely significant.

Acknowledgments

This volume is the result of many people's kindness and assistance. We thank Charles Collier of Wipf and Stock for believing in this project and for his help in bringing this volume to fruition. Since this is an anthology, it is a simple fact that this book would not be possible without all those who contributed chapters to the volume. We are grateful to Stanley Hauerwas for his foreword and to Charles Marsh for his afterword. We also appreciate our family, friends, and colleagues, who encouraged us throughout not only this project but our entire careers.

There are two people who deserve special mention. We thank Connie Goodson for transcribing Marsh's spoken afterword. We also acknowledge the steadfast work of Rebecca Dzida, an undergraduate English major and honors student at Loyola Marymount University, who assisted us at every stage of the process. She painstakingly edited every essay and provided comments to authors. She assembled the manuscript and performed the preliminary typesetting. The fact that she is an undergraduate speaks to her skill and professionalism.

Last but not least, we want to thank Richard Rorty. His work has presented Christian thinkers with much to consider. This volume speaks to the theologically rich ideas that he brought to the table, and it is our hope that the conversations will continue well into the future.

Contributors

Jacob L. Goodson (PhD, University of Virginia) is Visiting Assistant Professor of Religious Ethics in the Department of Religious Studies at the College of William & Mary. He serves as the General Editor for *The Journal of Scriptural Reasoning*. He has published scholarly essays in *The American Journal of Theology and Philosophy* as well as *Contemporary Pragmatism*.

Eric Hall has recently finished his PhD work in the Philosophy of Religion and Theology program at Claremont Graduate University. There he wrote his dissertation under the direction of Professor Ingolf Dalferth on the meaning of personal authenticity in the hermeneutic philosophical and theological traditions. Eric is also currently editing a volume exploring the idea of post-metaphysical philosophy of religion and theology and is working on several essays in Continental philosophy of religion.

Barry Harvey is Professor of Theology in the Honors College at Baylor University in Waco, Texas. He has earned degrees from the University of Colorado at Boulder and the Southern Baptist Theological Seminary, and was awarded the PhD degree in Theology and Ethics by Duke University. He is the author of three books, *Politics of the Theological* (1995), *Another City* (1999), and *Can These Bones Live?* (2008), and a coauthor of a fourth book, *Storm Front* (2003). He has published numerous articles in collections and scholarly journals, including *Modern Theology*, *Pro Ecclesia*, *Scottish Journal of Theology*, *Christian Scholar's Review*, *First Things*, and *Perspectives in Religious Studies*.

Stanley Hauerwas is the Gilbert T. Rowe Professor of Theological Ethics at Duke University. His work has centered on virtue ethics and how the cultivation of Christian virtue occurs through the faithful witness of the church. The focus on the church as witness has often led to polemics about the church's accommodation to secular politics and culture. His most recent books include *Hannah's Child: A Theologian's Memoir* and *War and the American Difference* (2010).

D. Stephen Long is professor of Systematic Theology at Marquette University. Previously, he worked at Garrett-Evangelical Theological Seminary, St. Joseph's University, and Duke Divinity School. He has published eight books: *Living the Discipline: United Methodist Theological Reflections on War, Civilization, and Holiness* (1992), *Tragedy, Tradition, Transformism: The Ethics of Paul Ramsey* (1993), *Divine Economy: Theology and the Market* (2000), *The Goodness of God: Theology, Church and Social Order* (2001), *John Wesley's Moral Theology: The Quest for God and Goodness* (2005), *Calculated Futures* (2007), *Theology and Culture* (2007), and *Speaking of God: Theology, Truth and Language* (2008).

Charles Marsh is Professor of Religious Studies and Director of The Project on Lived Theology at the University of Virginia. He is the author of seven books, including *Reclaiming Dietrich Bonhoeffer: The Promise of His Theology* (1994), *God's Long Summer: Stories of Faith and Civil Rights* (1997), and *The Beloved Community: How Faith Shapes Social Justice, from the Civil Rights Movement to Today* (2005). He was the recipient of the 1998 Grawemeyer Award in Religion, a 2009 John Simon Guggenheim Fellowship in the Creative Arts, and the 2010 Ellen Maria Gorrissen Fellowship at the American Academy of Berlin. His book *Strange Glory: A Life of Dietrich Bonhoeffer* will be published by Knopf in 2012.

David O'Hara is Associate Professor of Philosophy and Classics at Augustana College in Sioux Falls, South Dakota. His research areas include pragmatism and religion, environmental philosophy, and ancient philosophy. He is the author of several books and articles, including a book on the environmental vision of C. S. Lewis and a forthcoming edited volume of the religious writings of Charles S. Peirce.

Jason A. Springs is Assistant Professor of Religion, Ethics, and Peace Studies at the Kroc Institute for International Peace Studies at the University of Notre Dame. His research and teaching focus on modern religious thought and Christian ethics, and American pragmatism and postliberal theology, in particular, attending specifically to how these provide resources for mediating and transforming religiously motivated conflict in contemporary and North American and European contexts. His book *Toward a Generous Orthodoxy: Prospects for Hans Frei's Postliberal Theology* (2010) traces out and expands upon the uses of Wittgenstein, pragmatist insights, and socio-theoretical dimensions of Frei's engagement with Karl Barth's theology.

Keith Starkenburg (PhD, University of Virginia) is Associate Professor of Theology at Trinity Christian College in Palos Heights, Illinois. He is writing his first manuscript, which examines connections between Karl Barth's doctrine of glory and his ecclesiology.

Brad Elliott Stone is Associate Professor of Philosophy and African American Studies and Director of the University Honors Program at Loyola Marymount University. He has published several essays and book chapters on pragmatism, Continental philosophy, and Spanish philosophy. He is currently writing a monograph on Spanish philosophy of religion and a commentary on Heidegger's *Being and Time*.

Roger Ward is Professor and Chair of Philosophy at Georgetown College in Georgetown, Kentucky. His work focuses on American philosophy, from the Puritans to contemporary issues in pragmatism and religion. His books include *Conversion in American Philosophy* (2004) and two edited collections, *The Scholarly Vocation and the Baptist Academy* (2006) and *Tradition and the Baptist Academy* (2011).

Donald G. Wester is Professor Emeritus of Philosophy at Oklahoma Baptist University. His teaching was in Western philosophy focused on pragmatism, along with ethics, aesthetics, and modern philosophy. He has been retired the last ten years.

Introduction

Prior to his death in 2007, the self-described secular philosopher Richard Rorty modified his description of his personal view of religion. In his conversations with the Catholic philosopher Gianni Vattimo, Rorty stated that he was mistaken in considering his neo-pragmatism as a kind of "atheism"; rather, he continued, his personal view is better described as "anticlericalism." By describing his own philosophy as atheistic for most of his career, Rorty did not only mean that he did not believe in the existence of God. He also meant that positions and reasons determined by beliefs in the existence of God had no place in public debate because they are "conversation-stoppers." For Rorty, *conversation*—and its continued possibility—provides humanity's greatest hope for peace and solidarity. Whether Rorty remained to the end of his life atheistic or legitimately clarified his own position as anticlerical, he represents a concrete and substantial challenge to Christian belief and ways of life. One possible Christian response to this challenge includes dismissing or ignoring Rorty's philosophy, which would involve a defensive strategy of non-charitable engagement. Another possible response to Rorty's challenge to the Christian life requires constructive and serious engagement with Rorty's work, perhaps even attempting to find promising nuggets within Rorty's thought for addressing particular questions within Christianity. The essays in this volume represent this latter approach to responding to Rorty's work, through charitable yet fully confessional engagements with this impressive secular philosopher.

This collection of essays gathers the work of Christian philosophers and theologians. Denominationally, most of the contributors find themselves part of Baptist life (though, admittedly, in different degrees). We the editors grew up as Baptists, even attending Baptist colleges (Oklahoma Baptist University and Georgetown College, respectively), and the network formed in our young careers involves interesting thinkers within contemporary Baptist life—including Barry Harvey, Charles Marsh, Roger Ward, and Donald Wester.[2] Wester and Ward served as our undergraduate professors and mentors, and individually they introduced us to American pragmatism and the use of pragmatism (and philosophy more generally) within our Christian lives.

GOODSON: In my sophomore year of college (1999), Wester encouraged me to spend my weekends in two different ways: by studying Rorty's *Contingency, Irony, and Solidarity* as a constructive response to the problems worked through in *Philosophy and the Mirror of Nature*, and by attending First Baptist Church of Shawnee, Oklahoma, sitting in the balcony with him and his wife, Janie. Neither of these tasks was part of my undergraduate coursework, but both proved to be as formative as the classes I took, if not more so.

STONE: Ward joined the faculty of Georgetown College in my junior year (1996), so I did not have many classes with him. However, he was the moderator of the Brokmeyer Society, our college's philosophy society. After a Symbolic Logic class, I asked Ward if there was more logic I could learn and if he would be willing to help me with it. Only now can I understand and appreciate the fact that he gave me John Dewey's *Logic: The Theory of Inquiry*. Although I had studied Rorty in a postmodernism course and not with him, Ward exposed me to American philosophy as such, including the work of Cornel West and John William Miller. In my last years at Georgetown College and beyond, Ward inspired me to be an earnest philosopher who did not have to compromise belief in order to think. Outside of the classroom, he led the way in Georgetown College's relationship with Regent's Park, the Baptist College of Oxford University, and created the Young Scholars in the Baptist Academy program. An active member in and past president of the Baptist Association of Philosophy Teachers, he is also a member of the Executive Committee of the Society for the Advancement of American Philosophy.

Both Wester and Ward have inspired a generation (in Wester's case, generations) of Baptist philosophy. It is no surprise, therefore, that we wanted them to be represented in this anthology and to "set the theme."

---

2. Harvey, Marsh, and Ward have been involved in scholarship directly pertaining to the Baptist experience. See Harvey, *Can These Bones Live?*; Marsh, *God's Long Summer* and *Beloved Community*; Ward and Thompson, *Tradition and the Baptist Academy*; and Ward and Gushee, *Scholarly Vocation and the Baptist Life*.

In this regard, this anthology is also a kind of Festschrift, not in the traditional, ego-stroking manner where all the essays deal with Wester and Ward, but rather as a collection of essays about something that both Wester and Ward care about and taught us—that there are Christian ways to engage and appropriate non-religious philosophers.

Wester's essay addresses Rorty's private/public distinction from two different angles. First, Rorty's account of private self-creation takes the political edge away from modern art. Wester turns to Goya's art to display, against Rorty, that it cannot and should not be limited to the private realm of aesthetic experience. If it is privatized, then we deny its radical potential for political action. Second, Wester addresses Rorty's public/private distinction in terms of "equilibrium" and—with reference to the ecology-centered poet Gary Snyder—suggests that Rorty's distinction needs a third equilibrium: "the primitive." Without this third equilibrium, Rorty's work remains too anthropocentric and problematically ego-centered.

Through a comparative analysis of Rorty's and William James's philosophies, Roger Ward emphasizes in his essay "Therapy to Apocalypse" the "apocalyptic" character of their work. This apocalyptic tone serves as a representative of epistemology's (and philosophy's) "abyss" where our only hope is found in the other world that both James and Rorty actively construct and describe. Unfortunately, neither James nor Rorty displays sufficient patience in waiting for this other world: the history of philosophy has left us hopeless, and all we can do is mourn this world and conceptually or linguistically construct another one. Philosophy is therefore reduced to a kind of "therapy" against the coldness of the abyss. In this sense, Ward finds in James' and Rorty's work an apocalyptic tone without the strong eschatology of Moses or St. Paul. However, this lack of eschatology leaves us wanting, and the insistence on a non-eschatological apocalypse folds James and Rorty back into the very philosophical tradition they are seeking to overcome. Ward calls for a non-apocalyptic epistemology, one that believes that there is still something worth waiting for.

D. Stephen Long emphasizes what gets neglected in Rorty's defense of his own "methodological nominalism." In his essay in the anthology *The Linguistic Turn*, Rorty defends the significance of "methodological nominalism" for analytic philosophy and suggests that "the linguistic turn" is founded upon what he labels methodological nominalism (instead of metaphysical nominalism). Long's contribution illustrates how this methodological nominalism plays a continuous role within Rorty's philosophical career. Long contrasts Rorty's nominalism with Charles Taylor's realism in order to argue that Taylor, not Rorty, serves as the better philosophical companion for contemporary theologians. To the question, "Can (Analytic) Philosophers Tell Theologians the Truth?" Long answers both yes and no: yes, if the philosopher works from a methodological realism that allows room for robust theological claims; no, if the philosopher works from a methodological nominalism that renders theological claims problematic on an *a priori* basis.

An interesting contrast in approaches arises between Long's contribution to this collection and Barry Harvey's contribution, titled "For and Against Richard Rorty: Christian Convictions, Liberal Democracy, and the *Christenfrage*." Whereas Long addresses the question of what kind of philosophy theologians should trust, the question that Harvey raises is what kind of philosopher one should be. In answering this question, Harvey presents two ways of being a philosopher. The first kind of philosopher, exemplified by Richard Rorty, is one that keeps his theological convictions a "secret." The second kind of philosopher, which Harvey spends less time describing, is one that maintains his theological convictions as an explicit part of his philosophical work. According to Harvey, Rorty wants to show us what would really happen if we put all of our eggs in the basket of liberal democracy. For Rorty, liberal democracy might actually bring about the kingdom of God on earth. In this sense, Rorty stands as emblematic of the crisis between actual secular social hopes and their Christian underpinnings. In Rorty, there is always a theology—but it remains secret.

We chose to call the first part of this collection, "Reflections in Rorty's Mirrors," because we found that the essays of Wester, Ward, Long, and Harvey highlighted aspects of Rorty's work that Rorty himself had a difficult time seeing. We might say, then, that Rorty saw "in part," and these four authors help us see Rorty's work, as well as the world around us, more fully. The reflection(s) in Rorty's mirror identified by these four essays are ones that he might not recognize—and, possibly, might even deny. If Rorty posed the question, "Mirror, mirror on the wall: who sees the world best of all?" the answers of "politically charged modern artists," "ecological poets," "non-apocalyptic epistemologists," "methodological realists," and "philosophers who make explicit their theological convictions" might not be what Rorty expects to hear. But, according to the first four contributors, those are indeed the answers—at least in relation to the ways in which Rorty sees the world.

The next three essays, gathered under the title "Moral Dispositions and Religious Belief," address questions raised in the first set of essays. In this second set of essays, Rorty serves as a philosophical "hero" for particular movements and specific problems found within contemporary philosophical theology and the philosophy of religion. The movements or problems addressed in this part of the book are the following: (*a*) How does Rorty's social epistemology serve as a corrective to Alvin Plantinga's "Reformed epistemology"? (*b*) How does Rorty's strong plea for the avoidance of cruelty relate to John Milbank's—and Radical Orthodoxy's—understanding of Christian charity as the form of the virtuous life? And (*c*) how does Rorty's *Contingency, Irony, and Solidarity* provide a literary theory focused on the reader's dispositions toward both the text and others reading texts for the current interreligious practice of scriptural reasoning—as developed by Peter Ochs and others who work at the intersection of philosophy, politics, and practices of reading traditionally sacred texts?

Keith Starkenburg's "What the Apostles Will Let Us Get Away with Saying: Plantinga and Rorty on the Social Establishment of Religious Belief" addresses an often made criticism of Rorty's work: that when Rorty says, "truth is what our peers will let us get away with saying," he cannot but fall into incoherence and relativism. According to Starkenburg, however, this kind of claim lies at the heart of a Christian understanding of "belief" and how particular beliefs become established or gain their "warrant." In the developments of his "Reformed Epistemology," Plantinga continually addresses Rorty's understanding of truth as "what our peers will let us get away with saying"; Starkenburg, who remains sympathetic with Plantinga's "Reformed Epistemology," argues that the Christian understanding of belief and truth requires some version of a social epistemology where the communal ecclesiological development of convictions and doctrine remains at the center of the church's task. In this sense, Rorty's recognition of the significance of the role of the community ("our peers") for warrants concerning what counts as "true" is a legitimate—if not necessary—recognition of Christian epistemological standards. In this way, Starkenburg's engagement with Plantinga's work might be considered Wittgensteinian in the sense of bringing to light the ways in which "grammar" works for understanding the nature and purpose of beliefs. For Starkenburg, saying, "what the apostles will let us get away with saying" is not relativism but stands as an important part of the formation of Christian beliefs, because beliefs are governed by the grammar and ways of reasoning originated by the apostolic office of the early church.

Eric Hall's essay proactively synthesizes Rorty's politics with Christian charity, but without the underlying metaphysical core of the Christian understanding of charity. According to Hall, Christians participate in acts of charity, which is more than simply avoiding cruelty or suffering. Hall claims that Rorty never feels like he needs to sacrifice himself for others; however, Christianity requires us to pry into the business of other people. Rorty finds that this getting into the affairs of others is in itself an act of cruelty. Christianity, however, thinks that these relationships are acts of charity. Hall articulates how Christian charity not only avoids cruelty but turns Rorty's plea for the avoidance of cruelty into an active—rather than a passive—practice of charity.

In Jacob Goodson's chapter in this collection, "Contingency, Irony, Vulnerability: Richard Rorty and Scriptural Reasoning," new ways to think about the role of religious convictions within public, secular debates are proposed. Goodson argues that religious believers need to develop a particular sense of "vulnerability" in both inter-faith and secular engagements where religious believers argue from the wisdom of God rather than the will of God, because arguing from divine wisdom makes possible a healthy sense of the "contingency" of our convictions. At the same time, such contingency need not diminish the "love" one has for the particularities of their own religious tradition. Goodson shows how the practice of scriptural reasoning nurtures a healthy sense of the "contingency" of our convictions while requiring its practitioners to be fully committed to their religious traditions. Because of this, Goodson argues that the practice of scriptural reasoning represents (in Jeffrey Stout's terms) a "non-resentful" religious traditionalism.

The final set of essays form a group titled "The Philosophy and Theology of Social Hope." All three essays in this group attempt to use Rorty's view of social hope in spite of Rorty's own worries about religion. Indeed, Rorty fulfills the deepest meaning of pragmatism as a philosophy of hope. This hope, however, leads to many questions—namely, the question of "faith," understood by St. Paul as "the substance of things hoped for." Without doubt, Rorty has hope—but what centers or grounds that hope?

David O'Hara's essay, "Rorty's Religion," bluntly points out that Rorty is religious in spite of himself. Rorty's work has enough theological elements in it so as to have no problem being directly submitted to theological analysis. Claiming that Rorty's account of social hope is in no conflict with religion as traditionally conceived, O'Hara criticizes Rorty's desire for social hope to substitute for religion. The contradiction of Rorty's position, O'Hara claims, is that in arguing for social hope without rational underpinning, Rorty is preaching a faith-based belief system—one that is severely critical of other belief systems. As a result, in spite of Rorty's objections against religion as an intolerant force in society, Rorty's religion is itself intolerant. As a corrective, O'Hara re-emphasizes the centrality of community, love, and tolerance in religion in opposition to the fear-based religious politics found in society. In this sense, Rorty is a kind of prophet who admonishes the religious community to return to its beliefs and values.

Of course, Rorty would not consider himself a prophet. His critiques of the prophetic tradition, including the writings of his most famous student, Cornel West, shows that Rorty's anticlericalism spills over into a critique of anything deemed "prophetic," be it religious or not. Brad Elliott Stone's essay, "Can There Be Hope without Prophecy?," shows that, in spite of his disdain for prophecy, Rorty is himself a prophet whose message is the distrust of all absolutes in prophecy and violence done in its name. Focusing on Rorty's critique of prophetic pragmatism and its main influences, Marxism and Christianity, Stone shows how Cornel West's work should satisfy Rorty's fears about prophecy. In fact, Rorty's own expressions of social hope (that his, his writings on what is needed in order to have a better moral future) can be understood in terms of prophetic pragmatism, a fact that Rorty should have been able to see (except that he is too committed to being against it).

Continuing the theme of Rorty as a prophet of better moral futures, "The Difficulty of Imagining Other Persons, Re-imagined" by Jason Springs offers us a defense of Rorty's belief in the power of moral imagination and a call for more practices of moral imagination in a variety of areas. Connecting Rorty to Elaine Scarry, John Rawls, and other theorists from politics, literature, philosophy, and theology, Springs shows how Rorty contributes to the continuing conversation concerning moral imagination. Through developing stronger moral imaginations, especially as it pertains to imagining the experiences of other people, we could find solutions to several long-standing conflicts and become a stronger democracy. Rorty gives Christians a true way to determine who should "count" as a neighbor.

The afterword is a wonderful speech given by Charles Marsh, which we have transcribed and presented for publication in this volume with his permission. Marsh recalls a comment made by Rorty that things would be better if all theologians simply went away. Marsh imagines what would happen if Rorty's wish were fulfilled during the Civil Rights Movement. The Rev. Dr. Martin Luther King Jr., Marsh reminds us, was a theologian who correctly used religious thinking to bring about a better America. Rorty's views, as clever and postmodernly thought-provoking, are refuted—not by cleverer argumentation, but through reference to the lives of those whose faith improved the politics of the world.

It is our hope that this collection of essays will bring Rorty closer to the religious discussion he always tried to avoid, albeit unsuccessfully. Like it or not, Rorty will continue to inspire theists, atheists, and anticlerical thinkers for quite some time. These essays hopefully show how Christian thinkers can admire, while nonetheless correcting, Rortyan thought.

JACOB L. GOODSON, Williamsburg, Virginia
BRAD ELLIOTT STONE, Los Angeles, California
June 2011

Part I

Reflections in Rorty's Mirrors

CHAPTER ONE

The Priority of Democracy
The Public, the Private, and the Primitive

Donald G. Wester (with Jacob L. Goodson)

One can scarcely avoid an initial shock when Richard Rorty unabashedly proposes that since the justificatory projects pursued for centuries by Western philosophers now have come to a timely but unhappy end, philosophers might change their subject as well as their public function and engage with other intellectual ironists in the ongoing conversation of humankind.[1] The ongoing conservation that I find in reading Rorty is simply one that acknowledges the priority of democracy to philosophy. Rorty's distinction between the historic failure of diverse and prolonged epistemological quests for "foundations" and the new conversational function is not based on the outcome of logical arguments, but rather upon the critical dialectical play between "final vocabularies."[2] The philosophical project Rorty has in mind is a contingent version of Hegel's holding one's time in thought. A contingent version consists of a private sphere of self-creation distinct from an experimental public sphere of liberal democracy. This is the alternative that Rorty prefers among those currently available in our cultural situation.

In this paper, I focus on Rorty's rather novel advocacy of his liberal preference. Consequently, my questions are: (1) How can a public composed of contingent and idiomorphic final personal vocabularies

---

1. According to Wester, this is the thrust of Rorty's *Philosophy and the Mirror of Nature*. Concerning philosophers changing their subject matter, see 389–94.

2. See Rorty, *Contingency, Irony, and Solidarity*, 73ff.

"dwell" in solidarity? (2) Is Rorty's project an effective way for liberal "edification"? (3) Do my answers to the first two questions show a fruitful new course for philosophy as cultural criticism? My strategy is to concentrate on the first three chapters of Richard Rorty's *Contingency, Irony, and Solidarity*, interweaving other texts into my (re)description as they prove useful to do so.

The Contingency of Language

Rorty's project is contingent on a linguistic turn within philosophy.[3] In other words, our age is one of contingency through and through; we are constellated in our ethnocentric languages, our idiocentric private selves, and our desires for free liberal solidarity. Our culture's historic context is coherent only when inquiry is extended across the culture cohesively with the pivotal belief that democracy remains prior to philosophy.[4] I spell this out by retelling the dramatic narratives Rorty constructs in order to free us from our past hegemony of essentialist metalanguages, which continue to conceal the contingency constitutive in modern Western culture. For Rorty, the primary episode in his genealogy historically occurs when vocabularies created by democratic revolutions are blended with vocabularies of Romantic poets.

At the beginning of Rorty's story of modern democratic vocabularies, his initial description of "revolutionary democracy" calls attention to a paradigm shift incited by those intellectuals who adopted the language of utopian politics. The vocabulary change enables the cultural invention of truth in public and private life. The political act of truth invention is the creative act that engenders new liberal hopes that human life can overcome the essentialist vocabularies of supernatural interference. The cultural expectation swerves against all philosophical divinization through metalanguages. Solidarity is at risk with the holistic extension of the liberal revolution's final vocabulary of experimentation in private and public life.

---

3. Wester means that all of Rorty's work is an attempt to tease out the cultural and philosophical implications of taking language seriously for philosophical reflection, but Wester also gestures toward Rorty's editorial work and specific contribution to the collection of essays published under the title of *The Linguistic Turn*. Rorty's contribution to this collection is "Metaphilosophical Difficulties of Linguistic Philosophy."

4. See Rorty, "The Priority of Democracy to Philosophy," in *Objectivity, Relativism, and Truth*, 175–96.

The second event in the Western story of the Romantic poets equally portends expanded personal liberties. The accepted story is that democracies are imprisoned in *logocentric* reason, a metalanguage adopted from the "new science" during the Enlightenment. But reason so apotheosized merely hides itself through the recontextualization of the antithetic difference between "freedom" and "nature." This marriage of incompatibles is canonized in essentialist foundations for liberal democracy with the Cartesian-Kantian arrangement. The upshot of the Enlightenment solution is an impasse between the vocabulary of scientific objectivism and the contingent democratic vocabulary. Fortunately, the Romantic recontextualizations of nature and imagination nudged positivism from its initial exclusive hegemony over personal and public freedom. The only undesirable aspect of the Romantic vocabulary concerns its own divinization of the self as ground for the inversion of emotion and reason. The Romantic divinization of the self can be dissolved along with scientific positivism since both depend upon versions of philosophical essentialism.

The recontextualization of scientific positivism is possible because of new developments in recent analytic philosophy, namely through Willard Quine's and Donald Davidson's philosophical work. Quine ably undercuts the "two dogmas" of foundationalism.[5] His linguistic analysis dissolves the Enlightenment project of justifying belief by reference to one of two extralinguistic grounds: experience or reason. Further, Rorty tells how Quine's achievement is extended by Davidson's deconstruction of a third positivist assumption: the form-content dogma.[6] Davidson removes the Western distinction between appearance and reality. For our story's purposes, Rorty reads the upshot of the removal of the three dogmas as indicative that philosophy defaults on a projected extralinguistic theory of truth. He reminds everyone that the dissolution of the three dogmas does not deny that there is a world in addition to language; rather, it affirms that only language has truth-values. Language must resolve its shortcomings through the contingencies of redescription. We are at the cultural point where the Enlightenment project of discovering metalinguistic elucidation of epistemic justification is defunct. The Romantic quest for metalinguistic descriptions of the self and the imagination are dissolved in the same deconstruction. The contingency

---

5. See Quine, "Two Dogmas of Empiricism," in *From a Logical Point of View*, 20–46.

6. See Davidson, "On the Very Idea of a Conceptual Scheme," in *Inquiries into Truth and Interpretation*, 183–98.

of language alone remains, and it serves as the only pretext for Rorty's redescription of the hegemony of poetic democracy. By turning once again to Davidson's work,[7] Rorty recontextualizes utopian democracy.[8] Davidson takes coherence within a particular language as the truths available in linguistic practices and attributes it (the coherence) to the vocabulary's pragmatic survival—its causal linkage with the world. Cultural changes will occur simultaneously with significant changes in vocabulary. How these changes happen is laid out in Davidson's account of metaphor.[9] Normal language is the habitual corpus of usage built out of "dead metaphors." Abnormal usage occurs in the creative potential of "live metaphors." Metaphor is by definition an expression without meaning because to have a meaning is to have a place in a language game. However, when enough metaphors catch on in a particular language they become the catalyst of change.

The upshot of this is that Rorty links developments in language with cultural change, and he displays how the contingency of language overlaps with a pragmatic priority of liberal democracy to philosophy. It is pragmatic in that the priority is coherent with a contingent vocabulary.

The Contingency of the Self

The Rortyan self is not exactly straightforward. Although not yet canonical within philosophy, his description of the self as decentered is common enough. Nevertheless, the Rortyan self should be seen as standing within the Nietzschean-Freudian tradition. In this context, the self is held as antithetic to the traditional Platonic-Cartesian-Kantian reflections on the self within philosophy. For Rorty, this is simply saying that the latter view provides a metalinguistic account of the self, while the dissenting tradition offers an account of the self that remains engendered by its own contingent project of redescription. Arising from puzzles within the Nietzschean-Freudian tradition, the overlap between a contingent self and the contingency of language remains problematic. Rorty marks the distinction between the metalinguistic account of the self and the contingent self with a heavy hand: he reverses the ascendancy, originating in Platonism, of the priority of philosophy over

---

7. See Davidson, "Paradoxes of Irrationality."

8. See Rorty, *Contingency, Irony, and Solidarity*, 48–52.

9. See Davidson, "What Metaphors Mean," in *Inquiries into Truth and Interpretation*, 245–64.

poetry. As noted earlier, Rorty fidgets over the Romantic tendency to divinize the self and uses Davidsons' account of metaphor to show the fly the way out of the fly-bottle for this problem. Rorty diagnoses the tendency for giving divine status regarding the self as an anxiety concerning human mortality.

The Promethean Myth of the Self

Rorty's use of the word "anxiety" as sublimated into self-creation in relation to Harold Bloom's "anxiety of influence"—i.e., the poet's fear that one's own poems are "only a copy or replica" of past poets.[10] With Bloom's critical tools in hand, Rorty offers a strong misreading of the Romantic Hegelian-Nietzschean-Heideggerian narrative of poetic perfection. Rorty's story begins with Hegel, the original master of redescription through the dialectic, who partially overcomes—through his European and philosophic historicism—the ahistorical metalanguages. Hegel's heroic self finds immortality in the cultural destiny of Europe, but he succumbs to the "anxiety of influence" and apotheosizes his own narrative as the end of history. In order to overcome this Hegelian lapse, Nietzsche inverts Platonic essences such as "good" and "truth" into "the will to power." But failure to escape the desire to make humanity divine fails again when Nietzsche elevates the heroic self to a Übermensch.[11] Finally, as the latest advocate of self-completion, Heidegger uproots the onto-theological tradition and restores difference between individuals and the wholly other. Instead of inverting Platonic metaphysics as Nietzsche had, Heidegger dissolves ontologism altogether. Heidegger's project becomes compromised when he does not forego the apotheosis of a reconstructed Greek language as "the house of being."[12] Rorty connects Romanticism's fanciful quest for self-immortality with this dramatic narrative of the Promethean revolt against mortality.

---

10. See Bloom, *The Anxiety of Influence*.

11. Wester translated this as "Superman," but—given recent trends within Nietzschean scholarship—I am returning it to the original German.

12. See Heidegger, "Letter on Humanism," in *Basic Writings*, 213–66. (While I do not know for certain which edition of Heidegger's "Letter on Humanism" Wester read while writing this paper, in my studies under Wester he led me to this volume as well as Heidegger's *The Question Concerning Technology* for understanding Heidegger's thought.)

A Sisyphean Myth of the Self

Rorty's antithetical story of the self-creator is best understood in the role of Sisyphus perpetually pushing contingent redescriptions of the self up the slopes of finitude, nominalism, and historicism. This approach to the self remains content to stay within the limits of mortality. The shift in myths shows that, for Rorty, if metalanguages are to be avoided, then the redescription of the self cannot escape contingency. Persons survive idiosyncratically in self-narrations. *The self is safe as long as it owns and manages the story.* Rorty models this form of aesthetic self-creation upon a "strong misreading" of Proust's *Remembrance of Things Past*.[13] The narrator of the Sisyphus myth continues to self-create as long as his own storytelling controls the descriptions of the self. After that, why should a narrator care? At this point, we might say that Rorty's project depends too much on spreading descriptions of the self over poets, painters, scientists, and other intellectual groups. As I read Rorty, self-possessing individuals must sustain their solitariness in avoiding reduplication even as intellectual members of professional groups. Rorty's proposed ethnocentricity seems to roll back downhill as mere dysfunctional solipsism.

A Saturnian Myth of the Self

I now turn to the Saturnian myth to describe the difficulty of extending self-creation beyond the particular aesthetic practice favored by Rorty. An interminable conflict arises in "strong poets" who seek freedom from mere reduplication, which is a strong misreading (though easy to make) of the autobiographic narrative in Francisco Goya's graphic art.[14] Goya narrates conflicts engendered by an artist who wants to paint the soul of those individuals or groups; he does not want to be merely an understudy of Diego Velasquez. Goya wants to catch *his times* on *his canvas*. Goya's portraits of royalty show the hollow pretense he is able to describe from his stance as court painter. He puts himself behind the royal family as they face into a mirror posing for his unveiling of their

---

13. In order to describe Rorty's interpretation of Proust, Wester borrows the language of "strong misreading" from Bloom's *The Anxiety of Influence*, where Bloom argues that "strong" poetry results from creative and "strong misreading" of previous poets (see 30ff.).

14. Again, Wester is borrowing language from Bloom in order to describe Rorty's project.

mediocrity. Even his capricious treatment of the Spanish Enlightenment in his print *The Sleep of Reason* makes an ambiguous statement about whether "demons sleep in reason" or "demons play when reason sleeps."[15] Even his gruesome series of war prints ironically describe the liberal French liberating the politically unliberated and the very determined unliberatable Spanish.[16] As Goya portrays his times, he narrates a personal contingency that cannot sublimate or transfer redescriptions of the self into the personal equilibrium of a strong poet.[17] In other words: *Goya never owns the story.*

For Goya, the avoidance of cruelty and the affirmation of personal freedom remain hopelessly disjointed.[18] Throughout his different works, he presents his readers with alternate versions of a giant Saturn eating his children.[19] Cannibalism becomes the motif through which Goya holds his own time in thought. He has an extensive series of prints telling the ways of wars and bullfights. Goya desired to be a "liberal" and enjoy madness over the absence of continuity. Even the description that Goya presents concerning his work with the subtitle, "This I Saw," stands antithetical to the Nietzschian "thus I willed it." Granting the obvious, war is a public disorder trafficking on personal cruelty. Likewise, war is a trite metaphor only if tragedy is banal. How do metaphors of "bad luck" and tragedy catch on if they are restricted to redescriptions of the self in only personal or "private" "final vocabularies"?

Consider for the moment the possibility that Goya has lost himself through overextension. Has he simply confused the ordinary languages that are "public" with his own "final" vocabulary as an "ironic" painter? Let us try to rearrange these matters in the old demonized Goya. Consider the "black paintings" Goya put on the walls of his house: Quinta del Sordo's *The House of the Deaf Man*. Three of the paintings are useful: *Saturn Devouring His Children*, *The Cudgel Fight*, and *A Drowning Dog*. The latter is but the head of a dog at the bottom of a mostly blank canvas struggling to escape the quicksand. (I return to the role of non-language users within Rorty's project later in this essay.) As for the other two black

15. See Goya's painting titled *The Sleep of Reason*.

16. See the series of paintings by Goya, *The Disasters of War*.

17. I would argue that Goya's *Self-Portrait* displays Wester's point here in the sense that the painting is larger in stature than is Goya himself.

18. Note the connection to Rorty's concern with cruelty in his *Contingency, Irony, and Solidarity*.

19. See, for example, Goya's *Saturn Devouring His Son*.

paintings, I interpret them as Goya's suspicion that unchecked narration of the self leads only to melancholy and actually preys upon the self. Public ease is generally available to Goya. The only exception might be his poor health in his later years. Goya seems to have problems provoked by the irony he publicly paints. He is a "strong poet" who paints darkly.

Returning now to Rorty's understanding of the self: *Is Rorty escaping contingency by stacking the deck for a very privileged bourgeois liberal self-describer?* I think that Rorty is not unaware of the options I am listing, nor is his Bloomian poetics—that is, his tendencies as a "strong poet" intentionally providing "strong misreadings"—unable to accommodate my three mythical types. My criticism is of a different sort; I am suggesting that Rorty has non-pragmatically privatized irony into final vocabularies that are needlessly private. He is content with equilibrium in public normal or ordinary languages. Furthermore, his tendencies as a strong poet present a self-created equilibrium. In the three mythical groups presented here, there is a ratio or degree of continuity between light and dark irony. *Why then make the gap between the personal and the public unbridgeable?* It is my suspicion that Rorty is unable to dispel an analytic/synthetic metalanguage thinly disguised in his public/private distinction.[20] Rorty translates collapsed distinctions into a formula: irony is private because it cruelly bisects and humiliates while the public is less intellectual and thrives on synthetic nurture. I do not think Rorty wants to censor or conceal Goyan ironic public art, nor do I think that the public can do without such irony. To circumvent the dilemma, it is pragmatically useful—and perhaps unavoidable—for ironic creations to work across the cultural-linguistic continuum.

The Contingency of a Liberal Community

As previously noted, the Rortyan project wants to expunge any lingering traces of the divine or supernaturalism from natural languages. To accomplish such a project, Rorty presents a hard line between natural and supernatural by extending it to any and every case of theories of truth that fashion metalanguages. Although I remain sympathetic with Rorty's pragmatism, I find it difficult to adopt his narrow reading of the "self" as coherent with the contingency of language. I suspect Rorty is globalizing poetics in a thinly disguised scheme/content metalanguage.

---

20. In this sense, Wester applies Quine's critique of the analytic/synethetic distinction (from "Two Dogmas of Empiricism") to Rorty's private/public distinction.

Further, I suspect the difficulty lies with the use of the Nietzschean-Freudian arrangement of the "personal"—which Rorty problematically interchanges with the "private." The upshot, for Rorty, is an unbridgeable difference between the private and the public. But the problems are found in my descriptions of Goya's art—namely that the proper use of irony has much impact on the public and its problems.

My exposition of Rorty's notion of solidarity operates with three equilibriums rather than with the two that Rorty uses—the private and the public. All three are distinguishable only by the ease with which equilibrium stabilizes tensions between normal and abnormal, ordinary and technical languages. Instead of restricting cultural change to the creative elite as Rorty does, I build my exposition on a populist degree of stability between the old and the new. I call the three equilibriums (1) the private, (2) the public, and (3) the primitive. I use these three equilibriums in order to redescribe Rorty's notion of solidarity in the following ways: (1) the private becomes the Freudian equilibrium of the Ego or, in Rorty's terms, the self; (2) the public becomes the Rawlsian fairness equilibrium; and (3) the primitive becomes the indigenous as found in Kuhnian paradigm equilibriums. My extension of Rorty's inquiry is my attempt to expand pragmatic equilibriums based on "contingency" while sustaining "the priority of democracy to philosophy." My additional equilibrium raises the question of the real ecological or environmental limitations of Rorty's own account. In other words, solidarity itself becomes enhanced by adding the "primitive" to Rorty's ratio of the "public" and "private" within his understanding of how liberal democracy works; however, Rorty fails to account for it.

The Private Ratio

I remain inclined to agree with Rorty that the moral upshot of Freud's construction of the Ego displaces the Platonic-Cartesian-Kantian canonical arrangement of what constitutes the self as well as the ethical. Rorty overlooks the extent to which continuity in his Freudian ethics does not make possible a single self-creator who exhibits all mastery and control over his personal narrative. The "ghost" of the Übermensch in the Freudian-Nietzschean tradition eventuates in a metalanguage of possessive individualism through exclusive self-description and self-ownership.[21] As I understand it, the story Freud tells illustrates that

21. Wester employs Gilbert Ryle's language of "the ghost in the machine," found in

each human is a haphazard conglomeration of diverse self-descriptions accumulated incidentally and most often from insignificant happenings in a peculiar past. The incoherent pluralism of alternate self-descriptions that make up the complete life story of any human organism circumvents all essentialist projects of self-control, selflessness, or self-realization. The sane resolution comes about through such extensions and redescriptions, which reach some contingent stability or vulnerable equilibrium. The self becomes the free play of fantasy where continuity is minimal and fragile. This is the private ratio in which abnormal or technical languages function as open windows of change. I cannot constrict this vortex to a Freudian-Nietzschean-Bloomian avoidance of self-reduplication or any other metalanguage of self-proprietorship of change. Instead, I extend the play of fantasy to overlap the private and the public.

The Public Ratio

The Rorty-Rawls arrangement of pragmatic due process is antithetical to Kantian ethics. Due process as public protection against cruelty is the only public coherence Rorty seriously entertains. Rorty problematically ignores the lower pole of Rawls' fairness equilibrium as a scale between the optimum and the minimum. In my judgment, Rorty's concern for cruelty remains incomplete in relation to his interpretation of Rawls because it provides the only ground for stability within Rorty's priority of democracy to philosophy. There is no scale of mutual enjoyment in Rorty's anxiety of influence.

Rorty and the Primitive

Gary Snyder's *Turtle Island* presents a frontal assault upon the egocentric metalanguages of Western culture.[22] He is part of the Eastern turn in the San Francisco Renaissance poets, but he is at his best when he reflects upon the ecologies of the Native Americans. To read Snyder as stranded on scientific objectivity is to read Snyder as a poet of anthropological primordialism, which overlooks his poetic rejection of Western metalanguages. His indigenousness uses old tribal rituals to exorcise a globally extended cruelty resulting from bourgeois ethnocentricity.

---

his critiques of the Cartesian self, as a possible (and surprising) critique of the alternative account of the self in the Freudian-Nietzschean tradition.

22. See Snyder, *Turtle Island*.

Snyder is not trying to divinize a self beyond selfishness; in fact, he is not trying to sustain descriptions of the self at all. His poetic indigenousness, therefore, serves as a corrective to Rorty's use of self-creating eccentricity.

Traces of indigenousness occur in Rorty's overcoming of conceptualism through his own adoption of Freud for his moral philosophy. Although Rorty thinks culture is created with abnormal or technical language metaphors caused by sublimated desire, Rorty cannot escape the indigenous so easily. His use of Davidson's account of metaphors includes the concession that pragmatic holism is the process by which metaphors catch on. This is the way that Rorty's use of Kuhn and Rawls links up with the Quinean-Davidsonian tradition. A language is, holistically, connected with the world. But this does not gain verification as true in the particular description of correspondence. This holistic account is employed by some philosophers to include normal and ordinary languages within cultural arrangements. Changes in technology, habitats, normal science, and fairness occur by increments as well as by revolutions. His deep concerns to maintain the self at all costs display Rorty's ethnocentric tendency to be an aesthetic inversion of the generalized scientific method of objective science. *If abnormal or technical language use is restricted to personal proprietors, for instance, then how can Rorty keep his notion of solidarity from falling like a house of cards?*

Returning now to Goya's painting *A Drowning Dog*: we are in a position to see how this work is mutilated by the absence of something from the negative space above the dog. The surviving mutilated painting is mostly negative space in three-fifths of the upper canvas. The painting has become a nice reminder of Rorty's ethics: the advantage of Freud over Nietzsche is that the vast majority of humanity is not reduced to the status of dying animals. The upshot of Snyder's poetry is that all earthlings are included in solidarity. As far as Snyder is concerned, and unlike Rorty's use of Davidson's work, metaphors make change possible throughout the continuum between language culture in non-egocentric ways. If metaphors by definition are words outside of a language game, why do they have to go through the game of self-creation to change or sustain our culture? My engagement with Rorty merely wishes to replace a world limited to private self-constellation with a solidarity created through an inclusive constellation of equilibriums.

CHAPTER TWO

Therapy to Apocalypse
Encountering the Abyss of Epistemology in James and Rorty

ROGER WARD

It is easy to sympathize with William James' and Richard Rorty's responses to religious orthodoxy and Christian over-beliefs. In John McDermott's memorable image, hope for a divine clean-up crew that will right every wrong, address every pain, and in some way sum up all the mystery of human reality in one fell act seems not only anachronistic but childishly and foolishly simple.[1] Rorty advocates for "the end of redemption,"[2] and James asks, "May not the notion of a world already saved *in toto* anyhow, be too saccharine to stand? . . . Must all be saved?"[3] The sensitivity and challenge Rorty and James show to apocalyptic Christian hopes are similar to their responses to the promise that epistemology will overcome the gap that separates ideas and reality, and finally resolve the puzzle of knowledge. In this essay I explore some of the high rhetorical moments in James and Rorty that seem to invoke apocalyptic images of unveiling and transforming discovery, especially in the context of epistemology. I argue that their use of this rhetorical and religiously charged strategy transforms the question of knowledge into something more like an abyss than a philosophical project.

1. See McDermott, *Drama of Possibility*.
2. Rorty, "Decline of Redemptive Truth."
3. James, *Pragmatism*, 295.

Re-treading this rhetorical ground and delving into the meaning of the apocalyptic character of Rorty and James is necessary, I suggest, for both overcoming the tendency of pragmatists to discount the tradition of epistemology, and for locating the pragmatic challenge of transformation as the key to inquiry squarely in the wheelhouse of contemporary epistemology.

Gary Gutting in *What Philosophers Know* catalogues the most significant moments in the last half-century of philosophical history. In each case, the moment of transition in understanding arises not from within the normal operation of philosophical discourse, but by virtue of powerful metaphors or images that reshape the context of argument. For example, he says that Quine's radical empiricism is a "pre-philosophical conviction, not something [he] is able to support by philosophical argument."[4] In a similar way, James' and Rorty's radical transformations of philosophy also emerge from extraphilosophical convictions. By holding both of these together and calling this movement "therapy to apocalypse," I am suggesting that the reorienting arguments made by these two pragmatists trade on the religious ground of a striking revelation which they both ostensibly reject. This connection allows us to point out a significant division that then appears between them. James retains something of an image of "last things" that corresponds to an eschaton of final determination of character, albeit a private one. Rorty seeks the radical revelatory moment of an apocalypse, but one that is abstracted from any eschatological connotations or reflection. This move jeopardizes the consistency of his reliance on literature in the last section of *Mirror of Nature*, since, I will argue, all narrative forms imply some kind of end. Rather than reduce the problematic of epistemology, I suggest that James and Rorty freight these concerns with an additional problematic of transcendence and its rejection. For this reason, any approach to pragmatic epistemology will require an excursus into apocalyptic thinking and the abyss of understanding it limns.

Philosophy as Therapy

In the preface to *Philosophy and the Mirror of Nature*, Richard Rorty describes the discoveries motivating his work. He was inspired by Wilfrid Sellars and Quine, who "rendered doubtful" most of the assumptions

---

4. Gutting, *What Philosophers Know*, 23.

behind most of modern philosophy. Rorty says, "I have been trying to isolate more of the assumptions behind the problematic of modern philosophy . . . getting back to these assumptions, and making clear they are optional, I believed, would be 'therapeutic' in the way in which Carnap's original dissolution of standard textbook problems was 'therapeutic.'"[5]

This sense of therapeutic philosophy provides an analytic tool for unpacking the three pivotal thinkers for Rorty: Wittgenstein, Heidegger, and Dewey. These thinkers exhibit an internal dialectic by which they see their own constructive work as self-deceptive in later writing, which Rorty surmises is a "warning against the temptations to which they had once succumbed. Thus their later work is therapeutic rather than constructive, edifying rather than systematic, designed to make the reader question his own motivations for philosophizing rather than supplying him with a new philosophical program."[6] Rorty adds that he wants "to supply some ground that the problem of personhood is not a 'problem' but a description of the human condition, that it is not a matter for philosophical 'solution' but a misleading way of expostulating on the irrelevance of traditional philosophy to the rest of culture."[7]

The tagline here is important and compelling. Rorty subtly forces the judgment of irrelevance back on the philosopher concerned with solving problems of personhood: they are *choosing* to make themselves irrelevant to culture.

The therapeutic urge in James appears in quite a different tone. Rather than pursing movements in philosophy itself, James articulates the motivating urge he perceives in all people: "Men and nations start with a vague notion of being rich, or great, or good. Each step they make brings unforeseen chances into sight, and shuts out older vistas, and the specifications of the general purpose have to be daily changed. What is reached in the end may be better or worse than what was proposed, but it is always more complex and different."[8]

Therapy, in the Jamesean sense, is the movement out of a Cartesian block universe into a world of expanding complexities. The therapeutic orientation (nomenclature James does not use) is not seeking a teleological explanation of meaning but an expansion of experience. For this

5. Rorty, *Philosophy and the Mirror of Nature*, xiii–xiv.
6. Ibid., 5–6.
7. Ibid., 37.
8. James, *Pragmatism*, 141.

reason, religious experience exemplifies a vital opposition to the limits of scientific doubt. Rather than a fideistic adoption of doctrine or narrative, the religious moment entails the recognition that knowledge is bounded by formative experience. The distinctions within religious experience have deeply formative, perhaps even ultimately formative results. James says, "One sees at this point that the great religious difference lies between the men who insist that world *must and shall be,* and those who are contented with believing that the world *may be,* saved."[9] For James, therapy corresponds to the movement beyond the borders of personality, which is the possibility of transformed experience; however, such a transformation occurs within the definite content of the universe, all of which is experienceable, and the task at hand is to find the "workableness" of true ideas. This is not a "constructive philosophical project" but an approach to getting on with the ideas and connections necessary for living well. Just as with Rorty, a question arises about the motivation to take up this task of increasing complexity for the benefit of the "men and nations." What does this transition to philosophy as therapy satisfy?

Pragmatic Apocalypse

James and Rorty have powerfully shaped our received tradition of pragmatism. They both introduce and create pivotal philosophical moments. These are the points I call "apocalyptic," and I mean that in two ways. First, "apocalyptic" refers primarily to a literary genre. In this type of writing, a vision of another world often appears in parallel to that of our common experience. The root meaning of apocalypse is "to unveil," and the sense is primarily that some reality hidden in plain sight is now perceived with clarity. This unveiling is often attached to events in the future or at the close of the world, as in the Revelation of John, but not always. This distinction is important for what I am saying here about Rorty and James. There are moments that work apocalyptically in their arguments, moments in which emerges an entirely new way of seeing everything that has gone before, and future action (or philosophy) will have to take account of *this* difference that has been revealed. The second point is that the "unveiling" does not happen to a reader, but that through reading a pivotal and radically reorienting discovery is possible, one that realigns our experienced world with a world that is more stable. Although it may

---

9. Ibid., 282.

be more challenging and troubling, the new world is perceived as the truer sense of reality.[10] My larger claim in this section is that the movement to therapy described above depends on these apocalyptic moments, and so drives pragmatism from therapy to apocalypse.

"Far away, on the other side of our galaxy, there was a planet on which lived beings like ourselves." Rorty uses this visual and imaginative beginning early in the second chapter of *Mirror of Nature* to introduce the Antipodeans.[11] The thought experiment of the Antipodeans presents a description of people capable of intentions, motivations, and feelings, just not the notion of "mental states" or the notion of a "soul" which is separate from the body. In Rorty's wonderfully flowing prose, the image emerges of persons opaque to the philosophical powers of "tender-minded" and "tough-minded" Terran philosophers. The imaginative creation of a world with people but without the fragmenting puzzle of mental states *in addition to* feelings and thoughts enables Rorty to recapitulate the movements of Western philosophy against a different screen, where an obviously human reality has nothing added to its value of self-understanding by virtue of the philosophical tradition.

In summary, Rorty returns to the foundational difference between a people entranced by a gap between the knower and the known, and the Antipodeans. Terran philosophy, encountering the Antipodeans, comes to a standstill without any potential for progress. Rorty writes,

> The real difficulty we encounter here is, once again, that we are trying to set aside the image of man as possessor or a Glassy Essence, suitable for mirroring nature with one hand, while holding on to it with the other. If we could ever drop the whole cluster of images which Antipodeans do not share with us, we would not be able to infer that matter had triumphed over spirit, science over privacy, or anything over anything else . . . Only the notion that philosophy should provide a permanent matrix of categories into which every possible empirical discovery and cultural development can be fitted without strain impels us to ask unanswerable questions like "Would this mean that there were no minds?"[12]

The apocalyptic sense is generated in the subtle claims of wholeness and resistance carried in the story. The Antipodeans are discovered

---

10. Fiddes, *Promised End*, 24–26.
11. Rorty, *Philosophy and the Mirror of Nature*, 70–127.
12. Ibid., 123.

by Terrans (us) and exhibit no fragmenting philosophical problems of their own. Their reality has functioned in a parallel world with a full compliment of philosophers who mirror our struggle with notions of God and Pyrrhonian skepticism. More than a simple flight of imagination, though, this thought experiment produces real consequences. Since it is possible to conceive of human life without the founding philosophical problematic of the seventeenth century, the entire tradition and all its complexities are vain and useless, diligently working toward an ephemeral and impossible goal. Like all apocalyptic images, Rorty's story of the Antipodeans creates a shocking reformulation of the meaning of past efforts and future possibilities of human thought. What these philosophers *thought* they were doing was fundamentally mistaken, and the action of philosophy now needs to be completely refigured.

James is both subtler and more abrupt than Rorty. In his epochal essay "Does 'Consciousness' Exist?" James begins with a casual narrative: "One day Kant undermined the soul and brought in the transcendental ego, and ever since then the bipolar relation has been very much off its balance."[13] He then informs the reader that "'consciousness' is on the point of disappearing altogether, and has no right to a place among first principles . . . It seems to me that the hour is ripe for it to be openly and universally discarded."[14] James knows full well the significance of releasing the conception of consciousness, of the soul as a discrete and perduring entity. He speaks in the voice of readers holding on to the personal sense of consciousness: "We *feel* our thought, flowing as a life within us, in absolute contrast with the objects which it unremittingly escorts. We can not be faithless to this immediate intuition . . . Let no man join what God has put asunder." Rhetorical cleverness and power abounds with this phrase. James, in the voice of those holding to consciousness, articulates the belief that God produces the original bifurcation of thought and thing. The phrase is backwards—feels backwards. What God has joined let no man put asunder, namely, a man and woman bound in marriage. The person James is speaking for is worried about losing faith in our intuition. Yet how often are we precisely wrong when we follow such articles of faith and intuition? In this way James aligns holding on to a conception of consciousness with blind faith in an outworn cliché. He proposes an alternate origin: that breath is that

---

13. James, *Essays in Radical Empiricism*, 1.
14. Ibid., 2–3.

"out of which philosophers have constructed the entity known to them as consciousness."[15] This essay is apocalyptic in the sense of unsettling the otherwise steady ground of a personal conception of ourselves as entities distinct in kind from the things around us.

Once the ground is unsettled, essays like the "The Moral Philosopher and Moral Life" drive the consequences of James' vision to the extremes of reflection, especially given the demand of stabilizing moral epistemology without consciousness to anchor the ship. James dispenses with the psychological and metaphysical questions of morality in order to focus the reader on the point that "we see not only that without a claim actually made by some concrete person there can be no obligation, but that there is some obligation wherever there is a claim."[16] This concrete assertion of the moral demand clears the stage for the casuistic problem. What does action *mean*? What are the possible differences of meaning if action does not exemplify a divine and prior character? The entire undertaking obliges him to seek an impartial test: "How [to] avoid complete moral scepticism on the one hand, and on the other escape bringing a wayward personal standard of our own along with us, on which we simply pin our faith?"[17] The dilemma James brings to his reader's attention brooks no traditional safe answer. He offers the reader a possible way out: "From this unsparing practical ordeal no professor's lectures and no array of books can save us. The solving word, for the learned and unlearned man alike, lies in the last resort in the dumb willingnesses and unwillingnesses of their interior characters, and nowhere else. It is not in heaven, neither is it beyond the sea; but the word is very nigh unto thee, in thy mouth and in thy heart, that thou mayest do it."[18] These words conclude the essay, leaving the reader with an existential demand for action, heightened in significance to demarcating the separation of blind faith and a moral abyss of skepticism. As in "Does 'Consciousness' Exist?" James morphs a familiar biblical phrase, here St. Paul's translation of Moses' words to the Israelites. But rather than the Law, for Moses, and the Law of Love for Paul, James inserts the willingness of the interior character. The reader who has followed the argument is cast back upon the reality of his or her own willing acts as the fundamental meaning-giving character of the universe. The moral and Christian tradition is

---

15. Ibid., 36–37.
16. James, *Will to Believe*, 194.
17. Ibid., 199.
18. Ibid., 215.

reconceptualized as precedent to this discovery, and no searching for the heart of Jesus or following moral authorities can any longer provide a secure path. Only the radically emerging sense of one's interior character enables us to authentically respond to the moral weight of the universe. Apocalypse indeed!

After the Storm

Two main points emerge from this apocalyptic rereading of James and Rorty. The first is to indicate a level of complexity in the beginning of pragmatism and neo-pragmatism by paying careful attention to the kind of language used by these two tradition-making and tradition-changing philosophers. Their forceful claims do not simply emerge from a straightforward application of the pragmatic dictum. Rather, they perceive a troubled tradition, unstable in its origins and practices, and respond with discoveries that could not have been fully anticipated. These discoveries depend on a changed perception of the past and a radically altered conception of future possibilities.

The second point is that the apocalyptic challenge to philosophy in James and Rorty binds their thought even more tightly to modernity. They both respond to *the result* of modernity, which is, according to Fiddes, a "loss of self, without ideological alternatives for society, imminent apocalyptic disaster."[19] The modern world, in which transcendence is banished, is also a world without eschatology, because "there is no transcendence without oppression."[20] Instead of reestablished transcendence, James and Rorty create the philosophical desire for a "'place' or 'space' where there is fuller presence of persons to themselves and others, and a more immediate intuition of truth and universal access to reason."[21]

The final point in this mediation on apocalypse and pragmatism is to consider the differences that now can be assigned between James and Rorty. Their senses of the unveiling of philosophy are clearly very different. James' discovery that a separable and opaque "consciousness" does not determine the fate or good of the individual looks like an unlocked prison door. The collective fate of all souls in a world bound into one complete narrative unity disappears along with the expectation of an

---

19. Fiddes, *Promised End*, 227.
20. Ibid., 229.
21. Ibid., 235.

eschatological end of time in which we all share. But there are ends and *an* end. James escapes the oppression of the presence of Being, only to find an analogical demand that arises from the irremovable presence of personal character. James faces his own private eschaton, one in which the individual cannot count on the judgment of any other person to corroborate one's character or adjudicate one's intuitions. Cycling back to the epistemic ground of James' departure, it is clear that this result is perhaps less of an advance by avoiding mistaken goals than it is an expression of an overdetermining fear of a final articulation of one's character.

Rorty, on the other hand, turns to narrative constructions of identity and away from a philosophically defined problematic. This move away from the process of philosophical dialectic demonstrates the illimitable nature of time connected to Rorty's apocalypse. There is no "later" against which reflection works in the present, only a "now" that cannot be fundamentally distinguished from any other "now," from all other "nows." There is no eschaton, and without an end there is no possibility of progress, or at least any "progress" can only be considered so in a provisional and attenuated sense. However, even the sense of narrative identity collapses into a meaningless succession without a conception of an end, like the story of a human life that does not acknowledge the possibility of death. Conversely, an end provides access to the expression of human desire for a world that "hangs together," even if it is only a purely verbal reality. Our stories continue to tell us about the end we want, or want to avoid. Once again, for the epistemic origin of Rorty's philosophical picture, the apocalypse *sans* eschaton points to an interminable spinning of language about knowledge, but without the hope of any tractable transformation. In a surprising way, Rorty's end reproduces what he seems to challenge most about modern epistemology, which is that it has no hope of arriving at an end that matters.

There remains, of course, the notion of a return to epistemology through pragmatism. Any such return, though, will have to negotiate James and Rorty, not in the sense of dismissing them, but in reading through them to a place where conceptions of knowledge enable circumspection of the abyss I have tried to point out. This return also entails the recognition that religious myths and metaphors continue to exert extraordinary force on both our conceptions of truth and expectations of philosophical discovery.

CHAPTER THREE

Can (Analytic) Philosophers Tell Theologians the Truth?
Richard Rorty and Methodological Nominalism[1]

D. STEPHEN LONG

Introduction

In his *The Beauty of the Infinite: The Aesthetics of Christian Truth*, David Bentley Hart suggests that "modern Continental philosophy is very much the misbegotten child of theology, indeed a kind of secularized theology . . ."[2] Far from seeing this as a reason to eschew Continental philosophy, Hart finds it a reason for engagement. Continental philosophy needs theology in order to overcome its "internal struggle against itself." The consanguinity between them allows theology to be a resource to bring peace to philosophy's turmoil. "Theology," he states,

---

1. Some material in this chapter was previously published in *Speaking of God: Theology, Language, and Truth* (Wm. B. Eerdmans, 2009). Used by permission.

2. Hart, *Beauty of the Infinite*, 30. Hart finds the similarities between modern Continental philosophy and theology in that philosophy's "governing themes everywhere declare its filiation—ontology is concerned with the being of beings, phenomenology with truth as manifestation and the unity of knowledge and being, hermeneutics with interpretation and the transmission of texts; the questions of transcendence and immanence, the moral law, the transcendentals, the meaning of being, substance and event, time and eternity, freedom and fate, and the logic of history remain the essential matter of Continental thought."

"is always already involved in the Continental tradition—its longings and nostalgias, its rebellions and haunting memories, its interminable flight from the Christian rationality that gave it life." For Hart, however, no such "natural kinship" can be found between theology and analytic philosophy. He writes, "There are theologians who believe theology has something to learn from and contribute to the analytic tradition of philosophy (here I reserve judgment), but even if this is so the encounter would be a purely apologetic enterprise; there is no natural kinship."[3]

Hart does not explain why he finds no consanguinity between analytic philosophy and theology. But he immediately enters into a criticism of the so-called Yale school theology, which illumines his suspicions about the analytic tradition. "Narrative," he argues, is used as a "shelter against critique and against the ontological and epistemological questions that theology must address (inasmuch as it is a discourse concerning the Logos)." Hart finds narrative theology and the analytic tradition too trapped in language, too committed to "narrative," and incapable of developing an adequate aesthetics, ontology, and epistemology that would allow us to move beyond language.[4]

Hart does not dismiss the importance of language for theology; he makes something of a linguistic turn when he writes, "Christian rhetoric can be undertaken only from within Christian doctrine." But he does not want theology confined to language; it must also *"speak out of its story* in a way that is not 'narrative' only, in a simple sense, and in a way that can find resonances and correspondences in the language and 'experience' of those who are not Christian." Hart confesses that this assumes "the possibility of a consummation of all reason in a vision and a wisdom that cannot be reached without language, but is as much *theoria* as discourse."[5] Analytic philosophy lacks substantive engagement with beauty and truth beyond language. Is this an adequate description of analytic philosophy? Does it illumine theology's proper relationship to philosophy? I will argue yes and no, but first Fergus Kerr's very different account of the relationship between theology and analytic philosophy should be noted.

Kerr finds the dismissal of analytic philosophy among contemporary theologians shortsighted. He writes, "Analytic Philosophy—unbelievably

---

3. Ibid.
4. Ibid., 31. He states, "the Christian story is the true story of being. . . ."
5. Ibid.

—is regularly dismissed as nothing but 'talk about talk,' or deplored as reluctant or even impotent to discuss the Big Questions (evil, death, the meaning of life, etc.). Worse still, in the judgment of many Christian theologians, and Catholics especially, it is, in John Haldane's words, 'something to be avoided as a serious threat to one's grasp of God, goodness and truth.'"[6] Kerr seeks to rectify this mistaken view of analytical philosophy, encouraging theologians to spend as much time with Frege, Russell, Wittgenstein, Quine, Davidson and "their followers" as they do with Nietzsche, Heidegger, Levinas, Derrida "and their kin."

Is analytic philosophy mere talk about talk? Should theologians approach it only apologetically? Does it lack the "natural kinship" to theology present in Continental philosophy? If I read Hart's concerns accurately, I want to be both against and for him. I want to be against him in assuming some sharp distinction between analytic and Continental philosophy that privileges the latter as a theological conversation partner but sees analytic philosophy only in need of conversion. I want to be for him in the sense that the difficulty with some narrative theologians and analytic philosophers is related to their reception of the linguistic turn; the problem is not the linguistic turn, per se, but the methodological nominalism that comes along with it. Correlative to this methodological nominalism are four philosophical moves that, when adopted, make it difficult to do theology well: a designative theory of language; extensionalist theories of truth; verificationist holism; and beliefs embedded in sentences as the primary truth-bearing vehicles. Analytic philosophy is not one monolithic tradition. None of these moves reigns uncontested. In fact, these moves could be traced through one tradition of analytic philosophy from Frege through Quine, Davidson, and Rorty. Yet, there is another that goes from Wittgenstein to Charles Taylor that makes more space for theology than many theologians themselves set forth. Thus, I also disagree with Hart's assessment of analytic philosophy. The problem with certain strands of analytic philosophy is not that it lacks natural kinship to theology but that it only allows one form of theology to work: nominalism.

My argument proceeds through four steps. First, I will present an account of methodological nominalism, as it comes into the English speaking philosophical tradition through Hobbes and Locke, and its relation to a linguistic turn. Second, I suggest that deflationist theories

6. Kerr, "Aquinas and Analytic Philosophy," 123.

of truth are one logical consequence of this union between the linguistic turn and methodological nominalism. Third, I argue that this union does not work. An adequate theory of truth must exceed methodological nominalism; philosophy cannot work within its constraints. Finally, I discuss the best use of the Frege-Quine-Davidson philosophical tradition in contemporary theology by Bruce Marshall. My thesis is that once we recognize that the problem is not the linguistic turn but methodological nominalism, then the Wittgenstein-Charles Taylor tradition can help theologians do their work well within the context of a linguistic turn not tied to methodological nominalism and the four correlates noted above.

The Linguistic Turn and Methodological Nominalism

Fergus Kerr, drawing on Michael Dummett, states that the key difference between the Continental and the analytic philosophical tradition is that the latter, unlike the former, "took the 'linguistic turn.'"[7] For this reason Kerr finds theology, especially Thomism, and analytic philosophy "natural allies." Both help us see how "a picture held us captive." Language tempts us to see the world in terms of its own structure where subjects represent objects through mental events. We wrongly imagine that analyzing this structure into its most primitive elements will give us the securest form of knowledge of the world. This tempts us to a building-block theory of meaning and a correspondence theory of truth that cannot avoid redundancy. Attention to language can help us overcome our captivity. This common move finds general agreement among analytic philosophers and theologians today, especially those committed to holism or narrative, which is a salutary consequence of a linguistic turn. Despite the linguistic turn, a picture still holds us captive: the "picture that holds us captive is that *a* single picture holds us captive." In other words, the linguistic turn is content to free us from our captivity to intractable metaphysical problems by drawing our attention to language and overcoming epistemological foundationalism. This is salutary but insufficient, for this very attention to language tempts us to be held captive by another picture, meaning that by attention to language we can simply walk away from these problems and they will disappear. Perhaps we should call this "the linguistic overturn," where it

7. Ibid., 127.

is assumed that metaphysical problems are only problems of language. In this "overturn," being, and its transcendental predicates such as the good, truth, and beauty, are *reduced* to problems of language. Thus, philosophers are tempted to walk away from these problems without illuminating them for us because this linguistic (over)turn supposedly removes the questions we ask about them. Philosophy becomes a useless endeavor with no positive role to play other than telling us what questions we can no longer ask.[8]

Some analytic philosophers certainly take this route: deflationist theories of truth are one obvious example where "truth" is not illumined but simply avoided as a linguistic redundancy that we can do without, but redundancy theories of truth are not the only theories present in analytical philosophy; they are one position among contending positions. No one should dismiss the linguistic turn because it leads to deflationism. The problem is not the linguistic turn per se; in fact, I think linguistic philosophers overstate the disjunction between the modern linguistic turn and the preceding philosophical tradition, which also recognized language's role in illuminating questions of God, being, truth, goodness, and beauty. The difficulty with the modern linguistic turn is not that attention to language illumines metaphysical questions (Thomas Aquinas and the scholastic tradition recognized that much), but rather that the modern linguistic turn is a theological stance on those questions. It follows the late scholastics in denying the existence of subsistent universals as an a priori method.

The modern linguistic turn assumes methodological nominalism. Richard Rorty states this explicitly: "It is probably true that no one who was not a methodological nominalist would be a linguistic philosopher."[9] Rorty seems agnostic as to whether concepts and subsistent universals exist, but only one method can successfully be used to determine their existence: "the fact is that our only knowledge of these entities is gained by inspection of linguistic usage."[10] He seems to conflate these two claims: the linguistic turn requires methodological nominalism, and entities such as concepts and subsistent universals can only be known through linguistic usage. These two claims are not necessarily linked together. Because essential Christian doctrines like the Trinity and the

---

8. For a fuller discussion, see my *Speaking of God*.
9. Ibid., 11.
10. Ibid., 10.

incarnation entail the kinds of realities Rorty links with methodological nominalism, Christian theologians cannot be indifferent to his claims. We can agree that concepts and subsistent universals are only known through linguistic usage, but we cannot begin with methodological nominalism because it already takes a position on the question of concepts and subsistent universals. It denies or brackets out their reality in order to show how language itself can illumine why we should not ask the question if such entities exist. Methodological nominalism is not neutral toward this question; it assumes nothing fruitful can occur by asking it. It walks away from it. Thus, the game is rigged in advance.

Notice, for example, Rorty's claim for the "methodological revolution" linguistic philosophers bring to philosophy. It avoids the limitations of Kant's critique of metaphysics, which failed to see that in setting the limits to what we could know it already claimed to exceed those limits. Linguistic philosophy avoids this mistake by setting the limits not anthropologically, but, as A. J. Ayer noted, "from the rule which determines the literal significance of language."[11] By turning to language, Ayer and others posed a question to all theologians and metaphysicians; Rorty puts it this way, "tell us what counts for or against what you are saying and we shall listen; otherwise, we have a right to ignore you."[12] This question can also be put another way, one that takes the power of adjudicating verification away from the linguistic philosophers. We theologians can say to them, "Tell us what counts as a proper method for determining the rule that lets language use adjudicate what questions can be asked." If you insist that we must be methodological nominalists, then we will ignore you. Why should we be so limited a priori? Methodological nominalism offers us only three options for assessing the truth of what can and cannot be known: empiricism, science, or language use. It brackets out arguments that assume that beauty, truth, and the good can illumine our language just as much as language illumines them; however, as we shall see, analytic philosophy has never been able to pursue language usage without assuming these transcendentals. They cannot be successfully bracketed out. Methodological nominalism does not work.

Nominalism is a theology that states that essences or universals are not entities through which God creates, sustains, and redeems the world; instead, everything God does is particular. All universals

---

11. Rorty, *Linguistic Turn*, 5.
12. Ibid., 5.

or essences are mere names that help us negotiate among the various particulars. An individual cannot remember every particular human creature or chair or animal that God creates. Therefore, I use "names" like human creature, chair, or animal to help me recognize the particular object before me. These objects are all individual bits of data I input into my memory, which cannot hold all the data, so I produce "names" to encompass the data. These names act like placeholders; they have no existence other than their logical existence in my mind, and they have no function other than their usefulness in helping individuals construct and negotiate their own reality. They are logical concepts, not ontological. Since these logical constructions are nothing but logical constructions, we must always be willing to abandon them for better ones.[13] This does not apply only to persons, chairs, and animals; it also applies to goodness, truth, beauty, and even "Person" or "hypostasis." This is the reason nominalist theologians struggle in sustaining the truth of the Christian doctrine of the Trinity.[14]

Nominalist theology held sway over much of English thought in the fourteenth century.[15] Did it produce habits of thought that shaped not only theology but also philosophy? Its influence on two seminal English philosophers, Hobbes and Locke, is unmistakable and noncontroversial. What might be mistakable and more controversial is the extent to which these habits of thought continue to shape the tradition of analytic philosophy. For Hobbes, four principles constitute knowledge. First, "we have such and such conceptions." These conceptions are "motions in some internal substance of the head," which emerge from objects exterior to us. Second, "we have thus and thus named the things whereof they are conceptions." Third, "we have joined those names in such a manner as to make true propositions." Finally, "we have joined those propositions in such a manner as they be concluding."[16] Names identify

13. Michael Gillespie traces the radical innovations Ockham introduces into scholastic theology with his "rejection of realism." "The rejection of realism undermines syllogistic logic. If all things are radically individual, then universals are merely names (*nomina*), verbal tools created by finite human beings for the purpose of dealing with the vast array of radically individual things. Logic thus becomes a logic of names or signs rather than a logic that expresses the real relations among things." Gillespie, *Nihilism before Nietzsche*, 18.

14. See ibid., 24. Gillespie writes, "Ockham was able to sustain this doctrine only by contradicting his own theory of universals."

15. Ibid.

16. Hobbes, *Human Nature and De Corpore Politico*, 41.

particular conceptions. Language allows us to combine these particulars into universals and make judgments, but this is where language misleads us. Hobbes states, "The universality of one name to many things, hath been the cause that men think that the things themselves are universal." They "deceive themselves by taking the universal or general appellation, for the thing it signifieth."[17] The universal is no thing; it is a mere name.

Hobbes uses this account of language to explain and critique the notions of both truth and the good. Truth is a function of propositions (what we would today call statements), which must have an accurate, formal logic supported by evidence grounded in experience.[18] Truth *qua* truth does not exist as an entity; it only exists in the relation between a particular statement and the experienced reality to which it refers. Likewise, no such thing as the good exists. All good is simply goodness, a relation to us, as it pleases or displeases.[19]

Locke continued these nominalist habits of thought. Language begins with individual articulate sounds. These are then fashioned into words that "stand as marks for the Ideas within [one's] own Mind." These ideas are the consequence of sense-impressions from objects external to one's mind. They stand in for the object when it is no longer present. Words name those ideas, but this remains insufficient "for a perfection of knowledge." If every particular sensation was marked by a particular idea characterized by its own word, then "the multiplication of Words would have perplexed their Use." The "remedy" for this "inconvenience" is that "language had yet a farther improvement in the use of general terms, whereby one word was made to mark a multitude of particular existences."[20]

---

17. Ibid., 36.

18. Ibid., 38. Hobbes argues that this "invention of names" allows men to exceed beasts, but it also makes possible "error," the error noted in footnote 11 above.

19. Ibid., 44. "Every man, for his own part, calleth that which pleaseth, and is delightful to himself GOOD; and that EVIL which displeaseth him; insomuch that while every man differeth from other in constitution they differ also one from another concerning the common distinction of good and evil. Nor is there any such thing as agaqon aplwz, that is to say simply good. For even the goodness which we attribute to God Almighty, is his goodness to us. And as we call god and evil the things that please and displease; so call we goodness and badness, the qualities or power whereby they do it. And the signs of that goodness are called by the Latins in one word PULCHRITUDO, and the signs of evil TURPITUDO; to which we have no words precisely answerable."

20. Locke, *Essay Concerning Human Understanding*, 402.

To find a linguistic turn in Hobbes and Locke might be improper; they did not suggest that all metaphysical questions could be reduced to questions of language. Yet, Kant astutely acknowledged that Locke thought he could resolve metaphysical dilemmas by turning to common experience. Kant's own critique of metaphysics assumed Locke's project failed. He wrote,

> In more recent times, it has seemed as if an end might be put to all these controversies and the claims of metaphysics receive final judgment, through a certain physiology of the human understanding—that of the celebrated Locke. But it has turned out quite otherwise. For however the attempt be made to cast doubt upon the pretensions of the supposed Queen (metaphysics) by tracing her lineages to vulgar origins in common experience, this genealogy has, as a matter of fact, fictitiously been invented, and she has still continued to uphold her claims.[21]

Locke's turn to common experience was based on how our use of words misleads us. Therefore, it is proper to see in Locke the origins of the modern linguistic turn, especially as heralded by Rorty.

Hobbes and Locke share three basic moves in common with the modern linguistic turn. First, universal or general terms like "true," "good," and beautiful" are wrongly construed as metaphysical entities because our language betrays us. Second, meaning requires a careful and precise analysis of words as well as their complexes. We must begin with atomic inputs.[22] This does not prohibit positing abstract entities, but such "entities" lack existence unless they can be verified through methodological nominalism. They can only be logical concepts whose meaning depends on our use of them. Here true and good lack intensional meaning. They are primarily extensional, designating all the particular true or good things that the "general term" stands for. Third, meaning is composed of two elements: the object and its ability to be perceived by us, as well as our ability to name objects, associate them into complexes, and abstract from them to form generalities for our own use. This has significant consequences for how we render intelligible the good and the true. They primarily become "properties" or semantic features of particular linguistic constructions or statements about the beliefs of individuals. It is no surprise that, as occurred with Hobbes, the good

---

21. Kant, *Critique of Pure Reason*, 8.
22. As will be seen below, I owe this term to Charles Taylor's work.

is now necessarily related to an individual's preferences. Philosophical theories of the good in this tradition logically lead to theories such as utilitarianism, rational choice, or Bayesian decision theory: all theories that assume the normativity of marginal utility. It is also used for a theory of truth. As Donald Davidson puts it, "Decision theory, and the commonsense ideas that stand behind it, helps make a case for the view that beliefs are best understood in their role of rationalizing choices or preferences. Here we are considering only one kind of belief, the belief that a sentence is true. Yet even in this case, it would be better if we could go behind the belief to a preference which might show itself in choice."[23] We should not be surprised that the modern linguistic turn finds common cause with a rationality based on marginal utility.

Rorty's correlation between the linguistic turn and methodological nominalism bears many similarities to the tradition of Hobbes and Locke. For Rorty, methodological nominalism separates contemporary philosophy from the preceding philosophical tradition. It does not walk away from questions such as "Does God exist?" Such questions will continue to be posed, but it resituates the question within the context of a "methodological nominalism" and provides the only context within which a proper answer might be given. Rorty attributes this methodology to Wittgenstein, citing his claim, "When philosophers use a word—'knowledge,' 'being,' 'object,' 'I,' 'proposition,' 'name'—and try to grasp the *essence* of the thing, one must always ask oneself: is the word ever actually used in this way in the language-game which is its original home? What *we* do is to bring words back from their metaphysical to their everyday use."[24] Rorty takes Wittgenstein's question and turns it into an all-encompassing philosophical method in which "the view that all the questions which philosophers have asked about concepts, subsistent universals, or 'natures' which (a) cannot be answered by empirical inquiry concerning the behavior or properties of particulars subsumed

---

23. Davidson, *Inquiries into Truth and Interpretation*, 147–48. See also a more developed account of marginal utility as important for a theory of truth in his "The Structure and Content of Truth," 326–28. Marginal utility as rational choice appears to be the common basis for Davidson's so-called principle of charity. In "The Structure and Content of Truth," he states, "The possibility of understanding the speech or actions of an agent depends on the existence of a fundamentally rational pattern, a pattern that must, in general outline, be shared by all rational creatures. We have no choice but to project our own logic on to the language and beliefs of another" (320).

24. Ibid., 13.

under such concepts, universals, or natures, and which (b) can be answered in *some* way, can be answered by answering questions about the use of linguistic expressions, and in no other way."[25] What cannot be answered by empirical appeals or science can only look to language.

Deflating Truth?

Does the linguistic turn in analytical philosophy assume these nominalistic moves? If so, then perhaps we could reframe the different assessments of analytical philosophy by Hart and Kerr. The question is not whether theology and analytic philosophy lack natural kinship or can be natural allies; the question is whether these specific nominalistic theological moves permit the possibility of considering a truth such as God is Triune, or if they render such a claim arational a priori. Is analytic philosophy already too theologically partisan?

Three assumptions in some philosophies of truth seem to repeat these nominalistic habits of thought. First, truth-bearing vehicles are primarily linguistic—sentences, statements, utterances, which can be analyzed in terms of their syntactical components and semantic value. Second, truth is primarily extensional. Third, semantic ascent and the distinction between an object and metalanguage, which supposedly safeguards the unsavory implication of the first assumption, fails in its purpose. It does not give us participation in the world, but mediates between the world and our language by means of logical concepts alone. This raises the question whether, for good or ill, theories of truth that assume these nominalistic habits of thoughts inevitably lead to a deflationary theory of truth.

Deflationists argue that "true" in our language misleads us. We misunderstand it because we can only see it as a metaphysical entity based on the faulty notion of correspondence, but no such property exists. Thus, disquotationalism, prosentential, and performative theory all argue the true is not a property, and there is nothing that it sets forth which cannot be set forth without it. The sentences where we use "true" will not change their meaning if we do not use the term, for it is redundant. The question is if this is an inevitable trajectory once we begin with Tarski's notion of a formally correct theory of truth that eschews metaphysics a priori and seeks to develop truth only extensionally through

25. Ibid., 11.

the semantic notion of satisfaction? Then when we discover that Tarski simply assumed the truth and worked with it, and that Convention T can work when the truth predicate is eliminated, why do we need to continue to use the term "true" at all? We will then have to interpret it as redundant or as a matter of "force" (Strawson's performative theory); or we can develop the "weak thesis" of Ramsey where "true" has more of a pragmatic function;[26] or true becomes necessary not as a property, and certainly not as a transcendental predicate of being, but "true" allows—as Quine suggests—"semantic ascent."[27] It allows us to generalize, to point away from the sufficiency of any natural language to a metalanguage, and to move from the sentence to the world through generalization. If "true" only has the status of this "generalizing device," then it seems to do little more than repeat the nominalist impulse in Hobbes and Locke. If that is all our language does, can we speak well of God and truth? It becomes impossible.

Exceeding Methodological Nominalism

Intriguing in the analytic tradition, and its linguistic turn, is the recognition by so many philosophers that the methodological nominalism of the linguistic turn must be exceeded. Tarski's semantic conception of truth assumes the linguistic turn where metaphysical problems, in this case truth, are translated into questions of language. He notes that the word "true" can be a predicate of judgments or beliefs, sentences or ideal entities (propositions). For "convenience" sake he restricts his discussion to sentences and thus to language. Here one wonders if Tarski did not restrict "truth" to language because otherwise his semantic conception of truth would not work. Tarski's argument requires an "exactly specified language" which can "characterize unambiguously the class of those words and expressions which are to be considered meaningful."[28] This meets one of Tarski's two requirements for a "satisfactory definition of the truth"; it is "formally correct." Formal correctness brackets out all metaphysical questions because they lack any precise specification of language.[29] Formal correctness entails that we "replace a natural

---

26. I am indebted to Cristina Lafonte for this interpretation of Ramsey.
27. See Quine, *Philosophy of Logic*, 10–13.
28. Tarski, "Semantic Conception of Truth," 346.
29. Ibid., 347.

language . . . by one whose structure is exactly specified."[30] Truth becomes manageable, unmysterious.

What, then, is the status of concepts or subsistent universals in Tarski? His semantic theory does not eliminate metaphysical questions such as "What is truth?" but clarifies their meaning. He rejects the claim that it is metaphysical or ametaphysical. It is a neutral concept that does not entail a specific epistemology, which he says explicitly, or a specific ontology, which he does not explicitly state but which seems to be implied in his argument. He says, "Thus, we may accept the semantic conception of truth without giving up any epistemological attitude we may have had; we may remain naïve realists, critical realists or idealists, empiricists or metaphysicians—whatever we were before. The semantic conception is completely neutral toward all these issues."[31] Because Tarski began with Aristotle's definition and argued for something like a correspondence between a sentence and reality or states of affairs, critics accused him of naïve realism (F. Gonseth) and of being metaphysical (Nagel). To the first objection, Tarski states that a sentence such as "snow is white" "implies nothing regarding the conditions under which" it would be true; it only implies that someone "asserting or negating" snow is white must also "be ready to assert or reject the correlated sentence: the sentence 'snow is white' is true."[32] To the second objection, Tarski suggests that the term "metaphysics" is more of a "professional philosophical invective" than a precise argument. The term metaphysics can mean "a general theory of objects (ontology)" or the opposite of empiricist.[33] He does not reject the latter and suggests there are "needs" that the semantic conception of truth satisfies that are not pragmatic. They are more like "aesthetic" or "perhaps religious" needs.[34] How does the semantic conception of truth meet quasi-aesthetic or religious needs? To explain this, he appeals to an aesthetic argument: "I do not think that a scientific result which gives us a better understanding of the world and makes it more harmonious in our eyes should be held in lower esteem than, say, an invention which reduces the cost of paving roads

---

30. Ibid. The second requirement, "material adequacy," asks whether this formal correctness allows for someone to use this definition of truth in order to "fulfill its task."
31. Ibid., 352.
32. Ibid., 361.
33. Ibid., 365.
34. Ibid., 370.

or improves household plumbing." Yet, how can the semantic theory of truth speak of "harmony"? Would theologians like Aquinas, with their notion of truth as *convenientia*, not be able to help Tarski say that which appears as a gesture beyond his semantic conception of truth? Such a gesture is impermissible within methodological nominalism.

Tarski's linguistic turn gestures toward something other than methodological nominalism but never develops it. J. L. Austin assumes a similar method and remains within it more consistently than Tarski. He states that truth is "an abstract noun, a camel, that is, of a logical construction, which cannot get past the eye even of a grammarian."[35] Austin begins by assuming what should be examined: is truth a "logical construction" or an entity? Here again truth is understood primarily as a question of "grammar," answerable through attentiveness to language. In fact, Austin walks away from certain Aristotelian responses to truth. He recognizes that truth has been understood as a "substance (the Truth, the Body of truths), or a quality (something like the color red, inhering in truths) or a relation ('correspondence')." He correlates these to three uses of the word truth: as a "substantive"—true; as an "adjective"—truthful; and as a preposition—"true of." None of these will do. In each case, language misleads us, so he gives the counsel, "But philosophers should take something more nearly their own size to strain at."[36]

Two questions cut the question of truth down to a philosophically manageable size. First, "what is it that we say is true or is false?" Second, "how does the phrase 'is true' occur in English sentences?"[37] Because these two questions are the same for Austin, he provides a single answer to them, saying that a statement "is true" marks an "absolutely and purely conventional" relationship between a statement and a "historic situation" or event.[38] This denies that our statements represent some fact about the world, so it has the advantage of avoiding redundancy in our use of the expression "is true." Austin acknowledges that the term "true" is an extraordinary term that cannot be rendered "logically superfluous"

---

35. Austin, "Truth," 18.
36. Ibid.
37. Ibid., 19.

38. "The only essential point is this: that the correlation between the words (= sentences) and the type of situation, event, etc. which is to be such that when a statement in those words is made with a reference to an historic situation of that type the statement is then true, is *absolutely and purely* conventional. We are absolutely free to appoint any symbol to describe *any* type of situation, so far as merely being true goes." Ibid., 24.

by correlating it to how ordinary terms work like "red" or "growls."³⁹ In an opaque footnote, however, he suggests that the transcendental predicates of being "*unum, verum, bonum* . . . deserve their celebrity. There is something odd about each of them." For Austin, acknowledging their oddness does not make room for another question of truth beyond what a conventional use of language posits. Instead he states, "Theoretical theology is a form of onomatolatry."⁴⁰ To analyze "true" as something other than how it functions within sentences is to turn the name into an idol. The question is whether Austin's correlation theory of truth takes into account this kind of negative judgment on theology.

While Austin found metaphysical questions a species of "onomatolatry," Tarski remained agnostic toward them. William James establishes the debate on the question of truth between "pragmatists" and "intellectualists" and forces us to choose between them. He begins his account of truth by setting forth a "dictionary definition" both sides could accept: truth is "a property of certain of our ideas. It means their 'agreement,' as falsity means their 'disagreement' with reality."⁴¹ The question is, what divides these two schools of thought? What constitutes agreement or disagreement with reality? He attributes to the intellectualists the understanding that for agreement "a true idea must copy its reality,"⁴² but he finds this unsatisfactory. The "great assumption" for the intellectualists is "that truth means essentially an inert static relation,"⁴³ but who are these intellectualists? James does not name names, but his argument seems to tar idealists, Platonists, Thomists, and others with this brush.⁴⁴

He posits his own pragmatic notion of truth as verification against this intellectualist tradition. It asks the question, "Grant an idea or belief to be true, what concrete difference will its being true make in anyone's actual life?" The answer is, "True ideas are those we can assimilate, validate, corroborate and verify. False ideas are those we cannot." This leads to his thesis, "Truth *happens* to an idea. It *becomes* true, is *made* true by events. Its verity *is* in fact an event, a process: the process

---

39. Ibid., 26.
40. Ibid.
41. James, "Pragmatism's Conception of Truth," 96.
42. Ibid.
43. Ibid.

44. "Some idealists seem to say that they [our ideas] are true whenever they are what God means that we ought to think about the object. Others hold the copy-view all through, and the Absolute's eternal way of thinking." Ibid., 96.

namely of its verifying itself, its *veri-fication*. Its validity is the process of its valid-*ation*." However, the supposed novelty of this idea misleads James. Nicholas of Cusa made a similar claim, merging an idealist claim of truth with the notion of truth as making. Robert Miner calls this "image-making."[45] In fact, Cusa first used the term "verification" to explain truth. He did so within a conception of divine ideas, drawing on Thomas Aquinas, where the true as made could not be separated from its telos as an idea. We would not know to what purpose it is to be made, and this is a question that James' pragmatism cannot answer. His notion of "what works" appears to be self-evident, measured by something called "reality."

Notice his pragmatist account of "agreement": "To 'agree' in the widest sense with a reality, can only mean to be guided either straight up to it or into its surroundings, or to be put into such working truth with it as to handle either it or something connected with it better than if we disagreed."[46] This is a deeply problematic statement. It divides "reality" and our perception or working within it and uses the passive "to be guided" to the real without any sense of agency. Is it reality that guides us? What could that mean? Does it guide us to itself? What is the status of the real when it is guiding us to itself? Is it then the irreal? James rightly tells us that truth is "verification," that it is something made, but his rejection of "ideas" cannot help us answer the important question, "made for what end?" Theology can make better sense of his pragmatist account of truth because, apart from the nominalist tradition, it never assumed a stark division between ideas or forms and truth as the made.

The semantic, correlation and pragmatist theory of truth point in directions of the true that their own methodological nominalism cannot adequately follow. The prosentential theory of truth shows the logical consequences of this method. The prosentential theory argues that understanding truth as "a property of being true," as do correspondence and coherence theories, or as a response to the question, "what sorts of things are most fundamentally to be said to be true," as occurs when we examine propositions, statements, or sentences are both misleading. They remain trapped within the picture from which

---

45. Miner, *Truth in the Making*, 23. As Miner puts it, for Cusa, "Image-making is not inferior to the contemplation of originals. It is the closest approximation to the divine art."

46. William James, *The Meaning of Truth*, 4.

Wittgenstein attempted to free us. They are mistaken results of "a standard grammatical analysis of ordinary English sentences containing 'is true' where 'X is true' is analyzed into a subject 'X' and a predicate 'is true.'" Prosententialists seek to offer a "coherent alternative" to this "subject-predicate" logic.[47] They do so by developing the linguistic idea of anaphora where statement such as "that is true" or "it is true" do not refer "to some bearer of truth, whether it be a sentence, proposition or statement." Instead, such statements are a matter of "cross-referencing." They do not refer to something outside the sentence; they refer back to a previous antecedent and thus can be accounted for by replacing "true" with the prosentence that.[48]

The prosentential theory of truth seems to do away with it altogether. Its claims are not as modest as Tarski's. The prosententialists state, "In the spirit of Ramsey our claim is that *all* truth talk can be viewed as involving only prosentential uses of 'that is true.'"[49] The prosentential theory fits with certain elements of pragmatism because "in using a proform one makes it explicit that nothing new is going on, that (in the case of pronouns) one is not contributing anything new." The words "is true" do not actually do anything beyond the "core pragmatic feature of granting points, expressing agreement and so on,"[50] but the prosentential theory opposes realists: "We have purposed a semantical treatment of English truth talk that never construes any sentence involving true as involving reference to a proposition or anything to the sort."[51] Here "is true" is redundant. It produces nothing beyond what a sentence can do without it.

Truth and the Theologians

Deflationist theories of truth—whether they be disquotational, prosentential, or performative—prove Hart correct. Inasmuch as theologians find God and truth necessary terms for an adequate theology, this union of the linguistic turn and methodological nominalism threaten the viability of any theological claims. In this case, the true is nothing but

47. Grover, Camp, and Belnap, "Prosentential Theory of Truth," 73.

48. Ibid., 88–92; see their theory as an exposition of Wittgenstein's *Philosophical Investigations*, paragraphs 134–36.

49. Ibid., 92.

50. Ibid., 108.

51. Ibid., 112.

a generalizing device that can be replaced by a proform, rendered redundant by disquotation or understood as primarily a matter of force. However, are these theories compelling accounts of how the words "is true" function in English sentences, or are they the logical result of a methodological nominalism? Have they been attentive to how language works? Are they the inevitable consequence of the modern linguistic turn or are they only the consequence of a linguistic turn constrained by methodological nominalism? I think they are the latter and thus not a reason to follow Hart's counsel without reservation. Pragmatist theories of truth can replace "is true" with "what works," but they do not dispense with the true altogether. They cannot tell us "works for what," but they recognize that the true is a human construction; it is made and therefore intimately associated with language. Yet, their notion of construction cannot avoid modern technological reductions of the true to the efficient, to its cash value. A correlation theory of truth recognizes that it points to something other than sentences even while it only does so through sentences. It has a space for the true as "extraordinary." Truth is not logically superfluous, but truth can only be correlated to an immanent "historical event" because of its demonstrative character.[52] Tarski gestures toward a theory of truth that makes more modest claims for what our attention to language produces.

No one has developed Tarski's work more thoroughly than Donald Davidson. He presents a coherence theory of truth where all that can justify a belief is another belief, where a belief is a sentence that is held to be true. We cannot give the meaning of true, for truth is primarily extensional. In other words, rather than using the intentionalist analysis "truth means that . . . ," Davidson finds Mates' problem convincing and develops Tarski's extensionalist analysis: "S is true if p."[53] Thus, we cannot give the meaning to "true" and should not seek to do so. Rorty finds this convincing: "The greatest of my many intellectual debts to Donald

---

52. Austin states, "A statement is said to be true when the historic state of affairs to which it is correlated by the demonstrative conventions (the one to which it 'refers') is of a type with which the sentences used in making it is correlated by the descriptive conventions." Austin, "Truth," 22.

53. Lepore, *Truth and Interpretation*, 7. Mates' problem critiques Frege's intensionalism where "whoever believes D, believes D." In other words, D can be explained in terms of an "intensional isomorphism." Mates argued that no synonym for D holds in all cases and therefore intensionalism is incoherent. Jerrold Katz defends a form of intensionalism that does not assume Frege's "criteria for inference by substitution into opaque context." See Lepore, *Truth and Interpretation*, 60.

Davidson is my realization that nobody should ever try to specify the nature of truth." This has theological consequences, for Rorty claims that following Davidson, "truth, like the God of orthodox monotheism" is "tiresomely ineffable."[54] Analytic philosophers inevitably relate truth to God and beauty even when they cannot account for it. Can theology supplement this philosophical tradition to help it make sense of truth as something other than ineffable? If it is finally ineffable, all we can do is walk away from it.

No one has engaged the analytic tradition's theories of truth more thoroughly than Bruce Marshall. In *Trinity and Truth*, he examines whether this tradition can help us make sense of the epistemic requirements for truth. He uses it brilliantly to question tendencies in theologians to found Christian beliefs on interior epistemic conditions. He uses Wittgenstein's private language argument to challenge such epistemic grounding and develops a more "public" epistemic justification for theological truth claims. He does so by engaging Donald Davidson's coherence theory of truth.

For Marshall, the question of truth is related to the question of belief and therefore to the question, under what conditions are we justified in holding a belief? Even though Marshall maintains some distance from Davidson's coherence theory of truth, and from delivering theology to analytic philosophy, setting up the question of truth in this manner presents some problems for his analysis.[55] He does not distance the Trinity and Truth from a coherence theory of truth. He accepts the linguistic turn and does so for good reasons:

> [O]ur best hope of thinking well about God lies in thinking well about our talk of God. Semantic ascent in theology is not a trivial distraction from the real issue (God), still less a confusion or equation of God with our talk of God. Rather, it enables us to see the issue at hand—what God has to do with the truth and justification of our beliefs about God, and about anything else—more clearly than we otherwise could, and to handle the issue in more plausible ways than we would otherwise be able.[56]

---

54. Rorty, "Introduction," 3.

55. He states, "If analytic philosophy (or any other discipline) makes claims which are incompatible with Christian beliefs, then so much the worse for analytic philosophy." *Trinity and Truth*, 12.

56. Ibid.

He also adopts methodological nominalism, extensionalism, verificationist holism, sentences as truth-bearing vehicles, and semantic ascent.

I doubt Quine's "semantic ascent," with its "holism of verification," can achieve what Marshall wants it to achieve theologically. In fact, I fear that Marshall has already divided into atomic parts certain elements that can only be narrated holistically. We have God, truth, and justification—discrete elements that can be treated separately based on the sentences we utter. Consistent with Quinean holism and semantic ascent, only as we move from these atomic parts to the whole can we bring them together. Thus, Marshall also accepts methodological nominalism. He writes, "I willingly remain agnostic about whether concepts and propositions are eternal objects to which our words and sentences are variously attached."[57] He then pursues a strategy of empirical verification communally situated,[58] and he presents an extensionalist account of truth that finally requires a compendium of discernable properties to warrant assertions of truth.[59]

Marshall does not concede theology to an epistemic, coherence theory of truth altogether. He develops a "mixed" theory that acknowledges that theology requires a realist as well as an epistemic theory. He rightly notes that for Thomas, truth is both *conformitas* to the divine ideas as well as linguistic.[60] Truth is a function of both the forms and language-bearing vehicles. However, Marshall accepts Frege's critique of the forms and acknowledges the fruitfulness of the linguistic turn where "what truth is will profit from treating truth as at most a three-way affair, involving sentences, the world, and human beings."[61] With this view,

57. Ibid., 10.

58. Ibid., 18–20. This seems to overlook Gettier's argument that "it is possible for a person to be justified in believing a proposition that is in fact false." Gettier, "Is Justified True Belief Knowledge?" 122–23.

59. Marshall uses this basic analytical move to argue for Christ's bodily resurrection. He says, "To identify a person or object x is to succeed in distinguishing x from all other persons or objects. At a minimum this requires that we hit on at least one property of x which no other person or object has, one predicate true of x which is not true of any other person or object." Ibid., 26. Does this work? Can it make sense of the threefold form of Christ's body found in not only his historical body but also in the Eucharist and the Church? Is identity atomic in this sense, or is it more narrative? Could my appearance not be utterly changed due to some accident and yet, because of the narrative whole within which my identity is constituted, people would still know how to refer to me as Steve Long?

60. Ibid., 219.

61. Ibid., 222.

"non-linguistic mental contents" cannot be ruled out a priori; since we cannot be sure of their existence, neither are they useful. Marshall seems to have confused the "forms" in Thomas with "non-linguistic mental contents," which already concedes too much to the methodological nominalism in the analytic tradition. Why accept Frege's critique of the forms as truth bearers without first examining more fully what they are? Marshall explains the limitations to anti-realist theories of truth and concludes by tilting toward Davidson's extensionalist coherence theory. He raises the question whether this might be a fruitful way forward for theology: "Should this be right then truth, while not an epistemic notion, is also not inaccessibly divorced form belief (and so from justification) in the way it seemed to be in correspondence theories, which led anti-realists to go epistemic in their accounts of truth. If successful, Davidson's proposal is thus a genuine alternative to both realism and anti-realism."[62] This allows us to make sense of the truth or falsity of beliefs within a community, but does it allow us to speak truthfully of God? How does an extensionalist theory of truth avoid violating one of the basic rules of grammar of Christian theology: *Deus non est genere*? How can we speak truthfully of the Holy Trinity on these grounds? We might know that Jesus is risen, but can we know He is (as Truth) the Second Person of the Trinity? This is not possible through methodological nominalism. Some means to affirm Aquinas's divine ideas is necessary, even as we make the linguistic turn.

Marshall does concede that the Tarski-Davidson approach cannot render intelligible the basic Christian claim that truth is a Person. He works diligently to relate the two, saying that Tarski-Davidson provide the "sufficient created conditions for the belief that Jesus is risen to be true" but not the "uncreated" conditions. These we cannot "conceive of . . . except by qualifying and negating elements in our conception of created conditions."[63] He nevertheless works with the supposition that "a view like Davidson's, which accepts realism's fall but not anti-realism's rise, is the most plausible outcome currently available of the long philosophical debate about what truth is."[64] I want to challenge this supposition by arguing that Charles Taylor has already shown us the weaknesses

---

62. Ibid., 238.
63. Ibid., 257–58.
64. Ibid., 241.

in Davidson's account; it continues a "mediational" epistemology that loses our being-in-the-world.

Perhaps a better way forward is to turn from Davidson's coherence theory of truth to the philosophy of Charles Taylor. Taylor sets his own meaning of holism against that of the "verification holism" of Quine and Davidson.[65] He suggests that verification holism errs by continuing the epistemological tradition of finding some vehicle by which our relationship to the world must be mediated. Rather than through mental constructs, it thinks truth primarily through "atomic inputs" via the linguistic turn where "the basic unit has come to be something like sentences held true, or beliefs." This remains "representationalist," for it assumes that all that can justify beliefs are sentences, which can then only be justified based on the representation of other sentences. We are told we cannot "get outside" our beliefs, which reproduces the representationalist picture. We refuse to follow Wittgenstein, Heidegger, and Merleau-Ponty in acknowledging "the embedding of our explicit beliefs in our background grasp of things" and instead posit beliefs as present only in sentences.[66] Taylor finds an alternative tradition from Kant through Witttgenstein that opposes the nominalism of Locke and Hobbes. Kant begins this tradition by acknowledging that we have no representations, no perceptions, without an "object." For Kant, we are not trapped in our representations; we only have them because of the unity of a transcendental object that we cannot reduce to a datum or a "determinate intuition." It is neither a mere particular nor just an appearance. It is the "unity of apperception" that makes the object appear to us at all.[67]

Kant was unable to bridge the gap between the tacit "unity of apperception" always present in every appearance and the appearance itself, but he set us on a tradition of holism that does not begin with atomic inputs. Wittgenstein, Heidegger, and Merleau-Ponty developed that tradition and bridged the gap. Taylor describes the difference between the latter tradition and that of Quine-Davidson as different

---

65. Taylor, "After Epistemology," 6. Taylor defines verification holism as "supposing an atomism of the input, that is, it tells me how I have to relate a number of facts and suppositions, which can be identified (although not verified) independently of each other." Meaning holism assumes "the nature of any given element is determined by its 'meaning' (Sinn, sense), which can only be define in placing it in a larger whole. And even worse, because the larger whole itself isn't just an aggregation of such elements."

66. Taylor, "After Epistemology," 1.

67. Kant, *Critique of Pure Reason*, 137–38.

accounts of language. The former treat language primarily as "designative," the latter as "expressive."⁶⁸ Designative theories "make meaning something relatively unpuzzling, unmysterious," but expressive theories "manifest" things. For the former, the language is the only access to the thing. For the latter, the thing makes its manifestation in language possible; in so doing, it "maintains some of the mystery surrounding language." It is only the expressive theory of language that can render intelligible "semiological ontologies" where "everything is a sign." Nominalism rebelled against this, making possible the designative theory of language.⁶⁹

What does meaning holism make possible that Quine-Davidson-Rorty's verification holism denies? Rorty understands the difference well: "Taylor reads his favorite authors in the light of his conviction that 'the poet, if he is serious, is pointing to something—God, the tradition—which he believes to be there for all of us.' I read some of these same writers in the light of my conviction that seriousness can, and should, swing free of any such universalistic belief."⁷⁰ How shall we theologians think and speak well God as incarnate Word? How can we think a Hypostasis that always is and yet becomes fully creature without ceasing to be Divine? How can we think a *Processio* that is also *Missio*? Do Quine-Davidson-Rorty, with their methodological nominalism, produce the same theological problems the nominalists themselves have in thinking these thoughts? Yes. Their use of the linguistic turn does not trap us in talk about talk; their methodological nominalism does. No reason exists to think the linguistic turn is some methodological revolution that undoes all that went before us and teaches us what questions we can and cannot ask. As Taylor asks, "How did we slide to the sense that the secret of human nature was to be found in man as a 'language animal'?" He answers, "The slide was not all that great." We can find it in Aristotle. We can have the linguistic turn without methodological nominalism. Taylor's philosophy of truth, based on an expressivist theory of language, points out the limitations of methodological nominalism and points us in a fruitful direction to think God and Truth as Eternal Hypostasis. How can theology be theology and do anything less?

68. Taylor's "expressive" theory of language bears no relation to what Lindbeck rightly critiques as experiential-expressivism within modern theology; see Lindbeck, *Nature of Doctrine*.

69. Taylor, "Language and Human Nature," 223.

70. Rorty, "Charles Taylor on Truth," in *Truth and Progress*, 84.

CHAPTER FOUR

For and Against Richard Rorty
Christian Convictions, Liberal Democracy, and the Christenfrage

BARRY HARVEY

With apologies to Dante, and strictly as an exercise in imagination, I sometimes picture Richard Rorty in the first circle of hell, conversing with the great pagan philosophers and poets in limbo, where from time to time he engages the great minds of ancient Rome. "Those Christians," they say to him, "we could see immediately that they were a menace." Rorty, nodding in agreement, says, "You were so right, they have always been a danger to the good order of the republic, which must always come first. Pity you were unable to suppress them before they became so numerous they couldn't be contained." Satisfied that they have reached a consensus on this question, they then move on to other topics of conversation.

    This is an apt image for many reasons, not the least of which is the fact that there is no cruelty or suffering in limbo, and for Rorty there was no social goal more important than avoiding cruelty.[1] It is also apposite because, as I shall argue, Rorty did not flinch from the "imperialist" position he established and defended so eloquently. Finally, it is a fitting picture because Rorty understood the social ramifications of "religion" much better than do most others who identify themselves as liberals. More specifically, he understood that the gospel would not stay for long

---

1. Rorty, *Contingency, Irony, and Solidarity*, 65.

within the boundaries the earthly city tries to set for it. He recognized (far more clearly than even he gave himself credit for) that Christian convictions, when embodied in a community of life and language, do in fact pose a real and perennial threat to democratic polities in particular, because these beliefs demand that Christians must give their allegiance to Christ and his kingdom in a manner that requires them finally to renounce loyalty to any other sovereign, including a liberal democratic polity.

To a great extent, then, given his preferences, Rorty was right to insist that politics comes first, and only when the matter of our fundamental allegiance is settled do we tailor a philosophy or theology to suit. This of course presents a real problem whenever the church sees itself, as I argue it should, as a political body that relativizes every other social, political, and economic arrangement. Thus its doctrines are not "religious" beliefs that individuals can choose to believe as they engage in the private act of self-creation (a practice that Rorty was willing to allow), but rather serve to articulate the points of convergence, competition, and conflict between its distinctive form of life together and those of all other polities.

In what follows I shall endeavor to show why I, a Christian theologian, am both "for" and "against" the philosophy of Richard Rorty. I am for it in the sense that it brings to light important details of the social arrangements within which the church is required to operate in a liberal democratic society, details that I contend the church cannot in good faith accept, at least not at face value. Ultimately, I part company with Rorty on the question of which politics is basic; however, even that does not end the discussion, but refocuses it on the negotiations that must then ensue between the two cities that occupy the same space, each professing a different faith, pursuing a different hope, and practicing a different love. In the end, the church will be compelled to develop the politics of otherness.

Rorty on Religion and Liberal Democracy

It would be foolhardy to attempt to summarize in a few sentences the life's work of an important scholar such as Richard Rorty. I shall therefore limit myself to his views on the topic of religion as it relates to what was near and dear to his heart: the preservation and progress of democratic institutions and values. On this score he was notorious for his antipathy towards religion in general, and Christianity in particular, which he saw as a key figure in the development of the philosophical foundationalism he fought against for most of his professional life. For example, in an article that first appeared in 1994, he condemned religion as a conversation-stopper, because it fails what he regarded as the only appropriate test for a political proposal in a liberal democracy, which is the ability to gain assent from people who hold radically diverse ideas about the meaning of human life.[2] In an even earlier work he declared that the culture of liberalism, in its ideal state, "would be one which was enlightened, secular, through and through. It would be one in which no trace of divinity remained, either in the form of a divinized world or a divinized self." In such a world women and men would not have any use for the idea that finite, mortal, contingently existing human beings might look for the meaning of their lives in anything other than finite, mortal, contingently existing human beings.[3] And as late as 1998, Rorty affirmed his desire, with Dewey and Whitman, "to separate the fraternity and loving kindness urged by the Christian scriptures from the ideas of supernatural parentage, immortality, and providence, and—most important—sin." He contended that Americans should "take pride in what America might, all by itself and by its own lights, make of itself, rather than in America's obedience to any authority—even the authority of God."[4]

Some may contend, however, that there was a significant change in tone toward the end of his life, particularly in connection to politics and public policy. In an article first published in 2002, Rorty regretted having characterized himself as an atheist in his earlier writings. Instead he wanted to be counted among those who, instead of describing themselves as believing that there is no God, prefer to say that they are "religiously unmusical," a phrase he attributed to the German sociologist Max Weber. "One can be tone-deaf when it comes to religion," he wrote, "just as one can be oblivious to the charms of music." Being religiously unmusical is "no more important, when evaluating a person's intellect or character, than an ability to read fiction or to grasp mathematical relationships or to learn foreign languages." Religion is therefore unobjectionable (as long as it remains private), but it is also inconsequential.

2. Rorty, *Philosophy and Social Hope*, 173.
3. Rorty, *Contingency, Irony, and Solidarity*, 45.
4. Rorty, *Achieving Our Country*, 15–16.

Rorty labeled his revised view anticlericalism, meaning that religion could be tolerated, but only "as long as ecclesiastical institutions do not attempt to rally the faithful behind political proposals."[5]

In the final analysis, however, the change in Rorty's position is minimal at best. He had previously been willing to concede that women and men could develop private moral identities around any number of ideas, including the love of God, as long as they conduct themselves as "loyal citizens of a liberal democratic society."[6] But he was convinced that all who embrace beliefs in such a way that they subordinate every other end to this one dominant end—he cited Friedrich Nietzsche and Ignatius Loyola as examples—should be considered insane, not because their views are unintelligible or erroneous, but simply because there is no way to see them as fellow citizens of a constitutional democracy.[7] Any concession to religion Rorty made in later writings must be assessed in this light, because he continued to insist that religious institutions are dangerous to democratic polities.[8] He saw—rightly, in my opinion—that everything liberal society seeks to catalogue under the category of religion is always threatening to break out of its place of confinement as something strictly individual and private, and assume a corporate, public stance that he regarded as illicit.

Rorty's stance represents a postmodern updating of the popular view of religious freedom in the United States, which he traced back to Thomas Jefferson. According to Rorty, Jefferson believed that all people—theists and atheists alike—shared a moral faculty that rendered beliefs about ultimate matters extraneous to a democratic society, a sentiment famously expressed in his claim that "it does me no injury for my neighbour to say that there are twenty gods, or no god."[9] That said, Rorty acknowledged that Jefferson was unwilling to excise religion completely, allowing that it could be relevant and perhaps even essential to individual perfection. The Jeffersonian compromise was to privatize religion (as John Locke had recommended), such that citizens could be as religious or as irreligious as they wished, provided they were not "fanatical." Fanaticism in this case was defined as the refusal to abandon or

---

5. Rorty and Vattimo, *Future of Religion*, 30–31, 33.
6. Rorty, "Priority," 270.
7. Ibid., 266, 268–69.
8. Rorty and Vattimo, *Future of Religion*, 33.
9. Jefferson, *Notes on the State of Virginia*, Query XVII, 159.

modify individual beliefs about matters of ultimate importance if they entailed public actions that could not be justified to the majority of their fellow-citizens.[10]

Whenever citizens subscribed to religious beliefs that had direct bearing on public matters, but that could not be defended on the basis of beliefs common to all, they could safely be compelled to sacrifice their conscience "on the altar of public expediency." There was no perceived tension in making this request, said Rorty, due to a philosophical theory widely embraced in the aftermath of the Enlightenment that held that "there is a relation between the ahistorical essence of the human soul and moral truth that ensures that free and open discussion will produce 'one right answer' to moral as well as to scientific questions. Such a theory guarantees that a moral belief which cannot be justified to the mass of mankind is 'irrational,' and thus is not really a product of our moral faculty at all."[11]

Since Jefferson's time, however, the confidence that one could clearly distinguish between innate rationality and the effects of acculturation, between the permanent truths of reason and the temporary truths of facts, between religion, myth, and tradition, and something ahistorical, common to all human beings *qua* human, has been thoroughly eroded in philosophical circles. Rorty responded, "The result is to erase the picture of the self common to Greek metaphysics, Christian theology, and Enlightenment rationalism: the picture of an ahistorical natural center, the locus of human dignity, surrounded by an adventitious and inessential periphery." We are compelled to conclude that men and women are historical all the way through.[12]

With the Enlightenment conception of universal reason discredited, and with it the notion that all can agree, at least in principle, which "irrational" proposals should be excluded from the public square, Rorty returned to a view of the body politic that owes more to Thomas Hobbes than to Locke. Unlike his fellow Englishman, Hobbes vested the authority to limit what a person may or may not do, not in a theory about the self or the nature of reason, but in the untrammeled sovereignty of a commonwealth: "The liberty of a subject lieth . . . only in those things which, in regulating their actions, the sovereign hath praetermitted

---

10. Rorty, "Priority," 257.

11. Ibid., 257–58.

12. Ibid., 258.

[passed over]: such as is the liberty to buy, and sell, and otherwise contract with one another; to choose their own abode, their own diet, their own trade of life, and institute [educate] their children as they themselves think fit; and the like."[13] As Rorty put it, liberal democracy simply does not need philosophical justification. The limits to what can be proposed in public are set in this polity "by what *we* can take seriously."[14] Of course, much depends on who is included and excluded by this "we," and who is empowered to make this determination. It is at this point that Rorty's imperialist standpoint comes to the fore. In the end, then, the question of "which politics?" becomes one of "whose empire?"

For and Against Rorty

As I stated earlier, there is a sense in which I agree with Rorty's contention that we must start with politics and then fashion a philosophy to match, though the idea that the practices and institutions of life together are foundational to our understanding of our human existence is not exactly new. Plato and Aristotle said as much over two millennia ago. It is also an insight that is basic to the biblical witness. The ancient Israelites came to know God, not first of all through giving mental assent to an abstract list of divine attributes, but by the fact that, as Rowan Williams puts it, "he is the God of a people who live 'thus-and-not-otherwise' . . . the God of *this* community with its particular, socially distinctive features." God is thus revealed to Israel in the course of wrestling with their distinctive identity as a people, which they do whenever they ask what constitutes it as a polity in its own right.[15]

So the question really is, which politics? Those who consider the nation-state as the only legitimate form of political association will no doubt regard this question as absurd. For these folks politics simply *is* those activities and institutions having to do with the maintenance and operation of the mechanisms of the state. This presumptive definition confers on the state virtually unlimited political sovereignty over

---

13. Hobbes, *Leviathan*, II.xxi.6.

14. Rorty, "Priority," 267. John Milbank is correct when he states that "Hobbes was simply more clear-sighted than later apparently more 'liberal' thinkers like Locke in realizing that a liberal peace requires a single undisputed power, but not necessarily a continued majority consensus, which may not be forthcoming." Milbank, *Theology and Social Theory*, 14.

15. Williams, *On Christian Theology*, 134–35.

a geographically defined space, thus privileging it as the fulcrum of all substantive social change.[16] Underwriting liberal democratic statecraft, more specifically, is the absence of any substantive conception of the common good, which effectively reduces politics to a set of managerial and economic procedures for protecting and promoting individuals' pursuit of self-interest in the marketplace of desire and consumption, while simultaneously striving for a minimal level of peaceful coexistence between individuals and groups.

If liberal statecraft can achieve these ends, and things go at least passably well, with the state's populace remaining relatively docile, then Rorty was correct: it does not need philosophical justification. Should a substantial portion of the population become restless and raise the question of legitimacy in one form or another, however, the potential for fragmentation, dissension, and exclusion comes to the fore. In these circumstances, the state can easily become defensive, and without at least some kind of credible explanation in hand, it becomes more difficult to resist the temptation to respond with the only instrument left at its disposal: coercion.

To his credit, Rorty did not shy away from this conclusion. On the one hand he certainly wished to be "inclusive" and "tolerant" by cultivating what he terms "cultural diversity." He believed that this goal could best be accomplished by giving pride of place to "specialists in particularity" (historians, novelists, ethnographers, and muckraking journalists), who are uniquely able to expand the powers of imagination of those in power, resulting in "their gradual willingness to use the term 'we' to include more and more different sorts of people."[17] (I shall return to this matter of the imagination below.)

On the other hand, he insisted that "bourgeois liberals" who are both connoisseurs of diversity *and* Enlightenment rationalists, and thus continue to believe that there is a metaphysical substrate in which things called "rights" are embedded, forming the basis of a common human nature that takes moral precedence over all merely "cultural" superstructures, must abandon this belief. Clinging to it produces a self-referential paradox that arises whenever liberals wonder whether their preference for this belief is itself anything more than a cultural bias. Their liberalism forces them to label any doubts about human equality a sign of irrational

---

16. Skinner, *Foundations of Modern Political Thought*, 353.
17. Rorty, *Objectivity, Relativism, and Truth*, 207.

bias, yet their advocacy of diversity compels them to acknowledge that most of the world's peoples do not believe in human equality, thus exposing their belief as a Western eccentricity.[18] Rorty said that the source of their error is the distinction they inherited from the Enlightenment between rational judgment, which was deemed both necessary and universal, and cultural bias, which had to do with the contingent and particular. These otherwise good thinkers "who have not yet gone postmodern" should simply say, "So what? We Western liberals *do* believe in it, and so much the better for us." When it comes to cultural diversity, liberals and those whom they wish to include in the "we" of liberal democracy must work out the limits of what can be tolerated on a case-by-case basis, through hunches or conversational compromise.[19]

One of those limits has to do with those who insist that all our ends be subordinated to one dominant end. When addressing the question of what to do with such persons, Rorty replied that while the range of possibilities within a liberal democratic polity is quite extensive, individuals who attempt to raise questions and press for ends that are ultimately incompatible with its basic tendencies have no inherent claim on its citizens. "We heirs of the Enlightenment" must simply view such persons as mad. There is no place for them to participate in the political realm, not because their views are unintelligible, or because they promote a mistaken view of the human self, but simply because "there is no way to see them as fellow citizens of our constitutional democracy, people whose life-plans might, given ingenuity and good will, be fitted in with those of other citizens."[20] The suggestion that there might be another politics would be further evidence of complete and utter insanity.

The way in which Rorty made room as a creature of liberalism for inclusion, diversity, and tolerance thus requires closer scrutiny. He uncritically adopts the concept of culture as the principal category by which liberal society works constructively to differentiate and classify otherness.[21] This concept is not a given, but is a distinctive way of containing and managing difference, strategically positioning it vis-à-vis the

---

18. Ibid.
19. Ibid., 208.
20. Rorty, "Priority," 266.

21. Talal Asad takes issue with the claim that hegemonic power necessarily suppresses difference in favor of unity, or that power always abhors ambiguity: "To secure its unity—to make its own history—dominant power has worked best through differentiating and classifying practices." Asad, *Genealogies of Religion*, 17.

two most dominant powers organizing social space today: the modern nation-state and the global market. Considered in the abstract, such a move is not particularly noteworthy, since throughout history imperial regimes take upon themselves the task of constructing a "world" big enough to encompass all human beings. The poet Virgil, for example, claimed that it was Rome's destiny "to rule Earth's peoples ... to pacify, to impose the rule of law, to spare the conquered [and] battle down the proud."[22] How a society conceives of difference, however, makes all the difference for how it deals with difference.

Bernard McGrane contends that the peoples of Europe (and North America, I would add) have used four broad paradigms to describe and interpret non-European peoples. Up to the sixteenth century, the frame of reference was Christianity, and thus the other was a pagan who inhabited a space that lent itself to demonization, since the only space of salvation was in the body of Christ. During the Enlightenment, the Christian paradigm was supplanted by one that positioned otherness in terms of epistemology, using categories such as ignorance, error, and superstition to account for the difference between the European (who was the exemplar of all things rational, cultured, and civilized) and the non-European.[23] The Enlightenment paradigm eventually gave way as well, replaced in the nineteenth century by one that privileged a certain narration of time as the "scientific" arbiter of difference, arranging it in terms of past and present, stages of development, or the primitive and the advanced.[24]

In modern secular society, says McGrane, people are no longer encouraged to demonize difference as pagan, describe it derisively as primitive and superstitious, or relegate it to earlier steps in the inexorable process of social evolution. Instead the dominant paradigm is "culture." According to McGrane, "We think under the hegemony of the ethnological response to the alienness of the Other; we are, today, contained within an anthropological concept of the Other. Anthropology has become our modern way of seeing the Other as, fundamentally

---

22. Virgil, *Aeneid*, VI.850–53.

23. J. Carter has shown that the fundamental category for dealing with the other in this paradigm involved the ranking of peoples by race, i.e., by skin color. According to Carter, Immanuel Kant labored with his transcendental idealism to connect whiteness and the perfecting of human civilization. J. Carter, *Race*, 82–96.

24. McGrane, *Beyond Anthropology*, ix–x.

and *merely*, culturally different."²⁵ As a result of this development, says Kenneth Surin, difference has been "democratized," such that the non-European other is no longer a relic of another time. The radical democratization of difference permits us to insert the other into "our" present, to transform her or him into "our" contemporary, always of course on "our" terms: "The non-European 'other' is still 'different' of course, but now (s)he is *merely* 'different.'"²⁶ What was once embedded in a distinct polity, where it was part and parcel of an entire way of life—orchestrating the exchanges and relationships that took place within families and clans, villages and towns—is now consigned to the domain of culture. That which made the other truly different no longer exists as part of a living whole, but is now treated as an "artifact" that is preserved in a museum.²⁷

Rorty was content with describing all difference as cultural, that is, as *merely* different. He said quite plainly that moral progress and greater human solidarity could only be accomplished by learning to see all traditional difference (he specifically cited tribe, religion, race, and custom) as unimportant in comparison to our shared capacity for pain and humiliation.²⁸ One does not have to be a proponent of unmerited suffering to realize that this view of difference is a recipe for the disappearance of all historical traditions, again save for their preservation as quaint objects in a museum. For example, Lila Corwin Berman has recently traced the ways that many Jewish intellectuals in America tried to create a public identity around the notion that to be Jewish was fundamentally to belong to an ethnic group. In the end, however, this attempt could not say what was at stake in remaining Jewish.²⁹

Liberalism thus consigns to the concept of culture the field of beliefs and practices that have been disowned. Slavoj Žižek writes, "all those things we practice without really believing in them, without 'taking them seriously'" (or at least, which we should not take seriously). In matters of religion, though many no longer "really believe," they may still follow (some) traditional rituals and mores to show respect for the "lifestyle" of the community to which they belong. As Žižek puts it,

---

25. Ibid., x, my emphasis.
26. Surin, "Certain 'Politics,'" 74, author's emphasis.
27. See Grant, "Research in the Humanities," 97–102.
28. Rorty, *Contingency, Irony, and Solidarity*, 192. Humiliation in particular, wrote Rorty, is that kind of pain that humans do not share with the other animals.
29. Berman, *Speaking of Jews*.

"'I don't really believe in it, it's just part of my culture' effectively seems to be the predominant mode of the disavowed/displaced belief characteristic of our times." What *is* a "cultural lifestyle," he writes, "if not the fact that, although we don't believe in Santa Claus, there is a Christmas tree in every house, and even in public places, every December?" Žižek notes that we do not include science within the ambit of this concept of culture, because we view it as all too real, as something we cannot hold at arm's length, and thus it is not "cultural." Those who pride themselves on being cultured derisively dismiss fundamentalist believers as barbarians, as uncultured, as a threat to culture, because "they dare to *take their beliefs seriously*."[30]

As an exponent of what he called "light-minded aestheticism," Rorty's notions fit neatly into what Stanley Fish labels boutique multiculturalism—a way of treating difference that consists principally of ethnic restaurants, weekend festivals, and high-profile flirtations with the Other that Tom Wolfe once satirized as "radical chic."[31] Boutique multiculturalism does not take seriously the particularity of other traditions because it stipulates that their core convictions and practices be regarded "as icing on a basically homogeneous cake." It sees differences not as basic to who and what human beings are, but as commodities to be consumed, tourist stops to be visited, exotic cuisines to be sampled. Boutique pluralism rejects the force of diversity at precisely the point where it makes the strongest claim on its most committed members, insisting instead that whatever concerns they might have remain private.[32] This form of pluralism may be light-minded, but politically it must be iron-willed.

Fish identifies another version of philosophical pluralism that does attempt to value difference in and for itself. For these strong pluralists, nurturing particularity and diversity through tolerance, not adherence to some purported universal quality such as our metaphysical status as holders of something called "rights," is the first principle of both personal morality and public policy. Unfortunately, says Fish, the time will invariably come for a serious pluralist when a cultural or religious tradition will act in a way that will be judged intolerant by citizens of a liberal democracy: "[T]he distinctiveness that marks it as unique and self-defining will resist the appeal of moderation or incorporation into

---

30. Žižek, *Puppet and the Dwarf*, 7–8.
31. Fish, "Boutique Multiculturalism," 378.
32. Ibid., 378–79, 382.

a larger whole. Confronted with a demand that it surrender its view point or enlarge it to include the practices of its natural enemies—other religions, other races, other genders, other classes—a beleaguered culture will fight back with everything from discriminatory legislation to violence."[33]

By advocating light-mindedness, Rorty avoided the self-referential paradox that plagues serious pluralists, who must either stretch their tolerance to include the intolerance of a group they might personally abhor, or condemn the intolerance, in which case they no longer advocate pluralism at the point where it is most obviously at stake.[34] Rorty thus had no qualms about setting strict limits to what "we" should tolerate. Doing what is necessary to sustain a liberal democratic polity, not tolerance, was his first, nonnegotiable principle. He was not troubled by those who insist that once we give up the Enlightenment project of attaining universal agreement on important issues we shall have declared them mere matters of taste. In his estimation such descriptions perpetuate the erroneous Kantian notion that being rational is a matter of following rules.[35] As for being light-minded, he claimed that the willingness to discard the Nietzschean "spirit of seriousness" has been an important vehicle of moral progress.[36]

Rorty's light-minded "moral progress" comes with a heavy price, however, for it assumes that our primary task as human beings is to create a world that makes suffering and cruelty a thing of the past.[37] We strive to achieve this goal by inventing by our own wits a world of unencumbered freedom where the only limits are those that individuals choose for themselves. Twenty-first-century liberalism has dedicated itself to the creation of a world free of suffering, in part, and most ironically, by a commitment to include every voice in a story of moral progress in which no one should suffer for the actions of anyone else. To this end, it takes special care to invite all the excluded voices to see themselves as characters in a story that denies the reality and significance of sacrifice. The problem is that these excluded voices, when we

33. Ibid., 383.
34. Ibid.
35. Rorty and Vattimo, *Future of Religion*, 31.
36. Rorty, "Priority," 272.
37. I am indebted to Stanley Hauerwas for what follows. See his *In Good Company*, 165–68.

actually listen to them, seem almost always to tell of suffering that only makes sense as tales of sacrifice. Hence we find it necessary, as we tell this story, to relegate these sacrifices to a now superseded past as our specialists in particularity attempt to narrate a common story that no longer is dependent on such sacrifice.

The story that men and women can live without sacrifice by their own wits, at least from now on, creates false memories that instigate more sacrifices that are even more damnable, because these stories prevent us from acknowledging the suffering and death of the past that was offered up as sacrifice. We hope that our condemnation of prejudice, slavery, segregation, and genocide in the past is a sign of our good will and essential righteousness. And so we deceive ourselves by saying that, now that we have acknowledged our guilt about the sweat and blood of past generations offered up as sacrifices to the idols of Enlightenment rationalism and liberal democracy against their wills, we just need to be more inclusive. Though such measures are sincerely implemented, what is often overlooked by the inclusion of these stories within the metanarrative of liberal capitalism is that these excluded peoples become victims all over again, this time by being inscribed without their consent into a history narrated by those who profited either directly or indirectly by their suffering.

Idolatry is the setting of our mind and heart, loyalty and confidence, hopes and fears, on something other than the God disclosed in the incarnation of the Son and the sending of the Spirit on the church. In particular, it is when we become convinced that the present constellation of institutions, events, and persons truthfully exhibits the abiding nature of things, and we have no choice but to act in accordance with it, that idolatry takes it most virulent form as the worship of necessity.[38] To be human is to be constituted in no small measure by the limits that subsist in our relationships with our fellow creatures, and also to be constrained by the fallenness of the world. In this sense, limits are a sign of grace, and to reject them is a particularly virulent form of idolatry. Walter Lowe rightly suggests that the modern rejection of limits paved the way for the ironic "dialectic of Enlightenment" in which our attempts to master the world led to the would-be master's undoing. Quoting Theodor Adorno, Lowe rightly observes that "'the principle of human domination, in becoming

---

38. A phrase I take from Lash, *Believing Three Ways*, 108.

absolute... turned its point against man as the absolute object.' Hence the sense of entrapment, the 'iron cage.'"³⁹

Rorty understood, albeit implicitly, that the language of tolerance ultimately belongs to, and is guarded by, the realm of coercive power,⁴⁰ that those with the means in hand to do so could force others to conform, but will allow them to keep on doing what they are doing, provided they keep to the boundaries set for them. Tolerance is the velvet glove that conceals the fist within the iron cage of a liberal capitalist regime, confining what qualifies as acceptable difference to private choices. In the words of George Grant, "how we eat; how we mate; how we practice ceremonies. Some like pizza, some like steaks; some like girls, some like boys; some like synagogue, some like the mass. But we all do it in churches, motels, restaurants indistinguishable from the Atlantic to the Pacific."⁴¹

Rorty and "Human Nature"

Though he would no doubt have grimaced to hear me say it, Rorty has in actuality posited a *de facto* conception of human nature, albeit one that was not explicitly grounded in a philosophical theory of some sort (though this is somewhat misleading, as I shall argue shortly). What was "natural" is anything that is compatible with, and supportive of those "settled social habits" that create the kind of latitude for choices that are part and parcel of individual self-creation.⁴² The operation that defines what is truly human is thus the optimum exercise of freedom, which, as numerous authors have pointed out, is simply the spontaneous outward movement of the will, unprompted by anything that is either interior or exterior to the agent.⁴³ This conception, which privileges unfettered choice as the paradigm of freedom and not as its most obvious result,⁴⁴ stands in stark contrast to the traditional understanding of

---

39. Lowe, "Prospects," 21. The quote from Adorno only recapitulates an insight of Augustine in the opening lines of *The City of God*: "we must not pass over the earthly city... which, when it seeks mastery, is itself mastered by the lust for mastery [*libido dominandi*]." Augustine, *City of God*, I.Pref.

40. See Carter, *Culture of Disbelief*, 96.

41. Grant, *Technology and Empire*, 26.

42. Rorty, "Priority," 266.

43. See, for example, Murdoch, *The Sovereignty of Good*, 35.

44. Burrell, *Freedom and Creation in Three Traditions*, 92.

the will as rational appetite, ordered by means of the intellect by the objects of its desire.[45]

The origins of this conception of freedom can be traced to medieval nominalism, the fundamental premises of which were mediated to modern and postmodern thought through the writings of Hobbes and Locke (among others), constituting an intellectual tradition to which Rorty was an heir.[46] If one starts with a complex web of tropes and analogies that animates a liberal capitalist polity, and then crafts a philosophy to suit, as Rorty proposed, it is hard to imagine a system of thought other than nominalism that could fit the bill. I would submit that this is not an accident; the rules of the game are set up to ensure this outcome.

Charles Taylor has coined the term "social imaginary" to examine the genealogy of these "rules," which are not really explicit rules, but the tropes and analogies in terms of which the members of a group of people (in this case, the members of a liberal democratic regime) understand themselves and the world in which they live, move, and have their being. This network of images and similes generates a picture of how the world operates, how men and women ought to relate to one another, how they expect things to go on between them and their fellows, "and the deeper normative notions and images that underlie these expectations." This self-understanding involves "a wider grasp of our whole predicament" and thus extends beyond the immediate background assumptions for our particular practices.[47] In short, a social imaginary names the working understanding we have of ourselves and the world we inhabit, a tacit interpretive construal that, as members of a variety of overlapping communities, we just live in, initially without being aware of it as a construal (though once we become aware that we all live within some such construal, typically through the raising of interpretive doubts, we can never go back to our original naiveté).[48]

Taylor speaks about social imaginaries and not social theories in this regard for three reasons. First, he is interested in the way ordinary people "imagine" themselves, their social surroundings, and what constitutes human nature. These matters are typically construed, not in theoretical terms but in images, stories, legends, and rituals. Second,

---

45. See, for example, Aquinas, *Summa Theologica* Ia.IIae. 8.1.
46. See the excellent essay on this topic by D. Stephen Long in this volume.
47. Taylor, *Modern Social Imaginaries*, 23, 25.
48. Taylor, *Secular Age*, 30.

theory is customarily the possession of a small minority, whereas a social imaginary is shared by large groups of people, up to and including a whole society. And third, "the social imaginary is that common understanding which makes possible common practices, and a widely shared sense of legitimacy."[49]

It is important to see that philosophical theories about human nature not only grow out of shared social imaginaries, but also give rise to them. In other words, the relationship between social imaginaries and philosophical theories is often reciprocating. Taylor contends that what starts off as a theory held by a few may over time infiltrate the social imaginary, first, of intellectuals, then of a class of social elites, and eventually of a whole society. A case in point is the social transformation that has taken place over the last five centuries in Europe and North America. Taylor stresses the role that social imaginaries have played when he notes that in the year 1500 it was virtually impossible not to believe in God, while in 2000 many find it not only easy, but in some ways inescapable.[50]

That Rorty presupposed something like a social imaginary throughout his writings is readily apparent. As I noted above, he asserted that liberalism had given up on the idea that theology and philosophy would supply general rules for resolving wrenching social issues, and looked instead to writers and writings that specialize in "particularity." He did acknowledge, albeit reluctantly, that Enlightenment rationalism was essential to the beginnings of liberal democracy,[51] but now that this polity has gotten out of its diapers, so to speak, he then allowed it no continuing role for it as a political practice. Ironically, the sort of theorizing that gave birth to democratic societies is now considered an impediment to their preservation and progress. He maintained that liberal social theory does quite well without a model of the human self, for example. All that is necessary is "common sense and social science, areas of discourse in which the term 'the self' rarely occurs."[52]

It is, of course, simply false to assert that simply because a term does not often appear in a discourse, its influence is also missing. The absence of a term in the working vocabulary of a social group can just as

---

49. Ibid., 172.
50. Ibid., 25, 172.
51. Rorty, *Contingency, Irony, and Solidarity*, 44.
52. Rorty, "Priority," 270.

easily indicate an implicit understanding and acceptance of what it denotes. Words are coined and used to emphasize the striking, the exceptional, the novel, or the disputed, not the ordinary. This is certainly the state of affairs in liberal social theory, where a highly developed sense of the self—enthroned in the concept of the individual—is deeply embedded in what passes for common sense and social science.[53] What Rorty ascribed to the promptings of common sense and the deliverances of social science has the earmarks of such a social imaginary around which he placed brackets to protect it from any and all dissent.

The only way one could accept Rorty's proscriptions about theory at face value would be to attribute a strange, almost bizarre Fukuyama-like quality to the social imaginary of liberal democracy, confessing (no other word will do) that we have finally arrived at the end of history (not as an act of some transcendent reality, but as artifact of human design), and that with the establishment of the requisite institutions and procedures there is no longer any need for careful reflection on the nature of political discourse and practice.[54] Not only does this peculiar confession lack credibility, it perpetuates the alchemical fantasy of liberalism, the illusion that process can transform itself into substance.[55] What Taylor understands, but which Rorty did not seem willing to entertain, is the possibility that while a philosophical theory about the nature of humankind or political associations may not pass muster in a postmodern academic seminar, it may nonetheless perform vital and irreplaceable work in society.

Theories helped institute the social imaginary of liberal democracy and now may be needed to sustain it, reinvigorating a shared sense of the range of expectations they could make of each other as they participate in the common practices that make up social life. Though Taylor does not put it this way, one could reasonably argue from what he has said that the alchemical fantasy of liberalism is just that, a fantasy, and that without regular theoretical renewal, liberalism's social imaginary will begin to wilt and then collapse altogether. Though it may not "need" philosophical justification or conceptual foundations, it appears that liberal democracy does need this sort of lived understanding, an important

---

53. See in this regard Milbank, *Theology and Social Theory*, 7–144.
54. Fukuyama, *End of History*.
55. Mensch and Freeman, *Politics of Virtue*, 5.

source of which were the philosophical theories of the sixteenth through twentieth centuries.

If by "politics" we mean something like the art of identifying and achieving the common good (for which we need some understanding of the nature of that good), and by "philosophy" the shared wisdom about what is good and best, which is incorporated in the stories, rites, and convictions that animate a people (and which cannot be long sustained without the practices and institutions of a political commonwealth), I would contend against Rorty that it is impossible to distinguish between them as neatly as he tried to do. Philosophy, as a living discourse cultivated within and by a people about the goods they will pursue as well as the means by which they will pursue them, may indeed be a crucial political practice. There is little doubt that without Grotius, Lipsius, Hobbes, Descartes, Locke, Kant, Mills, and others, there would be no liberal democratic polity for which one could now craft a philosophy to suit. It would be ironic if Rorty's antitheoretical crusade becomes a contributing factor in the future to the demise of the very sort of society he cherished.

Refusing Mere Difference

And so once again we are back to the question of which politics, and it is at this point that I am mostly against Rorty. He said that "what counts as rational or as fanatical is relative to the group to which we think it necessary to justify ourselves—to the body of shared belief that determines the reference of the word 'we.'"[56] Considered in the abstract, that sounds right; however, the only "we" that counts in a liberal democracy, at least in Rorty's mind, is that which has been formed in and around the imagined community called the liberal nation-state.[57] All others need not apply, but must resign themselves to operating as a "cultural" or "religious"

---

56. Rorty, "Priority," 259.

57. The social imaginary of liberal democracy both presupposes and projects a sense of time in which every individual is linked with all those living and acting simultaneously within boundaries of a particular nation-state, even though none will ever know more than a handful of them over the course of his or her life. This story seeks to cultivate the picture of a stable community moving perpetually out of a heroic past (whether real or mythic), through the difficulties of the present, and into an unbounded future. See Anderson, *Imagined Communities*, 22–24, and Cavanaugh, *Torture*, 222–23.

institution within the confines set for such entities by the state, governed by the axiom of light-mindedness.

But what if a group refuses to play by these rules, and acts as a political association in its own right? To make sense of this question, we need to recover a conception of politics that predates its reduction to statecraft. In both Scripture and Greek and Roman antiquity, and extending through the Middle Ages, politics was first of all the art of human community, the end of which was living well. Political institutions were a means to this end, sustaining and promoting those practices and dispositions that directed its members toward that highest good.[58] At issue in such communities, then, were the shared practices, habits, and relationships that enabled women and men to flourish in accordance with their highest good. Truth be told, these communities regularly fell far short of this lofty goal, yet such were the working assumptions that informed them. (Truth be told, what passes for politics in the modern world just as regularly falls short of its ambitions.)

Historically, Jews have seldom seen their association as strictly "a community of faith," a concept that in modern discourse automatically defines it as "religious" and "cultural," and therefore nonpolitical. When diaspora Jews in the Hellenistic and Roman eras attended to the crucial matters of assimilation and identity, the classical tradition of the *polis* provided them with the terminology for discussing both their identity and their distinctiveness. Wayne Meeks writes, "Their organized *politeuma* (or whatever their immigrants' association might be called in a local instance) was for them an alternative city. Israel, not Alexandria or Antioch, was their ultimate moral reference point, and Israel was both the local embodiment of Moses' ideal *polis* and the company of God's people that transcended local boundaries and the boundaries of time."[59] More recently, the supposition that the Jewish community should think of itself as a principally religious body is disputed by several noteworthy voices. David Novak, for example, asks, "Is not our relationship with . . . God a covenant? And is not a covenant a political reality? And could there be any polity not governed by law?"[60]

---

58. See Aristotle, *Politics*, III.9, and Cicero, *De Re Publica*, I.25.39.

59. Meeks, *Origins of Christian Morality*, 44.

60. Novak, "Avoiding Charges of Legalism," 279; cf. Wyschogrod, "Theology of Jewish Unity."

As the sibling of rabbinic Judaism, the early church understood itself in similar terms. Indeed, George Lindbeck says that the early Christian movement is unintelligible apart from a politics and polity that were "more Jewish than anything else."[61] The Romans regarded this movement as self-righteous and fanatical, worshippers of a capricious deity, atheists, the enemy of humankind and of a just social order. Rome classified this new movement as a political society primarily because its adherents, similar to Jews, "regarded it as fundamental that their allegiance to Christ cut across any allegiance to Caesar." As a result, says N. T. Wright, "they were seen not just as a religious grouping, but one whose religion made them a subversive presence within the wider Roman society."[62] Christians did not give their allegiance to any political entity that belonged to this world, because they saw themselves as members of a commonwealth with its own peculiar polity. Within this city all authority in heaven and on earth had been transferred to the jurisdiction of the only true King. The body of Christ was, in short, "an 'outpost of heaven' on earth."[63]

From the point of view of Rome (and of someone like Richard Rorty, as I have been arguing), all of this could not help but appear seditious. Georges Florovsky notes that Rome viewed itself as "*the City*, a permanent and 'eternal' City, *Urbs aeterna*, and an ultimate City also. In a sense, it claimed for itself an 'eschatological dimension.' It posed as an ultimate solution of the human problem." Essentially, Rome claimed to embody the final expression of "Humanity." The Roman commonwealth was in effect a politico-ecclesiastical institution that could neither admit separation of competence and authority, nor tolerate division of loyalty or allegiance. The empire claimed to be omnicompetent, and the allegiance of its subjects had to be complete and unconditional. "The Church was a challenge to the Empire," writes Florovsky, "and the Empire was a stumbling block for the Christians."[64]

The early church thus constituted what Václav Havel calls a parallel *polis*, a distinct community that operated within the dominant structures of the empire.[65] It was this fact, says Robert Wilken, that led

61. Lindbeck, "The Church," 193, 190.
62. Wright, *Christian Origins*, 350.
63. Florovsky, "Empire and Desert," 133–34.
64. Ibid., 135, 137.
65. Havel, "Power of the Powerless," 101.

Roman authorities to label Christianity as a seditious and revolutionary movement: "The life and teachings of Jesus led to the formation of a new community of people called 'the church.' Christianity had begun to look like a separate people or nation, but without its own land or traditions to legitimate its unusual customs." The Christian community was suspect precisely because "it created a social group that promoted its own laws and its own patterns of behavior."[66] These Christians refused to play by the rules of the game, insisting with unparalleled audacity (and from a Roman viewpoint, utter absurdity) that the significance of every movement of history and the reasonableness of every assumption of how human beings should relate to each other and the world of which they are inextricably a part, could be truthfully assessed only in connection with the brief but intense flurry of events that swirled around one Jewish man and the motley band of followers he gathered around him.

Of course, many would no doubt argue that this conception of politics is a relic of a bygone era, but should anyone, much less Christians, consider such pronouncements as anything other than a self-legitimating promotion of what are by Rorty's own admission contingent social structures? What would be the effects in the twenty-first century of thinking of the church as a political association in its own right, one that can to some degree distinguish itself from the liberal nation-state, but also cultivate the skills needed to interact with it? The latter question is particularly crucial, because like everyone else, Christians have no choice but to "do business" in some manner and to some extent with the institutions of state and market, for we must eat and drink, make clothing, find or build shelter, till the land and fashion instruments, marry and give in marriage, and raise children and bury parents. Together with our non-Christian neighbors, we must obtain the material goods necessary to life, while at the same time refusing to abide by the *pax americana* whenever it conflicts with our worship of the triune God.

What is needed, then, is a type of politics according to its ancient definition, only now it must be defined as the art of human community as practiced by those who, in the words of Dietrich Bonhoeffer, have been caught up in the messianic event of Jesus Christ.[67] A primary aim of this messianic politics is the cultivation of the intellect so that we may discern the wisest ways to obtain and use the goods necessary to

---

66. Wilken, *Christians as the Romans Saw Them*, 118–19.
67. Bonhoeffer, *Letters and Papers from Prison*, 480.

mortal life. This is where the notion of "art" comes into the picture, for as Aristotle reminds us, it is a mode of activity having to do with those things that can be other than they are: "All art is concerned with the realm of coming-to-be, i.e., with contriving and studying how something which is capable both of being and of not being may come into existence, a thing whose starting point or source is in the producer and not in the thing produced."[68] There is also an aesthetic sense and sensibility at work here, because the act of the intellect in the process of discerning the use of goods involves a shared judgment about what is fitting for those called to participate in the life and work of the crucified and risen Christ.

Though Christians must cooperate with others in liberal capitalism in the pursuit of these goods, we do have a choice about the *manner* of their use, which is predicated on prudential judgments regarding what is "natural" for human beings. Bonhoeffer configures this notion as a mediating concept between the created as such, in order to take into account the fallenness of humankind, and the sinful, in order to include the created as that which God declares to be very good. By entering into natural life and its pursuit of the goods necessary for human life, Christ transforms it into the realm of the penultimate, that which is directed toward the ultimate, which for Bonhoeffer is the justification of all things in the messianic reign of God. The concept of the natural designates an element of independence and self-development for the created as such, with a relative freedom appropriate to natural life. Within this freedom, however, "there is a difference between its right use and its misuse, and this is the difference between the natural and the unnatural; therefore there is a relative openness and a relative closedness for Christ." The natural designates that which is directed towards the coming of Christ, while the unnatural is that which has closed itself off against Christ's coming.[69]

The formal determination of the natural is provided by God's intention to preserve the world and direct it towards Christ; thus, what is natural can only be discerned in relation to Christ. Materially it is the form of preserved life itself, embracing the whole of creation. Reason belongs to the material dimension of the natural as the source of knowledge of itself. It is not a divine principle that can elevate human beings

---

68. Aristotle, *Nicomachean Ethics*, VI.4.
69. Bonhoeffer, *Ethics*, 173–74.

above the natural to the supernatural, but is itself a part of creation that has been graciously preserved by God, participating wholly in the natural. Its function is to "take in" (*vernehmen*) as a unity that which is whole and universal in reality. The natural and reason are thus correlated with each other, the former as the form of being of the preserved life, the latter as the form of its awareness. Reason thus shares fully in the effects of the fall, perceiving "only what is given in the fallen world, and, indeed, exclusively according to its content."[70]

Such talk for Rorty, in which all ends are ordered to one transcendent good, would surely have been written off as a sign of madness. Though he might have wished otherwise, the conversation cannot stop there. The question then becomes, what happens now? Ironically, in the future, Christians may well find themselves in the social position Jews occupied for much of the time of Christendom, that is, in the role of the alien other within. Only now, instead of puzzling about the *Judenfrage*, the Jewish question, the problem to be dealt with by Rorty's heirs will be the *Christenfrage* (or better yet, the two will merge into one difficulty). Who says that God does not have a sense of humor? *Providentia dei, confusione hominum.*[71]

---

70. Ibid., 174–75.
71. God's providence, human confusion.

Part II

Moral Dispositions and Religious Belief

CHAPTER FIVE

What the Apostles Will Let Us Get Away with Saying

Plantinga and Rorty on the Social Establishment of Religious Belief

KEITH STARKENBURG

Since the publication of Richard Rorty's *Philosophy and the Mirror of Nature*, Alvin Plantinga has often engaged some of Rorty's claims about truth and justification as the offerings of a philosophical gadfly.[1] In particular, Plantinga has summarized Rorty as saying that "truth is what our peers will let us get away with saying."[2] Rorty often made this claim in various ways, and Plantinga is not alone in recognizing this as provocative. Indeed, a different summary of Rorty's claim was included in *The New York Times* obituary for Rorty.[3] In *Warranted Christian Belief*,

---

1. This essay was made possible by an Interim Research Grant provided by Trinity Christian College in January 2010.

2. Plantinga, *Warranted Christian Belief*, 439. This is a summary of the following passage from Rorty: "Shall we take 'S knows that p' (or 'S knows noninferentially that p,' or 'S believes incorrigibly that p,' or 'S's knowledge that p is certain') as a remark about the status of S's reports among his peers, or shall we take it as a remark about the relation between subject and object, between nature and its mirror? . . . The second alternative leads to "ontological" explanations of the relations between minds and meanings . . . The aim of all such explanations is to make truth something more than what Dewey called 'warranted assertability': more than what our peers will, *ceteris paribus*, let us get away with saying." Rorty, *Philosophy and the Mirror of Nature*, 175-76. Hereafter, I will refer to *Warranted Christian Belief* as *WCB* and *Philosophy and the Mirror of Nature* as *PMN*.

3. Cohen, "Richard Rorty, Philosopher, Dies at 75."

a work that culminates Plantinga's work in religious epistemology in the last forty years and completes his trilogy on warrant, Plantinga engages Rorty's claim as a representative of social, theological constructivism. For Plantinga, the claim that human beings construct the justification and truth of their beliefs presents a kind of possible defeater of the belief in God. My thesis about this relationship between Plantinga and Rorty is twofold. First, I argue that the challenge of Rorty's work is more profitably approached as an implicit theological query about the role of community in the formation of religious beliefs and as a question about the purpose of Plantinga's work in religious epistemology. Second, I argue that Plantinga can suitably respond to these challenges by making two important modifications to his epistemological work.

Plantinga's Theory of Warrant and Christian Belief

As mentioned earlier, Plantinga's work in *WCB* is particularly important because of its role within Plantinga's corpus. In Plantinga's work preceding the *Warrant* series, he defends the idea that belief in God is as rational as other kinds of beliefs (and not as irrational, as it is with Rorty), such as incorrigible memory beliefs or beliefs arising from sense perception.[4] In other words, belief in God is properly basic; belief in God can lie within the foundations of human knowledge. In this earlier work, Plantinga provided a number of arguments against classical foundationalism, but he also often implied commitment to some form of foundationalism. In the *Warrant* series, Plantinga explicitly commits himself to what he calls "Reidian foundationalism." Plantinga agrees with the foundationalist claim that a proposition has warrant because it gets warrant from another proposition upon which it depends or because it is "properly basic" (i.e., it is not dependent on other propositions for its warrant).[5] Plantinga, however, differs from classical foundationalism because he does not think that all beliefs, basic or dependent, "are formed on the basis of evidence."[6] Plantinga argues that this claim is self-referentially incoherent and that lots of ordinary, properly basic

---

4. See, for instance, the series of articles in *The Reformed Journal* in 1981–1982: Plantinga, "On Reformed Epistemology," 13–19; Plantinga, "Reformed Epistemology Again," 7–8; Van Hook, "Knowledge, Belief, and Reformed Epistemology," 12–15. Perhaps the best early statement is Plantinga, "Is Belief in God Properly Basic?," 41–51.

5. Plantinga, *Warrant and Proper Function*, 184.

6. Ibid., 185.

beliefs are disqualified as properly basic if this criterion obtains. For instance, the justification for our beliefs about the makeup of our breakfast does not arise simply from the evidential experience of remembering our breakfast experience. When we are warranted in taking it as true that we had such-and-such a thing for breakfast, the warrant for the belief is related to whether it actually happened. When I judge that "I had eggs," I am not saying that I am having the experience of remembering that I had eggs. I am saying that I had eggs.[7] It was not until *WCB*, however, that Plantinga provided a wider set of epistemological assumptions and arguments that support those earlier claims about the rationality or proper basicality of religious belief. In other words, in the trilogy of books that *WCB* completes, Plantinga displays and argues for a full-blown epistemological model. *WCB* completes the series because it is there that Plantinga applies his epistemological model to belief in God and uniquely Christian beliefs.

Plantinga's basic thesis in *WCB* has two parts. First, he argues that objections to the rationality of Christian belief are unsuccessful. For Plantinga, these objections to Christian beliefs come in two forms. First, some objectors attempt to separate the question of the rationality of Christian beliefs from the truth of Christian belief. In other words, they say that while Christianity might be true, it is simply not rational to believe Christian beliefs. All of these objectors, according to Plantinga, offer implausible objections. Second, other objectors, notably Marx and Freud, tie their objections to the truth of Christianity. For instance, according to Plantinga, Freud thinks that "theistic belief is produced by cognitive faculties that are functioning properly, but the process that produces it—wishful thinking—does not have the production of true belief as its purpose; it is aimed, instead, at something like enabling us to carry on in the grim and threatening world in which we find ourselves."[8] For Plantinga, Freud's idea that religion arises from wish fulfillment has no evidentiary support, and, even if it were true, Freud never showed that wish fulfillment mechanisms cannot produce true beliefs about God. While Marx and Freud are quickly dispatched by Plantinga, they are chosen because they present claims that clash the most with Plantinga's project, which will be discussed later.

---

7. Plantinga, "Is Belief in God Properly Basic?," 44–45.
8. Plantinga, *WCB*, 161.

The heart of Plantinga's argument in *WCB* is that there is a certain epistemological process—what he calls the "Extended Aquinas/Calvin model" (it is found in Aquinas and Calvin and is extended to apply to Christian belief)—that provides "a way in which Christian belief can have warrant in the basic way and . . . (a) this model is possible, both logically and epistemically; (b) given the truth of Christian belief, there are no philosophical objections to this model's also being not merely possible but true and (c) if Christian belief is indeed true, then very probably it does have warrant, and has it in some way similar to the extended A/C model."[9] In other words, the guts of Plantinga's positive argument for his claim that it is possible for Christian belief to have warrant is his presentation of this epistemological model. As the above quote intimates, part of what Plantinga argues is that the question of the rationality of Christian belief can be subdivided into three questions/objections: (1) Is Christianity justified? (2) Is Christianity rational? (3) Is Christianity warranted? Plantinga associates justification with classical foundationalism, and rehearses his old arguments against classical foundationalism—it is self-referentially incoherent and makes most of the beliefs we take to be true to be unjustified (such as memory beliefs). The question of rationality is generally a catch-all category without much content, other than William Alston's proposals in *Perceiving God*. In other words, the real challenge before him is not whether Christianity is justified or rational. Those challenges are quickly defeated if they are tied to classical foundationalism, or those challenges are easily satisfied once they are sufficiently stripped of classical foundationalism.

For Plantinga, the real question—the real *de jure* question regarding Christian belief—is whether Christian belief is warranted. What is warrant? Plantinga's theory of warrant is as follows: "a belief has warrant for a person S only if that belief is produced in S by cognitive faculties functioning properly in a cognitive environment that is appropriate for S's kind of cognitive faculties, according to a design plan that is successfully aimed at truth."[10] Again, note that Plantinga does not claim to demonstrate the truth of this account of warrant. He is merely claiming that if Christian belief is warranted, it is warranted because of what this model or some similar model describes. That is, he attempts to show the epistemic possibility of this model and that there are no viable

9. Ibid., 350.
10. Ibid., 156.

objections to it. More particularly, *Christian* belief is warranted because there is a process in which God reveals the great truths of salvation through Scripture and human beings receive those revelations through the internal work of the Holy Spirit.[11] If this model is true, when human beings have Christian beliefs that are produced by this process, those beliefs are warranted. Christian beliefs are warranted when they are produced by this process, if this process is functioning properly for human beings within a compatible environment, according to the divine design plan that is aimed at truth.

How Plantinga Does Interact with Rorty's Epistemology and How Plantinga Should Interact with Rorty's Epistemology

How is Rorty connected to this project? For Plantinga, Rorty presents a potential defeater for the warrant of Christian belief. Plantinga notes that it is possible that Christian belief is warranted "in the basic way . . . but the warrant in question is defeated."[12] Formally, Plantinga delineates defeaters such that "you have a defeater for one of your beliefs B just if you acquire another belief D such that, given that you hold that belief, the rational response is to reject B (or hold it less firmly)."[13] For example, the belief that the earth is flat had warrant for many people in the past, and Plantinga points out that the warrant for that belief has now been defeated by a wide array of evidence.[14] For Plantinga, Rorty's claim that truth is what your peers will let you get away with saying presents a possible defeater for Christian belief. As Plantinga notes, if this were true, it would "make the truth about God . . . dependent on what we do or think," but, as he says, "This is clearly incompatible with Christian views about God, according to which God is not dependent on anything at all."[15] Plantinga claims to have found Rorty's best attempt at an argument for the claim in Rorty's *Contingency, Irony, and Solidarity*. Rorty argues that truth cannot "exist independent of the human mind" because truth applies to sentences made by human beings.[16] Plantinga's

11. Ibid., chs. 7–8.
12. Plantinga, *WCB*, 352.
13. Ibid., 366.
14. Ibid., 352–53.
15. Ibid., 433.
16. Rorty, *Contingency, Irony, and Solidarity*, 5; cited in Plantinga, *WCB*, 434.

favorite way of arguing against Rorty's claim about truth is through a particularly striking *reductio ad absurdum* argument. If Rorty is right, according to Plantinga, then one way to solve problems such as AIDS or to deal with the suffering imposed by rulers such as Pol Pot is to convince your peers to let you get away with saying such things simply do not happen.[17] Plantinga also engages Rorty's so-called best argument for this claim by arguing that we make many sentences that refer to something other than those very sentences. For instance, when we say, "There once were dinosaurs," our sentence is made true not by its very creation but because there once were dinosaurs.[18]

This way of arguing with Rorty is common in Plantinga's work. Plantinga shows the ridiculous logical implications of Rorty's claim, or its inability to achieve its goal. Much could be said about what is lacking in Plantinga's approach. First, in a joint interview of sorts with Plantinga and Nicholas Wolterstorff, Rorty made plain that he was not offering a definition of truth. As Rorty said, "I do not think that you can define 'truth,' either as what your peers will let you get away with, or as correspondence with the intrinsic nature of reality or anything else. 'True,' like the word 'good,' is a primitive predicate, a transcendental term which does not lend itself to definition."[19] Rorty was not defining truth; he was talking about how the term describes how human beings act. Rorty's claim here is about what *counts* as truth. In practice, truth is a word that describes what happens when our peers let us get away with saying something. Human beings approbate as truthful what they will no longer challenge as rational. Properly speaking, that point is separable from the definition of truth. Rorty is doing social psychology of a sort; he is not offering a theory of truth. Second, on a related point, when Rorty does seem to be using the phrase "what your peers will let you get away with saying" as a descriptor of a theory, he seems to be offering a theory, not of truth, but of justification. For instance, he writes, "Truth is, to be sure, an absolute notion . . . 'true for me but not for you' and 'true in my culture but not in yours' are weird, pointless locutions . . . granted that 'true' is an absolute term, its condition of application will always be relative. For there is no such thing as belief justified *sans phrase*—justified once and for all—for the same reason that there is no such thing as a

17. Plantinga, *WCB*, 429–30.
18. Ibid., 435.
19. Louthan, "On Religion," 177–83.

belief that can be known, once and for all, to be indubitable."[20] In other words, justification is relative to a point in history, to points of interest, experience, and location. Justification is just what your peers will let you get away with saying. In the end, Plantinga has a point to make about the word "truth"—it tends to be used by its speakers as that which corresponds to reality—but he mistakenly regards Rorty's flat refusal to create a theory of truth. It is not that Rorty is rejecting a correspondence theory per se; he is rejecting all theories of truth.

If we interpret Rorty in this way, it helps clear the way for a deeper confrontation between him and Plantinga, a confrontation that would benefit Plantinga's work. At the center of Rorty's work is the contention that "we understand knowledge when we understand the social justification of belief, and thus have no need to view it as accuracy of representation."[21] In other words, Rorty holds to a social practice coherentism that makes representational theories of belief and correspondence theories of truth unnecessary.[22] For example, he writes, ". . . we would do well to abandon the notion of certain values ('rationality,' 'disinterestedness') floating free of the educational and institutional patterns of the day. We can just say that Galileo was creating the notion of 'scientific values' as he went along, that it was a splendid thing that he did so, and that the question of whether he was 'rational' in doing so is out of place."[23] Rorty uses whatever arguments or theorists he can find to undercut other theories of justification. For example, he uses Quine and Sellars to undercut the analytic-synthetic/necessary-contingent distinctions made in modern philosophy; however, he also often acknowledges that a full-blown argument in support of coherentism is difficult to make.[24] Thus, Rorty's arguments proceed along the lines of answering objections and modifying or repairing the works of others such as Quine and Sellars. Perhaps the most persuasive argument in favor of his social coherentism is the work of Thomas Kuhn, who, in Rorty's words, argues that "there is no commensurability between groups of scientists who have different paradigms of a successful explanation, or who do not share

20. Rorty, *Truth and Progress*, 2.
21. Rorty, *PMN*, 170.
22. Rorty also likes to point out that the issue is then about desirability.
23. Rorty, *PMN*, 170.
24. As an example, I refer to his "Is Truth a Goal of Inquiry?" in *Truth and Progress*, 19–42.

the same disciplinary matrix."[25] This led Rorty to utter another famous rhetorical question: "What could show that the Bellarmine-Galileo issue 'differs in kind' from the issue between, say, Kerensky and Lenin, or that between the Royal Academy (circa 1910) and Bloomsbury?"[26] Rorty's central contention is a commitment to a radical historicism. The justification of beliefs has little to do with comparing beliefs to a universal standard of rationality because the standards of rationality have to do with the historical conditions of the particular beliefs. That claim can be argued as part of a linguistic turn (à la Wittgenstein and Sellars) or as implication of the history of science (Kuhn). Either way, Rorty's questions for anyone working in epistemology are: How and where did this belief arise? What made it believable, if the "data" can be explained in any of a number of competing paradigms? What benefits does it offer, and for whom?

The First Form of Rorty's Challenge for Plantinga and How Plantinga's Work Should Be Reformed

Given these questions, Rorty's first central challenge has to do with whether Plantinga sufficiently acknowledges social causation within religious belief in general and Christian belief in particular. It is fair to say that Plantinga's epistemology does not deal effectively with social causation. Note how he describes the workings of his epistemological model, as it is relevant to Christian belief:

> What is really involved, in a believer's coming to accept the great things of the gospel . . . are three things: Scripture (the divine teaching), the internal invitation or instigation of the Holy Spirit, and faith, the human belief that results . . . We read Scripture, or something presenting scriptural teaching, or hear the Gospel preached, or are told of it by parents . . . or in some other way encounter a proclamation of the Word . . . What one hears or reads seems clearly and obviously true and (at any rate in paradigm cases) seems also to be something the Lord is intending to teach . . . there is the reading or hearing, and then there is the belief or conviction that what one reads or hears is true and a teaching of the Lord. According to this model, this conviction comes by way of the activity of the Holy Spirit . . . it is the instigation of

25. Rorty, *PMN*, 323.
26. Ibid., 331.

the Holy Spirit, on this model, that gets us to see and believe that the propositions proposed for our beliefs in Scripture really are a word from the Lord.[27]

On Plantinga's account, Scripture, or one's presentation of Scripture, is offered to someone, and the recipient comes to have faith because of the internal work of the Holy Spirit. Plantinga often mentions that scriptural teaching is presented by human beings to other human beings and that Scripture has human authors, but when those agents occur in his narrative, they play the role of occasions for the "teaching of the Lord." In other words, for Plantinga, the social context of one's belief formation is incidental. Human beings do not come to faith because they receive that faith from other human beings; they come to faith because the Holy Spirit creates that faith within them.

Indeed, what is interesting is how Plantinga clearly distinguishes this immediate testimony of the Holy Spirit from other normal, ordinary, natural means of belief in God. For Plantinga, the ordinary means of belief in God is the "*sensus divinitatis*." Plantinga describes the *sensus divinitatis* as "a disposition or set of dispositions to form theistic beliefs in various circumstances, in response to the sorts of conditions or stimuli that trigger the working of this sense of divinity."[28] For example, one climbs to thirteen thousand feet and one's awe becomes an occasion for belief in God (or the strengthening of one's belief). Plantinga goes on to describe the *sensus divinitatis* as "part of our original cognitive equipment, part of the fundamental epistemic establishment with which we have been created by God" which "would no doubt have been part of our epistemic establishment even if humanity had not fallen into sin."[29] In other words, all human beings have this sense; it is as universal and as normal as (perhaps more normal than) sense perception and memory, among other things. The *sensus divinitatis*, were it not for the disordering of human life (i.e., sin), would allow human beings to have beliefs about God and to know God. Yet, as Plantinga says, "the *sensus divinitatis* has been damaged and deformed; because of the fall, we no longer know God in the same natural and unproblematic way in which we know each other and the world around us."[30] In other words,

---

27. Plantinga, WCB, 250–52.
28. Ibid., 173
29. Ibid., 180.
30. Plantinga, WCB, 205.

knowledge of God is a matter of course for human beings, unless they somehow suppress that knowledge. Human beings have a God belief mechanism, which is triggered by the creation. This mechanism can be ignored, suppressed, and misdirected (and universally is, on Plantinga's account), but it is the normal state of affairs for human beings.

Thus, in response to sin, human beings require the internal testimony of the Holy Spirit. As Plantinga writes, "presumably it would not have taken place had there been no sin."[31] The internal testimony of the Holy Spirit "is a belief-producing process, all right, but one that is very much out of the ordinary. It is not part of our original noetic equipment (not part of our constitution as we came from the hand of the Maker)."[32] The internal testimony of the Holy Spirit produces Christian beliefs, and these beliefs "do not come to the Christian just by way of memory, perception, reason, testimony, the *sensus divinitatis*, or any other of the cognitive faculties with which we human beings were originally created; they come instead by way of the work of the Holy Spirit . . . these beliefs don't come just by way of the normal operation of our natural faculties; they are a supernatural gift."[33] For Plantinga, the internal testimony of the Holy Spirit is required because it does what the *sensus divinitatis* is no longer capable of performing, given human sin. The internal testimony of the Holy Spirit produces belief in God as it also produces particularly Christian beliefs. The internal testimony of the Holy Spirit is extraordinary because it overcomes the problems in the ordinary, run-of-the-mill human epistemic commitment and because it involves an additional layer of immediacy. It is extraordinary because the Holy Spirit becomes an immediate cause, as immediate a cause as other epistemic faculties, such as sense perception, memory, and the *sensus divinitatis*.

What is Rorty's challenge to Plantinga in all of this? The basic problem is that social identity and practice are entirely separable from belief in God. Plantinga does mention that human beings learn their beliefs from other people; but social practice, training, and formation are simply not constitutive of his epistemological model for either the *sensus divinitatis* or the internal testimony of the Holy Spirit. I am not saying that Plantinga separates social identity and practice from belief

---

31. Ibid., 180.
32. Ibid.
33. Ibid., 245.

in God; only that, given his model, they *can be separated*. As Plantinga mentioned above, one can view the horizon and use that experience as an occasion for belief in God. For the normal operations of that mechanism, no community is required. It might be that others also have that experience, but that fact is simply not relevant to whether another individual has this working mechanism. Belief in God and knowledge of God are entirely separable from social practice.

At times, it might seem that Plantinga's *sensus divinitatis* and internal testimony of the Holy Spirit are perfectly capable of dealing with social causation. Indeed, when he describes how the *sensus divinitatis* is distorted, he writes, "We human beings are deeply communal; we learn from our parents, teachers, peers, and others, both by imitation and by precept. We acquire beliefs in this way, but just as important . . . we acquire attitudes and affections, loves and hates. Because of our social nature, sin and its effects can be like a contagion that spreads from one to another . . . Original sin . . . is a cognitive limitation that first of all prevents its victim from proper knowledge of God."[34] Essentially, our sense of divinity breaks down—does not produce belief in God—insofar as we fail to teach and learn by imitation and precept. While Plantinga says this, it is difficult to know how our "social nature" makes possible the corruption of the built-in mechanisms that individual human beings have. Plantinga will often say that we do not choose our beliefs in God; they are "occasioned" by certain events as triggers.[35] How could social relationships affect something like that? On analogy, social relationships cannot remove sense perception or memory, since those cognitive faculties are part of normal epistemic equipment. If the *sensus divinitatis* is as much a part of the human epistemic equipment as sense perception is, for example, then we would expect, on his claim, that sense perception or knowledge of other people can be corrupted as neatly and as universally by social practice. Plantinga does not think that—he thinks that the *sensus divinitatus* is a distinctive epistemological faculty, which is entirely separable from other faculties and from social relationships. For instance, Plantinga writes that "because of the fall, we no longer know God in the same natural and unproblematic way in which we know each other and the world around us."[36] In other words, all human

---

34. Plantinga, *WCB*, 207.
35. Ibid., 175.
36. Ibid., 205.

beings share in original sin, and that original sin completely distorts our sense of divinity, but it does little to our beliefs in and our knowledge of other people or other creatures. Thus, the *sensus divinitatis* constitutes no relationship to social practice in its workings—knowledge of other people is untouched by original sin while the sense of divinity is almost entirely undone. While Plantinga does seem to want to acknowledge the social causation of belief in God, his overall epistemological model will not allow him to do so. It is an epistemological theory about the epistemic equipment of individual human beings.

Perhaps this is all to the good, but a Christian epistemology can and should be able to provide more. Indeed, Rorty's challenge is an implicit theological challenge to Plantinga's work. Of course, Rorty would not concern himself with this, but it would seem incumbent on Plantinga, if he is to provide a Christian epistemological model, to consider whether it is fitting in such a model for the social formation of beliefs to be inseparable from normal epistemic operations. In other words, is it more fully Christian to construct an epistemological model in which social practice is, in the normal state of affairs, non-optional or inseparable for its operation? Read charitably, that is Rorty's central challenge to Plantinga's work.[37]

I think that the answer to this question is, yes, it is more fully Christian to construct an epistemological model in which social practice is inseparable for production of warranted beliefs. I make this claim because that is the best way to make sense of the Christian tradition's own self-understanding. One classic source for this belief, as Augustine argued in his *Expositions of the Psalms*, is the story recounted in Acts 9—the story of Paul's recognition of the Christian community as having a more warranted account of Jesus' life and death than his own. The story recounts a vision to Paul in which Jesus says, "Saul, Saul, why are you persecuting me?"[38] Augustine argues that since Jesus Christ's

---

37. There is another severe theological problem with Plantinga's work. Belief in God, for Jews, Christians, and Muslims, is never a normal operation. That is, creatures do not have the capacity, as creatures, to know God unless they are given a "supernatural gift," as Plantinga calls it (see n. 32 above). If there is an infinite difference between God and creation, creatures simply cannot know God as a matter of their own powers. Of course, God can and does mediate that difference—that is also a belief common to Jews, Christians, and Muslims—but that is not simply because human beings sin; it is because they are creatures, not God.

38. Acts 9:4.

body is no longer spatially present, Jesus Christ has identified himself with Christian community.[39] Thus, Paul claims later in his letters that the Christian community is the body of Christ. Rorty's challenge to Plantinga is a theological challenge—a challenge to consider how beliefs are warranted by social practice and relationship. I say this because, according to Paul, Christians not only hold beliefs individually, they hold them as a body, as a group. Christians do not hold beliefs merely as individuals grouped together. The body of Christians believes beliefs as that body, not merely as a collection of individuals. A good example of this is Paul's letter to the church at Ephesus, where he writes:

> It was he (Jesus Christ) who gave some to be apostles, some to be prophets . . . to prepare God's people for works of service, so that the body of Christ may be built up until we all reach unity in the faith and in the knowledge of the Son of God and become mature . . . speaking the truth in love, we will in all things grow up into him who is the Head, that is, Christ. From him the whole body, joined and held together by every supporting ligament, grows and builds itself up in love, as each part does its work.[40]

The last sentence clarifies my point most poignantly. We might think that "we" refers to a collection of individuals; but Paul clarifies that it is "the body" that "grows" and "builds itself up in love." In other words, the Christian community believes in propositions about Jesus Christ as a group because, *as that group*, it is unified to Jesus Christ. Proper beliefs about Jesus Christ build up the body of Christ; improper beliefs do not. Why? The Christian community believes as a whole, as one.

More could be said here about other related theological limitations in Plantinga's work; but, I think the most beneficial and charitable thing to do is to suggest that Plantinga consider the following amendment to

---

39. For example, Augustine writes, "Were it not for the body's linkage with its Head through the bond of charity, so close a link that Head and body speak as one, he could not have rebuked a certain persecution from heaven with the question, 'Saul, Saul, why are you persecuting me?' Already enthroned in heaven, Christ was not being touched by any human assailant, so how could Saul, by raging against the Christians on earth, inflict injury on him in any way? He does not say, 'Why are you persecuting my saints?' or 'my servants,' but 'Why are your persecuting me?' This is tantamount to asking, 'Why attack my limbs?' The Head was crying out on behalf of the members, and the Head was transfiguring the members into himself" (*Ennarrationes en Psalms*, 30.2.3). This translation is from Augustine, *Expositions of the Psalms*, 1:323.

40. Eph 4:11–16.

his epistemological model.⁴¹ I propose that Plantinga add that Christian beliefs are warranted because they cohere with the core beliefs of other Christians. This is a kind of social coherentism. I am not talking about coherence with other beliefs within one's own epistemic processes; I am talking about coherence with other beliefs held by other Christians in whom the Holy Spirit works. Also, this does not mean that the belief must cohere with all beliefs of all other Christians. Instead, I mean to propose that certain core beliefs of certain other Christians provide warrant for Christian beliefs—by this I mean the apostles and those who continue to exercise apostolic authority. Given what Paul says about the body of Christ, Christian beliefs are warranted, given their coherence with the apostles' teaching about Jesus Christ, the Trinity, and the creation's relationship to Jesus Christ and the Trinity. Many different Christian traditions explain what apostolicity might mean, and it is not our task to mediate that discussion. All Christian traditions recognize that the apostles, due to their status as intimate eyewitnesses, exercise a sort of authority of precedent. All Christian beliefs are to conform to the core Christian beliefs of the apostles.

Let me get more specific and technical, given Plantinga's work. Plantinga claims that "a belief has warrant for a person S only if that belief is produced in S by cognitive faculties functioning properly in a cognitive environment that is appropriate for S's kind of cognitive faculties, according to a design plan that is successfully aimed at truth."⁴² As we have seen, Plantinga gives some Christian content to this—one such process is the work of the Holy Spirit, as the Holy Spirit testifies to the truths of the Gospel. I propose that, for Christians, Plantinga should claim something like "a belief has warrant for a Christian only if that belief is produced in S by cognitive faculties functioning properly in a cognitive environment that is appropriate for S's kind of cognitive faculties, according to a design plan that is successfully aimed a truth, and coheres with the core Christian beliefs of the apostles (and their successors)." This additional condition continues to honor Plantinga's arguments against classical foundationalism and his epistemological externalism. It

---

41. For instance, that the Holy Spirit's immediacy to human persons in testifying to Jesus Christ is not an addition to normal epistemic operations (Plantinga, *WCB*, 256, 269 [n. 214]). Instead, operations such as sense perception, memory, etc., are as much the work of the Holy Spirit as they are the activities of the individuals and communities who undergo them.

42. Plantinga, *WCB*, 156.

also honors Plantinga's arguments against Rorty's anti-anti-realism, but it does so while also answering the central challenge of Rorty's work—the ways in which beliefs emerge from social practice and are justifiable by social practice. In other words, truth is not what your peers will let you get away with saying, and justification is not what your peers will let you get away with saying. Warranted Christian belief is what the apostles (and their successors) will let you get away with saying.[43]

This move allows anyone who follows in Plantinga's train to discuss and elaborate on the means by which apostolic authority is exercised. In particular, it would allow those who want to build on Plantinga's work to interact with certain strands of sociological work. Some sociological work is not content merely to show correlations in data, but actually proposes social causes. For instance, Christian Smith, who currently conducts a longitudinal study of religious practice and belief in the United States, has recently proposed a number of social causes for the perpetuation of religious belief and practice.[44] Interacting with this sort of sociology, and sorting it out philosophically, allows those who sympathize with Plantinga's project to give more than lip service to history and social formation. Thus, it widens the potential audience of Plantinga's work.[45]

The Second Form of Rorty's Challenge and What Can Be Done about It

Second, it would be fitting for Plantinga's work to be confronted with the kinds of questions Rorty presents about the purpose of philosophy or inquiry in general. The conclusion of Rorty's arguments in *Philosophy and the Mirror of Nature* is that inquiry is about self-formation, self-creation, or edification. The best philosophy is the kind that tries to help systematic philosophers get over a theory of truth. More positively, philosophy helps to "keep the conversation going" as a "protest against attempts to close off conversation by proposals for universal commensuration."[46] In

---

43. Although not reductively so, of course, Plantinga has lots of other conditions in his definition. It is a necessary, but not a sufficient, condition.

44. Smith, *Souls in Transition*.

45. This is similar to the kind of work done by Justin Barrett in evolutionary psychology, in using Plantinga's work. See Barrett, *Why Would Anyone Believe in God?*

46. Rorty, *PMN*, 377.

later works, as Michael Williams points out, Rorty extended these ideas in order to make clear that philosophy is "conversation about what to have conversation about."[47] Philosophy is cultural commentary, with the health of the culture in mind (not simply the self-creative success of the philosopher). We see this at play when Rorty comments on the practice of religion. As he has said, his stance is more properly called anticlericalism than atheism: "Anticlericalism is a political view, not an epistemological or metaphysical one. It is the view that ecclesiastical institutions, despite all the good they do—despite all the comfort they provide to those in need or despair—are dangerous to the health of democratic societies."[48] Religion that occurs above the level of a local congregation is less desirable as social mechanism than science because "truth and knowledge are a matter of social cooperation, and science gives us the means to carry out better cooperative social projects than before. If social cooperation is what you want, the conjunction of the science and the common sense of your day is all you need."[49] Non-privatized science is useful for the growth of democratic societies; non-privatized religion is harmful for the nurture of democratic societies. Given the need to bolster democratic societies, privatized religion is desirable.

Rorty's claims about the purpose of philosophy, or inquiry in general, runs parallel to an impatience with the sort of epistemological work exemplified by Plantinga. This impatience becomes palpable when he discusses Sartre in *Philosophy and the Mirror of Nature*. When we make it a goal simply to nurture a human being "whose mind is an unclouded mirror, and who knows this," we seek to create a human being who "does not confront something alien which makes it necessary for him to choose an attitude toward, or a description of, it. He would have no need and no ability to choose actions or descriptions. From this point of view, to look for commensuration rather than simply continued conversation . . . is to attempt escape from humanity."[50] If human beings utterly mirrored the universe, what would we do once the universe was fully reflected in human cognition? For Rorty, to be human is to create as much as it is to find, and Plantinga's work attempts to eliminate

---

47. Williams, "Introduction to Thirtieth Anniversary Edition," xxix.
48. Rorty and Vattimo, *Future of Religion*, 33.
49. Ibid., 39.
50. Rorty, *Philosophy and the Mirror*, 376–77.

as much epistemic creation as possible. Basically, Plantinga's work attempts to strip human beings of their freedom.

A second central challenge for Plantinga, given the priority of democracy over philosophy for Rorty, is this: what is the purpose of Plantinga's inquiry, of the practice of philosophy? Plantinga often comments on the purpose of his inquiries, as he does in *Warranted Christian Belief*. In commenting on the purposes of *WCB*, he avers:

> It is an exercise in apologetics and philosophy of religion, an attempt to demonstrate the failure of a range of objections to Christian belief ... on the other hand, the book is an exercise in Christian philosophy ... The first is addressed to everyone ... it is intended as a contribution to an ongoing public discussion of the epistemology of Christian belief; it does not appeal to specifically Christian premises ... The other project ... is that of starting from an assumption of the truth of Christian belief and from that standpoint investigating its epistemology, asking whether and how such belief has warrant.[51]

What is interesting about Plantinga's statement is that it clearly exemplifies the goals of systematic philosophers: the self-provision of reasons to take as true what they regard as true and to seek to convince others of the truth of those held beliefs. Rorty's clear challenge to a project like this is, "Pragmatists think that if something makes no difference to practice, it should make no difference to philosophy."[52] Put in question form, the challenge would be: "What good do the intuitions you painstakingly salvage do us? What practical difference do they make?"[53] What difference would it make if everyone were to accept Plantinga's epistemological model? Now, an answer to this question cannot be exhaustive, and I suspect that Rorty's questions are a bit reductionistic. He seems to be working with the kind of pragmatism that makes the meaning of a concept absolutely identical to the activity of those who possess it. Against this form of pragmatism, Peircean pragmatism claims that the meaning of an epistemic habit is measured by "what effects that might conceivably have practical bearing."[54] In other words, the *meaning* of an epistemic habit (or belief) is measured by a tendency toward

---

51. Plantinga, *Warranted Christian Belief*, xiii.
52. Rorty, *Truth and Progress*, 19.
53. Ibid., 42.
54 Peirce, "What Pragmatism Is," 110

a range of actions that may or may not be concretely expressed in any given time or place. No one can be expected to take full account of the practical bearing of a concept—that would require an absolute social science that is not possessed by human beings.

It is interesting to note that Plantinga's work never takes account of the practical bearing of his work. While he associates it with Christian faith, it is difficult to know how assent to his epistemological model would bear on the practice of Christian faith, or the practice of philosophy or theology. Again, it is important to note that Plantinga is not presenting an argument for the truth of his model. Perhaps if he were to make such an argument, he would present an account of what this model would do for some possible range of practices. As in my first proposal about Rorty's challenge, I am uninterested in taking a crack at Plantinga's realism or at his desire to persuade his interlocutors of the truth of his model. Instead, as before, I wonder if Plantinga and his sympathetic readers might be aided by reading Rorty's work as charitably as possible, asking whether something about his approach would nurture a more fully Christian approach to doing philosophy—either as philosophy that does not assume Christian belief or as philosophy that does assume Christian belief. Similar to the question I posed above, is Christian philosophy more fully Christian if it is practiced with a bearing toward the practice of some particular community, other than the intellectual assent of some audience?

I believe the answer to that question is, indeed, yes. In this regard, it is interesting to note that the text from Paul's letter to the Ephesians I quoted earlier lists a number of capacities found within the Christian community that assist in the building up or edification of the Christian community. In other words, it is not simply for pastors or apostles to seek the truth in a way that aids the growth of the Christian community; it is for all who find themselves to be members of the group described as the body of Christ. Thus, Christian philosophers, as members of the body of Christ, if they are purporting to do Christian philosophy, are not required to aim their epistemic argumentation simply at the discovery of truth and the persuasion of its interlocutors. They are required to aim their argumentation at the edification of the Christian community and other interlocutors. Again, I am not saying that Plantinga's work is not edifying for the Christian community and a wider audience. Indeed, I am hopeful that it might be; however, Plantinga's work would indeed have a wider audience if he took his purpose to be not only seeking truth, but also the edification of particular communities. At least, it might offer a deeper connection to those who interrelate philosophy and practice at all levels, as do folks sympathetic to Rorty's work.

Let me conclude by mentioning what I take to be two layers of practical bearing for Plantinga's work. First, if one were convinced of Plantinga's model, it would not be fitting for someone to engage in evidentialist apologetic projects. In other words, it would not be fitting to attempt to find rational evidences in order to demonstrate the truth and warrant of Christian belief. If one is convinced that Plantinga's model is true (and that is one goal of his, for his Christian audience), then one would have to recognize that the testimony of the Holy Spirit cannot be controlled through rational means. Apologetic endeavors are to be commended, but only as the unfolding of Christian thought and practice or as an answer to objections. Second, Plantinga's model encourages new practices within pluralistic universities—intellectual practices that ensure that religious beliefs are not sequestered from consideration in any discipline. While religious beliefs and practice operate at all levels within research at pluralistic universities, they are rarely allowed to come to the surface as explicitly religious beliefs. For instance, it is a common (but of course not universal) assumption within economics that economists study the rational distribution of goods and services in circumstances of scarcity. This sort of assumption is as orthodox an assumption as any, but a religious challenge to this sort of assumption would be deemed an improper procedure in the discipline of economics. Yet, if Christian belief, and religious belief in general, arise in ways that Plantinga envisions, then it is hard to see how religious challenges to assumptions in any disciplines should be disqualified. In particular, if religious beliefs are due to processes, faculties, and social formation, then religious beliefs simply are not private beliefs—they are as public as any other kinds of beliefs. Given the amendment I proposed above, it allows Christian belief even more public access, since its epistemic structure operates socially. Christian belief operates, at least in part, on something like a precedent system, with all sorts of attendant practices. It is that social structure and formation that allows those who are not Christians access to those beliefs and their warranting features.

My conclusion that religious beliefs are as public as any other competitors' is probably not a conclusion that Rorty and his sympathizers would appreciate, but it makes for deeper arguments among those who want to make sense of the very different legacies of Rorty and Plantinga. I have hinted above that certain aspects of the chasm between Rorty and Plantinga simply cannot be crossed, but I also think that the concerns of Reformed epistemology intersect at many points with the concerns of the pragmatist tradition. In part, I have sought to use Rorty as a representative of that larger tradition. It may be that other representatives of the pragmatist tradition have more to offer Reformed epistemology, given a shared commitment to some sort of realism. In any case, it is time for deeper encounters between these two philosophical (and religious?) movements.

CHAPTER SIX

Pragmatic Charity
A Synthesis of Rorty and Milbank

Eric Hall

In this essay, I synthesize two social visions, both of which I find convincing in their own way. The first is the pragmatic vision offered by Richard Rorty. In many ways, this vision is a hyper-democratic one, bent on protecting private goods from public interference. The second is the charitous vision of John Milbank, which not only ignores the distinction between private and public affairs but also sees this distinction as contributing to the breakdown of social orders. As such, this paper presents no easy task; however, using Rorty's pragmatic insights as a basic political and legal framework of a social vision, I will incorporate Milbank's demand for the Christian virtue of charity within it as a personal project of self-creation. While at first a seemingly innocuous synthesis from a pragmatic perspective, it unfolds into a pragmatic admission to the *real* possibility of Trinitarian ontology.

At the same time, I will also present in this essay a two-tiered argument, the first—which I defined in the previous paragraph—standing as the content to the form of the next. I have just defined this first argument, but my second argument is that the above way of reading Rorty is a much better interpretation of Rorty than many of his contemporary atheistic interpreters. This point can only be shown to the reader solely by means of my performance, namely, if the essay successfully performs a redescription of Rorty and his project. In other words, I claim that my religious interpretation of Rorty is a better interpretation of him because it applies Rorty's own way of reading authors to Rorty himself (without, perhaps, the same wit).[1]

Pragmatism and Possibility

What precisely constitutes Rorty's pragmatic hermeneutic, by which I mean the basic categorical framework through which he interprets the world? One important way to develop an understanding of this framework is to look, like Rorty, at the political institutions and living conditions that persons lived under within, say, medieval Europe as compared to those we live under now.[2] In light of these changes, Rorty asks the question, what allowed Western society to move from that point to this point? More precisely, what allowed Western society to move from a world defined by the whims of nature to a world with penicillin? Finally, what allowed us to move from a world defined by fiefdoms to one ruled by organized, bureaucratic, and democratic states?

No doubt, one could develop several particular answers to the above questions. For instance, although Alexander Fleming first discovered penicillin by luck in a moldy petri dish, he developed it into an important pharmaceutical by means of experimentation and use of the scientific method. Again, the civic-minded, laissez-faire economists of the eighteenth century fought against, and gained powers from, the old absolutist states, securing the development of liberal democracy in the West.[3] While all these persons are concrete in their approach to the aforementioned questions, Rorty seems interested in a broader set of answers. Rorty wants to decipher the conditions for the possibility of these developments.

The first point is that this tricky transcendental claim must be stated with some care. "Transcendental" conditions here cannot be mistaken for "transcendent" conditions, as they are often interpreted. If the latter is asking what metaphysical structures allow x, y, or z to take place, transcendental structures in themselves are more neutral, asking

---

1. For an example of Rorty's method for interpreting famous authors, see any number of essays in Rorty, *Essays on Heidegger and Others*. Rorty's interpretation of Heidegger stands out as especially poignant, as I do not think he gets Heidegger right at all, even if he makes Heidegger extremely interesting. "Heidegger, Contingency, and Pragmatism," 27–49.

2. Rorty, *Truth and Progress*, 249.

3. Taylor, *Secular Age*, 181–85.

only what things condition x, y, or z, with no definitive transcendent or immanent end in mind. Rorty will only affirm an immanent answer to the question.

Accordingly, the second point is that Rorty seems to interpret the condition for the possibility of our social development as grounded in the category of immanent possibility. One of the most important reasons for the West's social development has been its ability to hold open true possibility as the primary category through which it interprets both itself and the world around it. The question, then, is what true possibility means. Rorty is a self-admitted nominalist.[4] As such, I have no problem moving back to this particular, theologically relevant, historical shift in Western thought to elucidate Rorty's position.

Once upon a time, the nature of modal thought made a dramatic shift. Classical modal thinkers, up through the height of Scholasticism, interpreted possibility as based on one set of eternal possibilities. There was one world, which, being created in and through the eternal ideas in the mind of God, was predetermined. This predetermination was not understood in terms of actual occurrences, but in terms of possibility. If an event were possible, then it would indeed eventually become actual, precisely because there was only one possible world. Modal thinking, however, made a turn with late scholastics such as Scotus and Ockham. Negating the idea that God created based on the eternal and preexisting forms, the late scholastics rejected the idea that there is one single possible world. The nature of the world was no longer set in such a way that there preexisted some set of possibilities, whose actuality in due time would come to fruition; rather, the notion of a single world was itself rejected. That is, these thinkers would have admitted that we live in a single and actualized world, but that this world does not comprise a necessary world. The world we live in is contingent. It constitutes only one possibility in many possible worlds, most of whose actuality will never come to fruition.[5]

In this shift from one possible to many possible worlds, one can see a shift in the development of the joint categories of *contingency* and *novelty*. For the first time, humans become free to think outside of, and beyond, an overreaching and undergirding actuality; humanity becomes free to think in terms of its own immanent good, redescribing

---

4. Rorty, *Contingency, Irony, and Solidarity*, 74.
5. See Knuuttila, "Time and Modality in Scholasticism," 168–257.

the world for the sake of gaining new and better social and individual options by bringing that world to actuality.[6]

In the meantime, Rorty protects precisely this kind of shift through his antimetaphysical rhetoric. In other words, a metaphysic envisions and systematizes the world not only as it is, but as it *must* be, based on an ordering of natural essences and their natural ends. It outlines the *one* world, its *one* set of laws and demands.[7] According to Rorty, a metaphysic cannot meaningfully imagine or realize any other world, precisely because only this one world exists. As such, metaphysical truth-claims stifle creativity by placing a wall between the world as it is and the world as it could be.[8]

On the other hand, the moment one drops the notion of a metaphysic, so, too, does one drop the notion of a singular world. This reason grounds why Rorty in his later years came to isolate and emphasize the role of contingency. A worldview determined by contingency holds that no-*thing*, no essence, is set in stone.[9] Essences are contingent, transitory, ready, and willing to change. Indeed, essences only stand for descriptions of objects onto which one can apply new, and perhaps more helpful, redescriptions. Furthermore, given the point that a world, for Rorty, comprises something like an integrated set of described objects, the principle of contingency creates room for redescribed worlds. From the standpoint of contingency, the one world that the metaphysician envisions comes to be understood as really only one of an infinite number of possible worlds—hopeful worlds, technologically savvy worlds—but each of these emerges as a world that, in light of the category of contingency, humanity will never find itself bound to for that world's own sake; one can always redescribe these worlds.[10]

Accordingly (and consistently), Rorty denies humans access to things such as truth, at least in terms of correspondence.[11] Truth presupposes essences, which in turn make demands of the way humans conceive of both these essences and the world they exist within and

6. If the reader is interested in linking this story more directly to the development of Western thought, he or she should read Taylor, *Secular Age*, especially ch. 2, "The Rise of the Disciplinary Society," 90–145.

7. See Rorty, *Contingency, Irony, and Solidarity*, 17, 23–43.

8. Ibid., 6–7.

9. Ibid., 8.

10. Ibid., 7.

11. Rorty, *Philosophy and Social Hope*, 27.

compose. In other words, truth denies humans the possibility of thinking in terms of possibility, the very category that gave us the power to envision (as indicated above) uses for penicillin.

In line with this logic, Rorty also denies something like a human nature, for this nature too would deny possibility its chance to redescribe the aspect of the world that is most important to humanity, namely, humanity's potential.[12] As I will show later, it would require of them a universal and ethical end, against which Rorty will unleash his most critical remarks.

In the end, Rorty states his position bluntly. The pragmatic hermeneutic stands as an entirely immanentist, anthropomorphic position that attempts to redescribe the world not according to its transcendent truth, but according to what might open up new possibilities for something better. To say the least, Rorty believes he consciously does what thinkers in the history of philosophy only latently sought to do: attempt to open up new possibility.[13]

Politics and Ethics

I have thus far presented the means by which Rorty's pragmatic hermeneutic works, only briefly talking about the ends toward which this hermeneutic strives; however, defining this end presents no easy task. Rorty's philosophical ends are by definition amorphous and uncongenial to definition.[14] At best, Rorty conceives of these ends most precisely in terms of "betterment," namely, "human betterment."[15] To the greatest degree possible, this concept will need defining.

Precisely what does "human betterment" mean? For one, this question is itself deceptive. Properly speaking, no such thing as "humanity" exists for Rorty. Again, Rorty admits to a nominalism that leads him to claim that the term "humanity" only denotes a convenient way to refer to a large number of individual beings, all of which share some sort of

---

12. Rorty, *Contingency, Irony, and Solidarity*, 8.
13. Rorty, *Philosophy and Social Hope*, 34 and Rorty, *Contingency, Irony, and Solidarity*, 76.
14. Rorty, *Philosophy and Social Hope*, 27–28.
15. Ibid.

common interest. No human essence stands underneath these things, just the prospect of mutual benefit.[16]

Secondly, this last statement forms an extremely important starting point for defining human betterment. No matter how one defines human betterment, one cannot denote by it something universal, ethical, Socratic.[17] Human nature does not exist in such a way that one could distinguish some universal human end, including any notion of "human betterment" as proposed above. As such, one finds only individual ends: one's own end and its possible relationship to all other beings' ends.

Rorty does have something of a strategy for pointing his readers in the right direction of what he means more generally. In fact, he intimates as to what it might mean in several different ways. At one point, Rorty talks about betterment negatively in terms of finding freedom from humiliation, gaining dignity in who one is.[18] At another, he speaks of betterment in terms of working out one's own private salvation.[19] Yet, perhaps the most important way that Rorty couches the term "betterment" is in terms of his vocabulary of self-creation.[20]

I will combine these latter two notions, defining betterment as somehow referring to one's private salvation as found in the activity of self-creation. I will, accordingly, develop what Rorty means by private salvation and how it relates to self-creation; it seems that Rorty offers a concrete starting point for an interpretation of each based on his reflections about wild orchids.

In his now famous chapter of *Philosophy and Social Hope*, "Trotsky and the Wild Orchids," Rorty sets out to clear up precisely what he means when he speaks of the notion of private salvation. At the very least, the chapter defends his previous book, *Contingency, Irony, and Solidarity*, and his absolute unwillingness in it to force a convergence between private ends and public goods; it seems, too, that Rorty manages to skillfully rebut both his conservative and liberal critics on this issue. No doubt, part of the skill of this rebuttal is found in the very concrete and personal account that Rorty was trying to defend. He writes,

---

16. Ibid., 72–73.
17. Ibid., 28.
18. Rorty, *Contingency, Irony, and Solidarity*, 92.
19. Ibid., 84.
20. Ibid., xv.

> [W]hen my parents began dividing their time between the Chelsea Hotel and the mountains of north-west New Jersey, these interests switched to orchids. Some 40 species of wild orchids occur in those mountains, and I eventually found 17 of them. Wild orchids are uncommon, and rather hard to spot. I prided myself enormously on being the only person around who knew where they grew, their Latin names and their blooming times. When in New York, I would go to the 42nd Street public library to reread a nineteenth-century volume on the botany of the orchids of the eastern US.
>
> I was not quite sure why those orchids were so important, but I was convinced that they were. I was sure that our noble, pure, chaste, North American wild orchids were morally superior to the showy, hybridized, tropical orchids displayed in florists' shops. I was also convinced that there was a deep significance in the fact that the orchids are the latest and most complex plants to have been developed in the course of evolution. Looking back, I suspect that there was a lot of sublimated sexuality involved (orchids being a notoriously sexy sort of flower), and that my desire to learn all there was to know about orchids was linked to my desire to understand all the hard words in Krafit-Ebing.[21]

What does not surface in this section is the sadness that implicitly contextualizes this story; and, frankly, that implied sorrow comprises the truly convincing justification of both the standpoint that Rorty wants to defend and the point I myself want to elucidate. Rorty was "nerdy," "bullied," "beat up."[22] Yet, in this place of alienation and rejection, Rorty established a point in his discovery of wild orchids that allowed him to gain some fleeting joy and meaning. Although Rorty undertook this interest with a sort of Freudian guilt (his Trotskian superego judging his non-socialist interests), Rorty was relieved enough by his discovery of orchids that he spent the first part of his academic career attempting to justify his personal interests in light of social necessities, a point that, admittedly, he ultimately failed at justifying, writing instead *Contingency, Irony, and Solidarity*.[23]

These concerns help formulate an important point: when Rorty speaks of personal salvation, he speaks of *this very moment* with the wild orchids that he himself experienced. The wild orchids form Rorty's

21. Rorty, *Philosophy and Social Hope*, 6–7.
22. Ibid., 7.
23. Ibid., 9.

salvific paradigm. More broadly, personal salvation refers to those times where Rorty found himself titillated by something—wild orchids, for instance—enough to relieve his mind of his current misery. He seems to hold to this understanding to such a degree that, if one attributes to Rorty the willingness to recognize one general element of existence, human and not, that element is that of misery, pain, and death. At least all those beings that can recognize this pain need something that stands as and remains *untouchable* by all other like-minded beings, through which these beings can alleviate their suffering.

Such is the meaning of personal salvation for Rorty. The idea is somber in tone; however, through it, the more joyful and positive counterpart also presents itself, namely, the idea of self-creation. If private salvation refers to the peculiar relief one finds from misery, self-creation refers to the hope and joy found in the new sense of freedom and possibility attained in the same move. While certainly no substantial and lasting self exists, according to Rorty, this temporal and contingent self (really, selves) can at least engage in projects that it finds interesting, personally worthy of attention.[24] Through these desires, it can formulate itself, redescribe itself, and find something worth positively living for. Rorty discovered one such project through his love of wild orchids, but he developed the project into an engagement with philosophy, literature, and poetry, the sum total of his books constituting the result of his self-creativity.

In this manner, Rorty in many ways emulates the insights of Heidegger and Nietzsche. Contrary to these two, Rorty makes no demand of this subject to adhere to a virtue of heroism, to be like Achilles or Odysseus—or even, for that matter, to comprise a unity.[25] In more of a utilitarian manner, one that both Heidegger and Nietzsche alike would despise, Rorty simply predicates the value of the project on the axiom that it must bring one relief, even pleasure; and if such a project includes heroism, so be it.

Historically, humans are not merely isolated individuals. In fact, humans *do* tend to need one another in order to achieve betterment, whatever betterment might be. For instance, without the collaborative efforts of engineers and scientists, humans would not be able to develop, among other things, the technologies that bring much comfort to human

---

24. Rorty, *Contingency, Irony, and Solidarity*, 99.
25. Fennell, "Harry Neumann and the Political Piety of Rorty's Postmodernism," 262.

life, such as home heat (which relies on highly complex power systems). Rorty could thus affirm (figuratively speaking, of course) that humans are "political animals," which seems to present Rorty with a paradox. That is, to no small degree, betterment rests not only on the notion of personal freedom and the ability to self-create, but also on the sociopolitical structures that create space for the development of personal freedom. How, then, does Rorty mediate these positions?

In answer to this paradox, Rorty's political reflections take on a radical proceduralist tone. No common political good stands as absolute for Rorty except the pragmatic and intersubjective good of lawful procedure, and this good always understands itself first within the context of self-creation. His understanding of politics as such is best exemplified in his vision of the Kuwaiti Bazaar.[26]

In this bazaar, persons of individually differing tastes interact with one another in the daytime, bartering and selling for mutual benefit the goods and services each has to offer. At night, these persons flock to different clubs and halls, arenas in which they can create themselves according to their own tastes while enjoying the company of like-minded persons in the process. Every once in a while, two persons from different parts of the bazaar—persons who do not usually see one another—find themselves in a dispute, and this dispute threatens to disturb the peace of the bazaar. Thus, the other persons in the bazaar come together and mediate the situation, establishing in this mediation certain rules for behavior within the bazaar. These rules both help prevent similar disputes from arising again and establish certain intersubjectively defined norms for dealing with these situations as they arise between disagreeing parts of the bazaar's constituency. The dialogue that takes place accordingly helps preserve both the peace and space necessary for all to go along their merry way, engaging in their own projects of self-creation.

What, then, can be said of Rorty and what he means by betterment? One can interpret Rorty as envisioning at least two levels of betterment: social betterment and individual betterment. In turn, to borrow conceptually from Aristotle here, he defines these notions of betterment *pros hen*, the second being definitive of the first—individual betterment in self-creation constitutes the end toward which the social betterment works.

---

26. Rorty, *Objectivity, Relativism, and Truth*, 209.

Social betterment can be understood through any of the advances with which I began this exposition of Rorty. For one, any technological improvement through which humans gain some distance from nature (e.g., penicillin) counts as social betterment.[27] In the same way, certain political developments can be interpreted as social betterments. That is, political ideas that allow humans to organize their lives in freer and more meaningful ways certainly better human living, but social betterment finds its end precisely in this latter purpose: any social betterment ultimately gives humans the space to work out their own salvation by engaging in self-creation.

The pragmatic judgment exposited here represents a view toward life and the world that establishes (1) a wider social space for engaging in projects of self-creation by (2) denying any metaphysical possibility of preset human ethical ends. Rorty's focus on the ultimacy (and there is little denying that this term sticks, here) of individual self-creation reflects itself in a hyper-secular politic. The common good can be circumscribed in general terms by means of Rorty's proceduralist views. Yet, this understanding sticks only because it stands as the best possible way Rorty knows to protect the individual's project of self-creation. The individual's project of self-creation constitutes both the means and ends for any politic.

Milbank, Rorty, and Peace

John Milbank shares many epistemic sympathies with Rorty. Both are historicist thinkers, avid redescribers, and are willing to push to the limits the language of postmodernity. Whatever sympathies Milbank might have with Rorty, one will find none in terms of Rorty's high-minded individualism and the secular political structures necessary to support this worldview. Politically speaking, Milbank is not so much interested in creating and preserving what the secular West calls "individual rights," the means and ends that create space for self-creation in Rorty's scheme. Instead, Milbank wants to unfold a politic of *true* peace. The notion of "right" is ultimately unnecessary, even counterproductive, for Milbank's ideal and peaceful political order.[28] The questions that come

---

27. Or at least counts as better in any particular social order telling itself a story of progress. See Rorty, *Contingency, Irony, and Solidarity*, 86.

28. Milbank, Pickstock, and Ward, *Radical Orthodoxy*, 193.

to the surface, then, concern the nature of peace, namely, what is it and what does it have to do with Rorty's rights talk?

In the first place, the pragmatist's secular, democratic political structures, and the absolute rights they afford to the individual, present, at best, a sort of negative peace.[29] This peace represents tolerant disagreement between persons' projects of self-creation, which allows all people to follow their own individuated paths—so long as such paths do not interfere with others. Perhaps the best known writer on this type of peace is John Mill and his *On Liberty*.[30] This manner of establishing peace has been developed and promulgated, for instance, in the US Constitution (it could be argued), which has sought vehemently from its inception to separate legal rights from ethical demands. Rorty moves along this same path, advocating for a social peace that has no truly communal element to it, where persons live under a united vision of a communal good.

Conversely, Milbank gives an entirely different social vision, one of positive peace. The chaotic Kuwaiti marketplace cannot represent this kind of peace; only the beauty and orderliness of a symphony can do so.[31] That is, the symphony is a harmonious flow of individual notes entering into and out of one another, not for the sake of themselves, but for the sake of the harmony created in the mutual relations between the notes. It takes individual notes to make the harmony, but the harmony is more than the sum of its parts; it emerges as a new property when the notes give themselves "in love" to one another for the sake of this harmony. Thus, Milbank's understanding of peace stands as a far cry from Rorty's pragmatic understanding of peace, defined by toleration. Milbank proposes an entirely positive understanding of peace, understood in terms of his reflections on the virtue of charity.

Many Catholic thinkers use the term *charity* to signify one of the three great Christian theological virtues taken from 1 Corinthians 13:13.[32] Love, then, stands as the later translation of the Greek term *agape*, which the Latin Vulgate translated as *caritas*, whose association

---

29. Milbank, *Theology and Social Theory*, 367.

30. Mill, *On Liberty, and Other Essays*, xix.

31. Milbank, *Theology and Social Theory*, 409 and Milbank, Pickstock and Ward, *Radical Orthodoxy*, 264.

32. "But now faith, hope, love, abide these three; but the greatest of these is love" (NASB).

with the term *charity* is fairly obvious; and at least in its earlier Catholic forms, charity comprises an aspect of God's gift of grace to humanity. More specifically, as God reveals Godself to the individual, God imbues the individual with faith, hope, and charity. Faith stands for the new willingness to believe in the mysteries of God (the Incarnation, the Trinity, the effectiveness of Communion) as taught in the Church; hope denotes the expectation of eternal life, whose sole guarantor is God in God's Church; love, charity, signifies a total willingness of the individual not only to submit to the Creator but also to willingly and entirely give over all of one's life to the Creator, living self-transcendentally in and through God's Church.[33]

Without desiring to unfold the value of the Catholic interpretation of grace, what is important for the purposes of this essay is how to interpret charity. Even if formulated only in terms of dedication to God, this virtue has had a long history of ethical interpretation as well, Milbank being a newer part of the history of this interpretation. To be more precise, Milbank understands the virtue of charity as rooted deeply in the early Christian narratives about Jesus, envisioning it as the ethic standing behind the notion of the kingdom of God, that peace and harmony rule the day, that love of neighbor outweighs the demands of justice.[34]

To no small degree, and unlike secular liberal social orders, charity stands unconcerned with the establishment of spaces for self-creation; rather, charity concerns itself with establishing a space wherein dedication to the positive good of another in God—the mutual giving of oneself to that other and that other to oneself—signify the primary attributes of the social order. Accordingly, charity, as a virtue and as a social ethic, presupposes the attempted and mutual indwelling of persons in one another, meaning that any individual cannot understand him or herself apart from the other in whom the individual has vested social identity.

One finds a good description of this idea of charity in the work of Catherine Pickstock, whose work concretely draws out the type of dynamic that Milbank, too, seeks to illuminate in his understanding of charity.[35] In her *After Writing*, Pickstock writes, "in the Middle Ages,

---

33. See Saint Thomas' interpretation of theological virtue in Kreeft, *Summa of the Summa*, 465.

34. Milbank, *Theology and Social Theory*, 400.

35. Radical Orthodoxy is a self-defined theological movement in the twentieth

there was no abrupt gulf between the familial on the one hand, and the social on the other."[36] This point is important because it implies that the sacred bonds of the family (the space in which God and person mutually create new life and jointly form social bonds) extend to the wider social order.[37] This extension, importantly, keeps all social bonds from falling into a system of formal contractual relations, which, in modern developments, break apart the sacrality of the social order and the world. In the latter world, those who were once perceived as brothers and coworkers in a guild become competitors, issuing after the same contract for the sake of an increased bottom line. This vision of the world as filled with competitors constitutes a vision of social violence, a war of all against all that necessitates the external power of a state to keep relative peace. For Milbank and Pickstock alike, this social order ought to be seen as the organic bond of mutually indwelling family whose source and ground is the Church in God.

Here, then, a major difference between Milbank and Rorty emerges. Their visions of peace lie in the role of the common good (so long as this term is used loosely).[38] For negative peace, the common good stands as a good of limitation, of negation, only allowed to define the limits of state power. Therefore, the state cannot interfere with certain fundamental rights given to humanity by its nature, including how individual persons define their ultimate and religious beliefs. Citizens of nation-states enacting such constitutions are allowed to interact at the political level however they individually see fit, so long as these interactions do not harm fellow citizens. (No doubt, Rorty differs from these past opinions insofar as he defines "rights" language, not by means of a human nature, but as having produced good results.) On the other hand, Milbank defines a positive common good with a positive human end, neither of which signifies a "choice," *per se*, of individual human

---

century. For a basic understanding, see Milbank, Pickstock, and Ward, *Radical Orthodoxy*, 1–20.

36. Pickstock, *After Writing*, 140.

37. At this point in my argument, I am for rhetorical purposes trying to leave out the theocratic implications of the notion of charity. All of these relationships are only possible because of the liturgical direction extended to the social family from the sacred family of the Church. Pickstock, *After Writing*, 142–43.

38. Common good usually refers to the good of the state, but the role of the state is precisely what is often called into question by both Milbank and his Radically Orthodox cohort.

beings. Rather, these ends are given not through the external decrees of the state, but through natural familial relations as grounded in the Church, which makes present a living vision of the source of Goodness itself in God.[39]

Thus, Milbank wants to put forward a view partially akin to what the West rejected during and after the Enlightenment. His task is a difficult one, precisely because it seems that the positive peace he hopes for resulted in, for instance, the "wars of religion."[40] No doubt, it will take a bit of an explanation to defend Milbank's view, but, as much as one might ultimately disagree with Milbank (and I do), the reasoning behind his understanding of peace compels. I will try to do it some justice.

Theory, Practice, and Self-Creation

To begin a justification of Milbank's understanding of social peace, I need to take several steps. First, I must give Milbank's axial proposition an account, namely, that "theory" and "practice" are intrinsically interrelated. Second, I need to show the distinction between charity as a practice and self-creation as a practice. With these two points clarified, I unfold the ontology that latently lies behind Rorty's pragmatic hermeneutic.

First, a practice in this context refers to a way of being in the world, one's directed and ethical (in a very loose sense) movements.[41] These ethical movements usually derive from some tradition, either cultural or philosophical, and they presuppose certain ends to be relatively (perhaps absolutely) worth more than others.[42]

Second, a practice always intrinsically relates to a particular interpretation of the world; so Rorty's understanding of self-creation, or any other term referring to an ethical end, alludes to ethical and ontological meanings. According to Milbank, practices and ontologies contain a relationship of correspondence; both presuppose and ground one another. This relationship is similar to Wittgenstein's understanding of a language game, namely, that certain vocabularies only make sense in

---

39. Milbank, *Theology and Social Theory*, 382 and 230.

40. Rorty himself refers to the wars of religion as the "so-called 'wars of religion,'" which seems to accurately signify the ideological bent of his writings. Milbank, Pickstock, and Ward, *Radical Orthodoxy*, 11.

41. Milbank, *Theology and Social Theory*, 454.

42. Ibid., 241–42.

relationship to certain ways of doing things. Again, it could also make sense in terms of the Hegelian and Marxist category of praxis: actions and environment determine thought as much as thought determines actions and environment.[43] Either way, Milbank understands thought and practice to have a dialectical relationship, both thoroughly penetrating one another in such a manner that all practices condition ontology, and all ontology conditions practice.[44]

Both charity and self-creation, then, signify practices of a sort. Each term stands for a specific way of ordering one's individual life within society; they signify a way of being present to one's community. As to the second point, the proposed ends of each of these practices illuminate their mutual exclusivity. Charity means an ordering of oneself, as a relationally defined individual, to the common good of the immediate community (which will eventually include the cosmos as a whole, for Milbank); self-creation means the use and toleration of the community insofar as it creates the possibility of individually defined ends. As to why this second point matters in the least, the third point (that these ontologies are mutually exclusive) needs addressing.

Once again, if Milbank's understanding of the relationship between practice and ontology stands, one must search for the terms that can reveal the relationship between Rorty's liberal democratic social ordering and its implied ontology. Milbank would argue that an intrinsic relationship resides between the terms *self-creation*, *absolute freedom*, and *nothingness*.

Once again, the notion of self-creation, at least as understood by Rorty, grounds itself in a proud Western tradition that holds to an ethical principle of absolute freedom. I have already laid out the basic premises of what such freedom means, so I will draw out the meaning of absolute freedom more precisely over and against a notion of "conditioned freedom"—the type of freedom that, if modified, could be ascribed to Milbank's understanding of charity. In other words, conditioned freedom signifies a positive metaphysic. It holds that a cosmos enfolds certain natures with certain pre-given ends, all of which can be known.

---

43. While I will use the term *praxis* out of ease instead of Milbank's own "theory/practice," one ought to be aware of the difference between the two. The main difference is that praxis, as used by liberation theologians, presupposes something like a stagnant and knowable order rather than an ontology that is indistinct from divine action. Milbank, *Theology and Social Theory*, 256.

44. Ibid., 254.

For instance, human nature symbolizes an actual structure inherent to that group of beings that are bipedal and display intelligence. As signifying an actual nature, humanity also comes, therefore, to signify certain ethical trajectories, that to be human means to exist in certain pre-given ethical ways.

Much of the history of Western philosophy concerns itself with prodding humans to live by that which differentiates them from other animals, namely, to live by their intelligence. In fact, figures such as Aristotle will argue that the "is" of human intelligence produces a natural "ought"; that because intelligence is humanity's specific difference, it ought to emphasize this fact over all other aspects of its animal genus.[45] Conditioned freedom stands for a choice, then, between what gives itself as more human and less human.

Certainly a figure such as Rorty, as a proponent of the notion of betterment, has no problem with the qualitative use of the terms *more* or *less*. However, these terms have no intrinsic meaning or absolute telos to them, precisely because neither the universe nor the beings in it have anything like intrinsic meanings or absolute aims to them; no natural ends exist that demand absolute allegiance. Value, then, is understood as absolutely created—a point that begins to truly get to the gist of the meaning of absolute freedom. Absolute freedom signifies a freedom from the illusion that being has any intrinsic value, and that there is such a way that, as a part of the universe, the human being ought to live naturally. Absolute freedom subsists as a freedom to interpret the universe as individually seen fit, to define the scope and ends of being without regard to the intrinsic meaning of being.[46]

This last statement points this discussion toward an interpretation of that ontology corresponding to the practice of self-creation in absolute freedom. Being, from this standpoint, means nothing; or, more directly, nothing is the meaning of being. When being has no intrinsic meaning, being is held out over a nothingness that creates the ontological freedom for any particular being to interpret the being of beings as it wants. Accordingly, nothingness and the nothingness of being comprise the conditions for the possibility of self-creation in absolute freedom.[47]

---

45. Aristotle, *Nicomachean Ethics*, 1139b.

46. Milbank, *Theology and Social Theory*, 279.

47. Take note of the relationship of nothingness to the will-to-power. See Milbank, *Theology and Social Theory*, 290.

Only if being has no meaning at all, only if ontology signifies a pure will-to-power, does a person have the space to create him or herself without regard to any intrinsic functions and meanings in the self or being as a whole. Absolute nothingness produces absolute interpretability.

So it is with Rorty's self-creation. This manner of self-creation presupposes being to have no intrinsic meaning precisely because being constitutes no ultimate end towards which beings strive. The being of beings is a nothing; it is empty, a mere concept, defined only by means of the flux of sensation that traverses in and out of one another, upon which persons apply various self-created meanings.[48] Thus, to presuppose self-creativity as an absolute end presupposes that the use of concepts, the production of language, signifies not the intellection of the world as it is, but a violent projection of possible worlds onto the nothingness that remains a flux of sensation, the most favorable of which (for Rorty) ought to be chosen and developed. That most favorable world elucidated by Rorty is the world that grants to the individual self a manner in which to find meaning, to create itself in such a way that allows the self to find relative meaning in a violent world.

The problem with this nihilistic position is twofold. In the first place, individuals become bound up in a hell of themselves. The "I" becomes all-pervasive and all-interpreting, imposing a conceptual frame on all being and beings according to its needs, wants, and desires. Lacking the omnipotence to absolutely fulfill these yearnings, the "I" tethers itself to continual wanting without having, reminiscent of the hole-filled jars in Plato's *Gorgias*.[49] Nothing stands beyond the individual except his or her own happiness, which can never actually be attained.

Second, and because of the bounded individuality, the immanent projects of self-creation that Rorty would seem to want to encourage, the projects that have made people historically the happiest, have been shut off.[50] Projects that involve the co-living and mutuality of being with another have no Other to make these projects actually meaningful;[51]

---

48. James, *Essential Writings*, 110.

49. Plato, *Gorgias*, 493a-c.

50. See Bragues, "Richard Rorty's Postmodern Case for Liberal Democracy: A Critique," esp. 179, for a take on this perhaps unconventional view of self-creation.

51. From this point forward in this essay, when I write "Other" with a capital O, I am signifying the absolute irreducibility of this "Otherness" to the self. Accordingly, when I use "other" with a lowercase o, the term signifies a broader notion of otherness that remains more ambivalent on this point, working in any number of contexts.

the meanings are simply forced onto a flux by individuals. Love of, and making love to, a beloved no longer retains the mutuality, the shared sensuality and meaning; they become something like acts of mutual rape as two isolated individuals impose their bodies and minds upon the other. Familial relations are reduced to economic and self-interested ends, and childbearing becomes a matter of enslavement.[52]

With these reasons in mind, Milbank begins to develop a justification for his rejection of any social order predicated on the notion of absolute freedom. As Milbank would claim, such orders espouse a nihilistic praxis, which result in an ontology defined by violence; Milbank's very purpose, however, is to reject and counter this kind of praxis. Yet, there is some caution to be had in Milbank's counterproposal, both in terms of its theological suppositions and its political application.

Starting Point in a Synthesis: Milbank or Rorty

One of the most important reasons for my skepticism over Milbank's project stems from his rejection of the pragmatic stance that violence seems *really* to constitute a part of the world as we know it. For instance, violence displays itself every day in the seemingly benign process of consumption called eating. Through eating, we gain vital nutrients for our bodies, supplying its demand for carbohydrates, proteins, and vitamins; however, through this process (or usually before), we kill something—a chicken, a spinach plant, a basil leaf—and consume the carcass of our prey. While neither Milbank nor Rorty would be particularly pleased with the more realist sense in which I am using this term here, the quasi-realist insight into violence seems at least latently presupposed in each thinker's basic judgments: Rorty in such a way that his pragmatic judgment attempts to dull the violence, and Milbank in the sense that he tries to reinterpret the violence.

Milbank attempts to achieve this reinterpretation through the charitous giving of the self for the good of another in relationship to a whole. While this understanding of harmony may well have some excellent social applications (to which I will come back), and while it may even have some application to the *idea* of violence, I fear that it does not have the power to overcome the all-too-real violence suffered in the created order. In other words, Milbank's notion of harmony, when applied

---

52. What I am trying to point out here is something similar to what Conor Cunningham is attempting in his *Genealogy of Nihilism*, 174–79.

to created violence, survives as one close to an older argument: that the seemingly tumultuous processes experienced in the created order remain, from a distance, viewable as well ordered, the giving of life for life, the parts for the whole. However, this "harmony from a distance" never really becomes comforting to the ones being eminently turned into food.

It seems that only in his book *Being Reconciled*—where he takes seriously the cosmological senselessness of fallenness—does Milbank *begin* to take seriously the fact that the end of violence and its earthly instantiation may not simply be a matter of perceptive redescription.[53] For now, violence constitutes part of the cosmic makeup, the overcoming of which stands out as part of the Christian hope; as hope, this overcoming is not yet fully realized. Perhaps Milbank would also agree that one must acquiesce theologically to the grip of violence on the created order, that one must recognize and deal with violence at a serious theological level as a real threat to the goodness of the created order. This threat no redescription can undo, although it might have a limited effect. Therefore, given the violence experienced in this order of things, Milbank's charitous hermeneutic falls short. Accordingly, Milbank's charitous hermeneutic cannot ground a basic synthesis between him and Rorty. Too much is at stake.

Aside from the theological indictment that Milbank's charitous hermeneutic fails to take violence seriously enough, Rorty's pragmatic hermeneutic seems more duly equipped at a basic level to deal with the phenomenon. As I have already argued, one can see the entirety of Rorty's project, defined as it is by the goal of betterment, as a way to cope with the violence that alienates humanity from the world in which it lives and the people with whom it shares this world. Moreover, based on the two levels of betterment outlined above, Rorty's pragmatic hermeneutic itself acts as a coping mechanism on two more intertwined levels.

For one, the pragmatic judgment recognizes that, frankly, nature subsists as no benign force. Nature, analogically understood or not, is filled with floods, hungry animals, and microbes. Really, the only defense that humanity can summon against these threats is found in the power of redescription and the new possibilities such redescriptions bring. The sciences develop technologies based on new understandings of the world, understandings that allow humanity to manipulate its environment in such a way as to negate some of the undue violence

---

53. Milbank, *Being Reconciled*, 29–30.

inflicted upon humanity. I cannot help agreeing with Rorty when he writes, "We should not try to pull the blanket over our heads by saying that technology was a big mistake, and that planning, top-down initiatives, and 'Western ways of thinking' must be abandoned."[54]

Second, Rorty properly recognizes that human organizational capacities have, to no small degree, been of extreme importance in creating possibilities for funding and implementing technological advancements. Central planning and collective action present themselves as the best means by which to ward off nature's menaces.[55] For example, while I was first writing this essay, we had a very big swine flu scare. Whether the swift and bold actions of world governments resulted in the flu's containment, I do not know; however, these governments managed to quickly channel vaccines into the hands of doctors who used them to undercut the virus' ability to wreak total havoc. At least some credit seems due to these governmental moves.

Similarly, we must use the power of human organization also to fight off human threats. Humans collectively pool their resources together into government bureaucracies so as to organize police forces, which fend off internal human threats of criminality, and militaries, which defend or offend other threatening societies. This list could produce a number of different ways in which humans rely on collective organization.

Regardless of the benefits of such organization, Rorty properly recognizes the negative toll that such organizations can take on individuals.[56] Since the nation-state's invention, absolutist states have plagued their citizens with overtaxation, conscriptions, and social repression. While establishing organizational bureaucracies capable of dealing with (and possibly creating) large-scale threats to human life, these same bureaucracies themselves became threats to the livelihood and happiness of the citizenry. The problem found a partial solution through the invention of the liberal democracy.[57]

---

54. Rorty, *Philosophy and Social Hope*, 228.
55. Ibid.
56. Rorty, *Objectivity, Relativism, and Truth*, 194.
57. One of my major disputes with Milbank, which I have not adequately brought out in this essay, concerns his causal explanation of modernity's faults. Secularity and its nihilistic vision cause the West's problems by misarranging order, drawing it toward the wrong end. He wants to claim that, out of a love of God, the church as an institution is less likely to fall prey to sin and its violent tendencies than secular regimes (Milbank,

Accordingly, the liberal democracy functions as, and stands for, a manner of organization that ideally does not attempt to sublate its citizens into a collective whole (which is often metaphysically defined).[58] Rather, the government runs as a functionalist government, operating in such a way as to *serve* its people rather than some positive common good external to the people.[59] The liberal democracy is for, by, and of the people, receiving legitimacy and sovereignty in the people's vote, all the while protecting the freedom of information through which the citizenry creates values in civil dialogue.

The freedom offered in the liberal democracy, at the end of the day, paradigmatically defines the way through which Rorty defines the ends of his pragmatic judgment, namely, individual betterment. The liberal democracy *is* the pragmatic judgment functioning at a legal level, despite any problems that Rorty would have with such a statement.[60] The liberal democracy, while providing the same protections and organizational utilities of more absolutist social structures, fends off the threat of absolutist tendencies in these social structures. It charts a legal course through which to permit citizens to individually cope with violence, allowing them to define for themselves life, liberty, and happiness and thereby gain some relative contentment.[61] In other words, the pragmatic standpoint must form the legal framework from which all other secondary hermeneutics find personal application. So long as persons stand willing to live by just such a pragmatic hermeneutic legally, they remain equally free to think and interpret the world as they want personally—as long as they cause no harm to anyone else. Such is Rorty's solution, too. All hopes and dreams of something utopian can be openly engaged and

---

Theology and Social Theory, 439–40). He says this despite his own engagements with Augustine's failures in this manner (ibid., 423–29). I claim, however, that proclivities to sin reside just as much in church bodies as secular ones, with the added fright that church bodies come to believe that they are above sin. Only a governmental structure that is grounded in the recognition of sin, holding open the meaning of sin in all of its manifestations, can properly seek to make itself structurally accountable to itself, through checks and balances, and to the people represented, through elections; only this form of government can provide stability and peace, stuck as we are between the "already" and "not yet." That government is only found in a liberal democracy and not clerical rule.

58. Rorty, *Objectivity, Relativism, and Truth*, 178–79.
59. Rorty, *Contingency, Irony, and Solidarity*, 66.
60. Rorty, *Philosophy and Social Hope*, 23–24.
61. Rorty, *Objectivity, Relativism, and Truth*, 194.

believed by the citizenry, even if these utopian dreams cannot make a legal-political foundation for the politic.

At this point, I have already pinned down the broad outlines in which to synthesize pragmatic and charitous social visions.[62] This above synthesis rests on the idea that one can conceive of Rorty's and Milbank's hermeneutics together on the basis that they apply to two relatively different social spheres. On the one hand, Rorty's pragmatic hermeneutic has formed the legal-political framework upon which a society builds its formal bonds. This framework allows both for the reign of possibility at a social and private level, not to mention the protection of the private citizen from the violence of nature and the state alike. On the other hand, Milbank's charitous hermeneutic constitutes the private vision and hope of the individual. Charitous living itself stands as a worthy project of self-creation. Even if such a project is non-constitutive to the social order as a whole, it comprises a fine and symbolic way of living in a world that unfortunately is a war of all against all.

Toward Overcoming Nihilism

In this final section, I make a more controversial claim. It forms a point to which I have already alluded above, namely, that the charitous hermeneutic could, under certain conditions, constitute a real hermeneutic possibility from the pragmatic perspective. The conditions are twofold. First, the pragmatic standpoint, as I have unfolded it, presupposes that (1) certain social conditions create the possibility for (2) individual betterment in self-creation. Thus, the point of betterment at a legal-political level is to open up the possibility of individual betterment, and to open this possibility without making a value judgment whether any particular project exists as more worthwhile than another, so long as the project causes no harm to anyone. Therefore, individual betterment constitutes the primary concern.

Second, many persons have historically defined their self-creative projects in terms of charity: projects dedicated to caring for, and receiv-

---

62. This particular synthesis is nothing new. Certainly Rorty himself sees religion as holding open a possibility for a project of self-creation, but rejects religiosity as constitutive of self-creation for a number of different reasons. See Rorty, "Religion as a Conversation-Stopper," in *Philosophy and Social Hope*. While this stance forms Rorty's initial and most basic assessment, he seems a bit more conflicted in his discussions with Vattimo. See Rorty and Vattimo, *The Future of Religion*.

ing care from, others. In this point lies an important argument. The very language of self-creation strays toward a solipsistic understanding of living, one that instrumentalizes the world as a whole (including others) for the sake of appeasing the self.[63] However, one cannot necessarily reduce the meaning found in charitous projects to the solipsistic projection of self-concern, if one intends to retain any semblance of actual, meaningful self-creative potential for those engaged in charitous projects. If these projects lose any such possibility of engaging with the other as really Other, they no longer hold the same meaning precisely because they were always already predicated on the actuality of an Other with whom to corelate. In other words, if the self believes and takes relief in the fact that it relates to another as an Other, then the only condition for allowing it such relief is the other's actual Otherness. The content of the notion of the Other, as Levinas is prone to argue, demands the overturning of solipsism in the self. Thus, the power of these charitous projects lies in the fact that one can potentially engage in *real* charitous relationships where the Other is not the self and the self attends charitously to the needs of the other as Other.

One concerned to hold to the pragmatic hermeneutic in its purity might fight back and argue that the underlying motives of such projects really have only the self in mind—the self and its frantic needs and passions constitute the world as a whole. In holding to such a point, however, the pragmatic hermeneutic would have to deny the conditions under which people *actually* tend to self-create, meaning the pragmatic hermeneutic engages in a performative contradiction. By trying to deny the otherness of the Other, the hermeneutic ends up taking away precisely that which the people have given it—the ability to meaningfully and privately self-create. The pragmatic hermeneutic functions for this reason and this reason alone; if it denies the validity or meaningfulness of any peaceful self-creative projects, it denies its own legitimacy.

In order to avoid this performative contradiction, the pragmatic hermeneutic must admit to the real possibility that the charitous standpoint stands as an immanent reality, a facet of the concrete pragmatic horizon. If a charitous hermeneutic, however, makes a stand within these private projects of self-creation as making room for an Other—making room for real differentiation—then one can begin to include

---

63. In terms of this notion of instrumentalization, Charles Taylor draws this point out at some length in *The Ethics of Authenticity*, 59–60.

Milbank's theological inclinations more definitively by grounding the Otherness of the other in the Trinitarian God. That is, if Milbank's interpretation of the correspondence between theory and practice holds, the practice of charity implies an ontology that contains a unity within differentiation, that is, the Trinity.

Once again, charity itself signifies the practice of giving oneself to another in mutual relationship. About this practice, one can elucidate several ontological points. First and foremost, the Christian practice of charity demands that secular ontology be fundamentally reinterpreted. Christian practice refuses to see the world as a pure and violently instantiated contingency, conditioned by nothing whatsoever, and so, too, must its ontology. There remains no ultimate room for the violence this secular ontology allows. Instead, for the Christian tradition, the world is reenvisioned as a pure gift, the result of a totally charitous outpouring of the infinite and necessary into the finite and unnecessary. While still contingent, the world no longer stands as meaninglessly contingent.[64] Rather, the world is drawn from and directed toward the gracious act of its creator, even if only eschatologically such that this gift has *not yet* come to full fruition.

This point means, secondly, that something stands beyond the world that gives of itself. For the Christian tradition, the world cannot be understood as conditioned by nothingness, for nothingness can give no gift.[65] The world must accordingly be conditioned by being—by pure beingness.[66] Thus, the Christian tradition in some way latently presupposes something like what Saint Thomas says, namely, that God is the act of being in which, by which, and through which all finite existence is granted its own limited being. No longer, then, does an empty space exist through which to defend absolute freedom; no, the pure beingness of God—whose mystery conditions freedom, drawing the world ever nearer in its search for its divinely rendered meaning—remains definitive.

Third, this position requires an analogical, rather than univocal, understanding of God. One cannot understand God as merely a being among beings, namely, as the highest being. This way of defining God presupposes the nominalism initiated by Scotus and perfected by

---

64. Milbank, Pickstock, and Ward, *Radical Orthodoxy*, 3.

65. This question would need to be taken up with Derrida. See Derrida, *Gift of Death*, 40.

66. Milbank, *Theology and Social Theory*, 296–97, 430.

Ockham.⁶⁷ In Milbank's reading of the nominalist tradition, these thinkers hold that the term *being* applies generically to all beings, including God.⁶⁸ The only difference between God's being and, say, a dog's being is the quantitative degree by means of which God has God's being. According to such views, however, the being of God must be conditioned by that which lies beyond being in the nothing, for being is "not-nothing" according to Scotus.⁶⁹

Yet, the truly Christian tradition (at least Milbank's interpretation of it) distinguishes between finite recipients of being and the pure and infinite act of being, which is identical to God.⁷⁰ The distinction constitutes a qualitative one, necessitating that God not be understood as an entity, albeit one containing quantitatively infinitely more being. Rather, God becomes the infinite act of being itself who charitously decides, for no reason other than the generosity of God's own being, to share and grant this being to a finite other.⁷¹ Accordingly, from the analogical perspective, this world must be understood as an imperfect reflection of its giver, but this reflectivity in turn means that the purpose of the world ought to reflect the self-giving nature of this *gifti*ng God.

Finally, in this gift of creation, God gifts—rather God is—the difference between Godself and creation.⁷² Accordingly, God creates something both truly other than God, which exists in God, and through which God relates back to Godself. Essentially, by giving something truly different, God must exist as internally capable of giving and giving to difference, meaning that God must subsist in Godself as internally differentiated, relating to Godself. God in God's self must internally be understood as charitous and gift-giving, which necessarily brings forth a discussion of the Christian understanding of the Trinity.⁷³ As such, the logic of charity stands intrinsically linked to the logic of Trinity, whom

---

67. Or at least Scotus causes all nominalist shortfalls, according to Milbank, whose position I am trying here to sympathetically reconstruct. See Milbank, *Theology and Social Theory*, xxiv.

68. Ibid., 305.

69. Copleston, *Mediaeval Philosophy*, 503.

70. Milbank, "Can a Gift be Given?" and Milbank, *Theology and Social Theory*, 297.

71. Milbank, "Can a Gift be Given?" 124, and Milbank, *Being Reconciled*, 66–67.

72. Milbank, "Can a Gift be Given?" 153.

73. Milbank, *Theology and Social Theory*, 430.

Milbank describes as "the harmonious ordering of difference," "the infinite series of differences," or again "the distinction of the different."[74]

Unlike what Milbank sees as the trajectory of the Anselmian Trinitarian tradition, Milbank refrains from beginning a discussion of the Trinity with respect to the unity of the divine essence.[75] The reason for this refusal stems from the Trinitarian logic of what Milbank believes originated in the early West and East alike, namely, that the divine unity of the Godhead establishes itself only in the willful perichoresis of different and differentiating Trinitarian persons. This point signifies that the Divine persons truly stand as distinct from one another, relating in freedom and love, mutually indwelling as a community that is both infinitely passive and simultaneously active.[76] Indeed, while rejecting the divine and Plotinian simplicity of the West's Trinitarian theology, Milbank takes up the language of pure relationality.

In this sense, Milbank does not define Fatherhood substantially, but with regard to Sonship. Thus, affirming with all Trinitarian traditions that the Father is the fount of all divinity, the love of the Father generates a difference by generating the Son as Other. Father and Son accordingly coexist, without substance in their own right, but as pure relations: between the two, a relationship of pure generator to the purely generated exists. While such a relationship, as Milbank explains, can appear "locked" within itself as two poles—as a power over another and as another under power and thus ultimately the subsumption of the Son into the Father's self-identity—one need not view it this way.[77] This image of domination ignores the willing love of the Son for the Father and the Father's reception of that love. From this mutual love proceeds the Holy Spirit; a relation within two relations, the Spirit constitutes the difference that breaks apart this self-identity, reversing the relative identities while producing a harmony within diversity.[78] The Spirit is the unity of the Godhead.[79]

Thus, the unity of the Trinity is a unity found not in its divine and absolute simplicity, but in the Godhead's ability to generate difference.

74. Ibid., 404, 429.
75. Milbank, "Second Difference," 231.
76. Milbank, *Theology and Social Theory*, 430–31.
77. Ibid., 430.
78. Ibid., 430–31.
79. Ibid., 430.

This unity within difference—produced by the reciprocal love of the Father for the Son and the Son for the Father through the Spirit—makes for a divine community of charity.[80] The community's unity (if that is even the appropriate word) is not defined by self-identity but, like the relationship between notes in a symphony, by harmonious difference.[81] It comprises an ontology of difference that can ground the practice of charity.

Conclusion

I have drawn out a possible synthesis of two social visions that I find particularly appealing, the pragmatic argued for by Richard Rorty and the charitous argued for by John Milbank. I have generally contended that one can synthesize these two hermeneutics in terms of the private-public distinction of Rorty's pragmatic hermeneutic, the public defining the boundaries of the legal-political order and the private defining personal aspirations. In light of the violence of the world as we currently experience it, Rorty's hermeneutic vision seems a necessary inclusion in any overarching political framework. It allows for collective, albeit limited, political and legal organization, defining the social order's common good as tightly bound to the individual goods of the persons who comprise the order. The order staves off tyranny and grants better possibilities. But this vision of the social order seldom constitutes the sole vision of the persons living in it. Rather, these persons concretely engage with their fellow citizens and friends not as objects for their own self-creative projects, but as Others who are valuable in their own right. Therefore, the fact stands that this legal vision cannot constitute the personal visions of most of the persons who make up the social order, if any of them engage in projects of self-creation defined by the Other, which is always charitous.

Through this manner of argumentation, I have also put a rather tricky spin on Rorty's hermeneutic assumptions, one that makes such an essay perhaps worthy of inclusion in a volume on Rorty and religiosity. The spin is the following: that so long as charity remains a real possible mode of self-creation from the pragmatic necessity, then, ontologically speaking, the pragmatic hermeneutic must itself confess

---

80. Ibid., 429.
81. Ibid., 431.

to the real possibility of a Christian ontology, defined by an analogical relationship to a Trinitarian God who gifts this world and its salvation. When one takes the language of charity seriously, one opens up the real possibility of eschatologically grounding the pragmatic social vision in a Trinitarian God, all by means of the middle term of charity. At least this point seems to hold as long as the pragmatic vision takes seriously its own aims: to protect individual and collective possibility.

I do not doubt that Rorty would himself be aghast by such a statement, especially considering his rather elementary views on the nature and structure of the Christian faith, not to mention his condescending attitude toward it. I would rely on Rorty's sense of irony and, again, willingness to enter into redescriptions of the world. I would hope that, in his death, he could possibly smile at the prospect that someone was, if not clever enough, then at least audacious enough to redescribe his project in such a way that it brings out precisely that which he most abhorred.

CHAPTER SEVEN

Contingency, Irony, and Vulnerability
Richard Rorty and Scriptural Reasoning

Jacob Goodson

Introduction

Jeffrey Stout, in *Democracy and Tradition*, develops typologies that he labels as "secular liberalism," "new traditionalism," and "democratic traditionalism." Democratic traditionalism arises as a possible third way between secular liberalism and new traditionalism. Representatives of secular liberalism consist of John Rawls and Richard Rorty while representatives of the new traditionalism include Stanley Hauerwas and John Milbank. The secular liberalism of Rawls and Rorty prevents religious reasoning in public, secular debates. This prevention, on Stout's account, creates "resentment" among the new traditionalists. This "resentment" leads to confusing the actual virtues of democracy with the inaccurate descriptions and theories of democracy provided by the secular liberals. Democratic traditionalism, therefore, offers a way to appreciate and understand the actual virtues of democracy. Stout recommends a democratic traditionalism where (a) secular liberals do not control our cultural understanding of democracy and liberalism and (b) religious reasoning remains a necessary part of public, secular debates. However, the latter is only fruitful if religious reasoning is not based upon "resentment" towards the secularity of that debate.[1]

1. See Stout, *Democracy and Tradition*.

In this essay, I forward Stout's proposal while simultaneously complicating his typologies.² I forward Stout's recommendation by offering the practice of scriptural reasoning as a way to form the necessary habits of religious traditionalists to reason properly in public, secular debates.³ I complicate Stout's typologies by employing the work of one of the secular liberals, Richard Rorty, to describe exactly how the practice of scriptural reasoning contains the ability to form such habits in religious traditionalists.⁴ I am not challenging Stout's democratic traditionalism with my reading of Rorty;⁵ rather, my claim is that religious traditionalists have a surprising ally in Rorty's *Contingency, Irony, and Solidarity* when it comes to locating a description for the practice of scriptural reasoning—a practice, as developed in the next section, that requires strong religious commitment in order for it to work well.⁶

Nicholas Adams observes that given "the religious difficulties surrounding foreign policy, school education and domestic and international law, it is surely a significant problem if the deep reasonings of religious traditions are not made public."⁷ Although I agree with Adams' observation, I also think religious traditionalists need to cultivate par-

---

2. For more on my appreciation of Stout's *Democracy and Tradition*, see my review of it in *The American Journal of Theology and Philosophy*, 185–91.

3. A description of the practice of scriptural reasoning is developed in this essay, so for now all that need be said about it is that it is a practice that involves members of the three Abrahamic traditions studying their sacred texts together. Furthermore, it should be noted at the outset that by offering a description of the practice of scriptural reasoning, I hope to remain in the parameters of Nicholas Adams' insight concerning scriptural reasoning: "Scriptural reasoning is a practice which can be theorised, not a theory which can be put into practice" (Adams, "Making Deep Reasonings Public," 43).

4. It is interesting to note that toward the end of his life, Rorty admitted that he was not against religious traditions per se but rather certain forms of religious rhetoric—such as the rhetoric of the so-called religious right. See Rorty, "Religion in the Public Square," 141–49.

5. Indeed, my reading of Rorty partly depends on Stout's own method of reading Rorty; see Stout, *Democracy and Tradition*, 85–91. Stout's section titled "Is Religion a Conversation-Stopper?" stimulated much of my own thinking for this essay.

6. In this sense, this essay addresses those whom Stout labels as new traditionalists for the purpose of arguing that the right questions to ask in this debate, rather than should religious traditionalists resent secular liberalism, are (a) what kind of reasonings should religious traditionalists employ in public, secular debates, and (b) how should religious traditionalists approach such debates?

7. Adams, "Making Deep Reasonings Public," 55. It should be noted that Adams footnotes Stout's *Democracy and Tradition* as offering a "timely argument for this view" (57).

ticular dispositions of reasoning in public debate.[8] Surprisingly, Rorty's work offers ways to think about how scriptural reasoning forms such dispositions.

Deep Reasonings and Rorty's Private/Public Distinction

In the conclusion of his book *Habermas and Theology*, Adams claims that the practice of scriptural reasoning (hereafter, SR) offers a way to make traditional "deep reasonings" public.[9] Adams understands the practice of SR to serve as a corrective to Jürgen Habermas' tendency of not taking religious discourses seriously on their own terms. Rather than offering a theory as a corrective to Habermas' tendency, Adams describes "an already-existing practice" that provides for "good-quality argument in the public sphere."[10]

By "deep reasonings," Adams means "the written record of arguments from the past, perhaps including minority positions that did not win the day, but which have been preserved."[11] They involve "actual chains of reasoning, argumentation, and conclusions" rather than "definitions, axioms, and presuppositions" or "logics and rules for reasoning."[12] Adams

---

8. In other words, religious traditionalists need to cultivate particular dispositions in order "to make their reasoning publicly accountable to those who reason differently," which is what C. C. Pecknold suggests is "one of the promises of the practice of 'scriptural reasoning'" (Pecknold, "Augustine's Readable City," paras. 6–7):
The thesis is simple: reading skills are political skills, and the reading of scripture is the training ground for reading the political. That is to link scriptural hermeneutics and reading practices with the generation of political culture . . . [that] encourages faithful Christians to make public their deepest reasons, which is also to say to make their reasoning publicly accountable to those who reason differently. This is to look forward to a different form of civic life than we presently face.
One of the promises of the practice of "scriptural reasoning" is that it may help model a different relation of unity and diversity in which traditions and the sources of traditions can fully face one another and converse in political friendships that seek political wisdom together.

9 Though different in its emphases, Pecknold offers a parallel account of scriptural reasoning to the one offered in the present essay.
See also Adams, "Making Deep Reasonings Public": "Scriptural reasoning models a practice of making deep reasonings public, by offering a forum, in which mutual learning of languages takes place, unpredictably, among friends, to which an open invitation is extended to those who are interested to participate" (54).

10. Adams, *Habermas and Theology*, 239, 238.

11. Ibid., 241–42.

12. Ibid., 242.

emphasizes: "*Scriptural reasoning makes deep reasonings public.*"[13] SR understands deep reasonings in terms not of "obstacles to debate" but rather "as conditions for conversation, friendship and mutual understanding."[14]

SR is the practice of "scriptural texts from at least two traditions being read [together] by members of at least two traditions."[15] Ideally, SR involves members of the three Abrahamic traditions (Jewish, Christian, and Muslim) reading and interpreting their scriptural texts together. Adams elaborates, "Each of the three Abrahamic traditions has its own rules for interpreting scripture (and internal disagreement about these rules), and even if there is overlap between them, it is not the overlap [itself] that makes scriptural reasoning possible."[16]

Furthermore, according to Adams, "Scriptural reasoning models the discovery that making deep reasoning public is . . . risky—because one makes oneself vulnerable when revealing what one loves."[17] The only necessary and common working assumption among practitioners of SR is "a shared desire to study scriptural texts."[18] Even within the practice, it is not "consensus" that serves as the goal but rather "friendship." The kind of friendship that comes from the practice of SR is a result of the vulnerability that comes from making deep reasonings public through shared textual study.[19]

While I think Adams' description of SR (and how it functions as a time and place to make deep reasonings public) is quite accurate and helpful,[20] there needs to be a clarification concerning what *kind* of

13. Ibid. Italics in original.
14. Ibid.
15. Ibid.
16. Ibid., 242–43.
17. Ibid., 242.
18. Ibid., 243.
19. For clarification on Adams' understanding of friendship, see his "Making Deep Reasonings Public"; for example, "Scriptural reasoning displays the characteristic of a society of friends, in the public sense" (53).
20. I find this paragraph from Adams' "Making Deep Reasonings Public" especially rich:

> Scriptural reasoning is a model for making deep reasonings public because it fosters discussion between members of different religious traditions with respect to their most important sacred texts. Precisely because it is not primarily oriented to particular agreements or outcomes that are clearly identified in advance of study, it offers a resource for discovering deep reasonings in ways that are not subject to severe pressures of time or other constraints imposed

deep reasonings SR actually nurtures or ought to nurture. I turn to the work of David Novak, who does not seek to answer this question for scriptural reasoning, per se, but does offer an answer to the question of what kind of religious and traditional "reasonings" ought to be a part of public debate.[21]

In his book *Natural Law in Judaism*, Novak defines natural law in these terms: "the idea of a reality that is less exalted than direct divine revelation and more exalted than merely local human arrangements."[22] In his elaboration of what he means by "less exalted than direct divine revelation," he engages the work of the American secular philosopher Richard Rorty. In particular, he suggests that Rorty's famous comment that religion is a "conversation-stopper" in public debate provides an opportunity for religious traditions to articulate precisely the kind of reasonings involved concerning religious convictions in "secular space."[23]

---

by mass media. Because of its *chevruta* approach to study, it is not reducible to the transmission of information by religious experts. Scriptural reasoning is probably not the most efficient means for conveying such information, or for generating agreement on important issues of the day. But that does not mean it serves no purpose with respect to these important purposes. Rather, it draws attention to the prior formation that may be required for things like transmitting information or coming to agreement. The practices of scriptural reasoning suggest that making deep reasonings public is not primarily a matter of transmitting information or reaching agreement. Making deep reasonings public may be a matter of being open to surprises, and fostering forms of collegial friendship, by deepening relations between persons with respect to sacred texts. This process cannot be rushed. That means that the urgency of contemporary questions, and the urgent need for consensus, should not be allowed to force the pace for making deep reasonings public. It is the attractiveness of study, not the threat of political disaster, that offers the most promising conditions for this time-consuming but urgently needed process.

(Adams, "Making Deep Reasonings Public," 55–56).

21. Except when quoting a source, I deliberately avoid using the phrases "public sphere" and "public square." Both rely on shape metaphors in order to offer an image of public debate, and both are tied to particular conversations about what that debate ought to look like. I use the less descriptive and more generic phrase "public debate."

22. Novak, *Natural Law in Judaism*, 3.

23. Interestingly, Novak claims that his reason for engaging Rorty on this question is that they came together in a public exchange over Rorty's comment that religion is a "conversation-stopper" in public debate. About that exchange, Novak remarks: "As someone who believes in the authority of God's will as I believe it to have been revealed to the Jewish people, and as someone who is convinced that there are no acceptable alternatives to democracy in the world today, certainly for Jews . . . I could not allow myself to leave such a challenge unanswered" (Novak, *Natural Law in Judaism*, 12). The exchange took place at the University of Virginia in the fall of 1994.

Rorty borrows the language of religion as "conversation-stopper" from Stephen Carter.²⁴ Carter argues that the problem with liberalism is that it does not allow religious convictions to have a substantial place in "the public square." In the second chapter of his book *The Culture of Disbelief*, Carter writes, "One good way to end a conversation—or to start an argument—is to tell a group of well-educated professionals that you hold a political position (preferably a controversial one, such as being against abortion or pornography) because it is required by your understanding of God's will." ²⁵ Rorty disagrees; he thinks that the virtue of liberalism is that it makes religious convictions a "conversation-stopper."²⁶ Rorty's problem is that this is not enforced enough in America.

Novak's engagement with Rorty results in two important observations. First, it displays the importance of how one reasons in public. Rorty's problem is not that one is against abortion or pornography. Rather, Rorty's problem is that one is against abortion and pornography because it is based on one's theological reasoning concerning the will of God.²⁷ Second, Novak, unlike Jeffrey Stout (among others), neither criticizes nor disagrees with Rorty's argument. Rather, he says that Rorty is right: reasoning based on the will of God in "public" is and ought to be a conversation-stopper.²⁸ In fact, Novak says that Jews cannot speak "persuasively in secular public space" about prohibitions that are based

---

24. See Carter, *Culture of Disbelief*; quoted in Rorty, *Philosophy and Social Hope*, 171.

25. Carter, *Culture of Disbelief*, 21.

26. In a later essay, Rorty clarifies his disagreement with Carter: "Some years ago I wrote a response to Stephen Carter's book *Culture of Disbelief* (1994). Carter had argued that it was unfair to religious believers to try to keep religious convictions out of the public square. I replied that such exclusion was part of a reasonable compromise between secular democratic governments and ecclesiastical organizations." Rorty continues his summary a paragraph later: "In my reply to Carter I urged that democratic societies should, in the manner of [Thomas] Jefferson, think of themselves as having exchanged toleration for an assurance that believers would leave their religion at home when discussing political questions in public" (Rorty, "Religion in the Public Square," 141).

27. In his later essay, "Religion in the Public Square," he confirms my judgment here: "It is OK for Christian believers to have Christian reasons for supporting redistribution of wealth or opposing same-sex marriage" (Rorty, "Religion in the Public Square," 147).

28. "Richard Rorty is right about the invocation of God's will being a 'conversation-stopper,' that is, in a conversation conducted within the confines of a democratic society and observant of its criteria of discourse" (Novak, *Natural Law in Judaism*, 16). Also see Novak's essay "Religious Communities, Secular Societies, and Sexuality": "I agree with Richard Rorty when he argues that those who speak of 'God's will' are 'conversation stoppers' in a democratic society" (287). Notice that the title of Novak's "reader," which was determined by the editors of the volume, is *Tradition in the Public Square*.

on arguments from "the will of God" because such prohibitions require "special revelation to a singular community in history."[29]

Novak does not stop there; he thinks we need to make a distinction between "the will of God" and "the wisdom of God."[30] He remarks, "If a Jew who is religiously committed to his or her tradition is going to be able to participate in a democratic conversation, he or she will have to speak of the wisdom of God."[31] What is the difference, he asks, between the wisdom of God and the will of God? He says, "To speak of the will of God, when 'will' functions as a transitive verb, is to speak of an object which cannot be separated from its subject at any time, even conceptually." In order to illustrate his point, he employs the prohibition of eating pork: to prohibit eating pork based on Leviticus 11 "is to assert that the very meaning of the prohibition of eating pork is a direct response to the will of God as revealed in the Torah."[32] In other words, to prohibit the consumption of pork is to make explicit the source of that prohibition and to reason only from that source. Novak continues, "to speak of the wisdom of God, when 'wisdom' functions as a predicate, is to speak of a state which can be spoken of, at least initially, apart from the subject of whom it is predicated. For when we speak of something as being the product of the wisdom of God, we can see its meaning, at least initially, in and of itself."[33] Novak's example for the wisdom of God is the prohibition against murder, which can be articulated without reference to its source (the Decalogue). Then Novak gets to the point that serves our purposes: "All of this, to refer to the respective examples just cited, is why Jews can speak persuasively in secular public space about the prohibition of murder in a way we cannot (and should not) speak about the prohibition of eating pork there."[34]

At this juncture, then, we have a pretty good idea of what Novak means by natural law being "less exalted than direct divine revelation." Claiming to know the will of God is reasoning from "direct divine

---

29. Novak, *Natural Law in Judaism*, 18.

30. Ibid., 16–18; see also Novak's essay "Religious Communities, Secular Societies, and Sexuality": "I disagree with Rorty's apparent belief that this is the only possible mode of religious conversation in public. One may also speak of the wisdom of God, and that is a different mode of discourse" (287–88).

31. Novak, *Natural Law in Judaism*, 17.

32. Ibid., 17–18.

33. Ibid.

34. Ibid., 18.

revelation."[35] While the wisdom of God is "less exalted" than the will of God, it has to remain primary in order for traditional Jews to "speak persuasively in secular public space."[36] Thus, for Novak, reasoning from the will of God is a "conversation-stopper" in public debate, whereas reasoning from the wisdom of God is not.[37]

35. Significantly, for the purposes of scriptural reasoning, I find a possible parallel to this claim in a medieval Islamic description of justified warfare. See Shaybani, *Islamic Law of Nations*, 76–77:
"If you besiege the inhabitants of a fortress or a town and they try to get you to let them surrender on the basis of God's judgment, do not do so, since you do not know what God's judgment is, but make them surrender to your judgment and then decide their case according to your own views [not what you consider God's views to be]. But if the besieged inhabitants of a fortress or a town ask you to give them a pledge in God's name or in the name of God's Messenger, you should not do so, but give the pledge in your names or the names of your fathers. For if you should ever break it, it would be [better] if it were in the names of you or your fathers [and not in the name of God or God's messenger]."

36. The primacy of the wisdom of God over the will of God is not without its Christian parallels. For example, John Milbank argues that William of Ockham is the one within the Christian tradition to wrongly describe the primacy of the will of God over the "intellect" of God. Before Ockham, on Milbank's account, the Christian tradition always prioritized the divine intellect over the divine will. See Milbank, *Theology and Social Theory*, 13–18. The danger of prioritizing the divine will over the divine intellect is that God's action becomes arbitrary and disordered. With Milbank's help, we better understand the significance of Novak's description of the natural law in terms of divine wisdom. Novak wants to maintain the theological origin of natural law *contra* modern secular politics, which divorces the natural law from eternal law. For St. Thomas Aquinas, natural law is participation in the eternal law; eternal law remains in the mind (intellect) of God. For modern secular politics, natural law becomes divorced from eternal law and finds its grounding in either "the sealed-off totality of nature" (Hugo Grotius) or "the state of nature" (Thomas Hobbes); see Milbank, *Theology and Social Theory*, 9–13.

37. Through an engagement with Plato's *Euthyphro*, Novak clarifies his distinction between divine wisdom and the divine will. In this engagement, he also addresses the importance of reasoning from God's will within one's own tradition: "I agree with Plato that it is better to argue for a practice based on *why* it is to be done (its wisdom) than simply on *who* originally authorized it (its will). However, unlike Plato, being a believer in divine *creation ex nihilo*, I thereby believe that God is the source of both wisdom and authority, and that the relationship with this God that revelation enables is the highest good. Therefore, although in secular society one need not mention the divine source of wisdom, since secular society is itself not concerned with the God-human relationship, the religious person must never forget the divine source of any wisdom. For the religious person comes to secular society out of a prior community in which he or she is forever rooted and to which he or she must ever return. The essential purpose of that community is to proclaim the name of God" (Novak, "Religious Communities, Secular Societies, and Sexuality," 288). While it is not within the scope of this essay to address

Scriptural reasoning offers a way for religious traditions to distinguish reasonings based on God's wisdom or God's will.[38] In this way, it is a practice or training ground for the kind of public debates that both Novak and Rorty envision.[39] Therefore, SR serves as a practice for establishing the significant habits for a public theology that engages different traditions.[40] In short, SR does this by training us how to distinguish our deep reasonings based on God's wisdom or God's will.[41]

---

the possible virtues of reasoning from God's will for arguments within one's own religious tradition, Novak provides a fruitful starting point for such an investigation. In order for "the religious person" to not "forget the divine source of any wisdom" yet not reason from the divine source in diverse contexts, we need to articulate the specific dispositions required within "public" arguments; filling in these details is what I hope to accomplish in this essay.

38. For an example of how scriptural reasoning offers a way for religious traditions to distinguish reasonings based on God's wisdom or God's will, see the essays that comprise the section titled "Spirituality and Social Responsibility," 89–183. In his introduction to these essays, Kevin Hughes remarks: "It is precisely in our reading of scriptures together, with an eye toward the economics and politics of late modernity, that we may liberate ancient insights for a new, transformative, theopolitical vision, one not possible for any one tradition to propose alone" (90). This last part of the quotation displays why the communal aspect of the practice of scriptural reasoning remains so important for how it trains people to reason.

39. I am aware of D. Stephen Long's argument that the church constitutes the highest "public" (see Long, *The Goodness of God*). Long might say that for the Christian, my use of "public" remains too determined by secularism; however, I would warn against Long's tendency toward both a binary and univocal use of "public" within his reasoning. Unlike Rorty, my use of "public" does not monopolize what constitutes "public." In this sense, the potential risk of Long's description of the church shares in Rorty's reasoning concerning the public and the private: they represent two sides of the same logical coin. Furthermore, the practice of scriptural reasoning offers a way to conceive of the "public" both in terms of degrees and with multiple layers depending on whom one engages at particular times. Within a non-binary reasoning, then, we could say that the church remains the highest "public" for a Christian practitioner of scriptural reasoning while other publics emerge through the practice of scriptural reasoning (a public consisting of Jews and Muslims and a public determined by shared textual study), through participation in the kind of public debates that Novak and Rorty describe, etc.

40. This thesis should not be read in a way that necessarily entails that SR, as a practice, is not a good in and of itself. Adams' own emphasis on the practice of SR, in relation to Habermas, suggests that it is both a good and an end in itself. I think that both are right: SR is a good and an end in itself, and it trains us for other ends and goods as well—such as engagement in broader public debates.

41. Talking about the practice of scriptural reasoning in terms of "wisdom" is not new. For two examples, see the following: Hardy, "Reason, Wisdom, and the Interpretation of Scripture," 69–88; Ford, "An Inter-faith Wisdom," 273–303. I hope this essay contributes to Ford's observation: "One promise of scriptural reasoning is the

In this sense, SR satisfies Rorty's worry with reasoning from the will of God but also challenges Rorty's privatization of religious convictions that remain grounded in scriptural texts.[42] In the next section, I develop Rorty's descriptions of final vocabularies, ironists, and redescription for the purpose of describing the practice of SR in these Rortyean terms.[43]

Final Vocabularies, Ironists, and Redescription

Rorty's understanding of "redescription" is couched in his account of what an "ironist" looks like. He attempts to describe an ironist rather than prescribe what an ironist ought to be or should do.[44] Within that model, he describes an ironist in the following ways. First, the encounter with and knowledge of other "final vocabularies" makes an ironist doubtful about his or her own "final vocabulary." Second, an ironist realizes that his or her final vocabulary contains no kind of absolute certainty in response to that doubtfulness. Third, the more an ironist reflects on his or her own final vocabulary, the more he or she recognizes that it is not closer to describing reality any better (or worse) than other final vocabularies. In summary, we might say that an ironist is someone who recognizes his or her interpretations of the world exactly as

---

formation of people through collegial study, wise interpretation and friendship who might be exemplary citizens of the twenty-first century, seeking the public good for the sake of God and God's peaceful purposes" (301).

42. In other words, this essay provides three different clarifications and corrections. First and foremost, while Rorty is right about certain types of deeper reasonings being a conversation-stopper, not all deeper reasonings are subject to Rorty's criticisms. Second, while Adams is right that scriptural reasoning provides a practice for publicizing deep reasonings, not all deep reasonings need to be publicized. Third, while Novak offers a helpful clarification to both Adams and Rorty on the same points discussed here, Novak's argument concerning the wisdom of God not involving revelation begs for clarification. The practice of scriptural reasoning itself clarifies Novak's argument. In Novak's own terms, SR can be a training ground for formulating the wisdom of God out of a theology of revelation—that is, through reading scriptural texts with participants in different religious traditions. Additionally, the strength of Adams' argument is that he offers an "already-existing practice" rather than a theory—which offers a correction to Novak's own proposal. This last point is emphasized toward the end of this essay.

43. See Rorty, *Contingency, Irony, and Solidarity*.

44. I take this move to be part and parcel with the overall tone of his book: not to offer any kind of philosophical theory to justify his arguments but rather to point toward what people are doing even if those people may not recognize Rorty's terms for what they are doing (it is for this reason that Rorty does not talk about "ironism" but rather "ironists").

interpretations and not as necessarily the way the world is. The result of these three descriptions is that an ironist remains aware "that the terms in which they describe themselves are subject to change, always aware of the *contingency* and *fragility* of their final vocabularies, and thus of their selves."[45]

Later in this essay, we will return to Rorty's uses of "contingency" and "fragility." More immediately, the question is, what does Rorty mean by doubt? Does he risk a kind of Cartesian use of doubt? Should we doubt all that we can? Should we doubt the undoubtable, such as our final vocabularies—which contain and include the very language we would have to use in order to doubt? Does Rorty recommend that we doubt for the sake of doubting? Charles Sanders Peirce calls these "paper doubts" and contrasts them with the real doubts that result from concrete problems and real situations.

Rorty's concern here is not with doubt, per se, but rather how people attempt to overcome their doubt. When someone asserts or assumes his or her own final vocabulary as the resolution for doubt, Rorty wants to call foul and impose a time-out. Final vocabularies do not resolve doubt. An ironist doubts her final vocabulary not because, in Cartesian fashion, doubt is the name of the game; an ironist doubts her final vocabulary because she recognizes that the final vocabulary is simply an interpretation of one's self and the world. It is one language game among many. The finality of a final vocabulary is not final in any metaphysical or ontological sense; it is final in a functional or pragmatic sense. In other words, Rorty wants to stress what final vocabularies are *not*.[46] He wants to address the question, what are the limits of one's final vocabulary? Those limits can be described as "poetic achievements" instead of the result of inquiry with

---

45. Rorty, *Contingency, Irony, and Solidarity*, 74; emphasis added.

46. This claim does not entail that Rorty is against "final vocabularies." Indeed, I find the opposite to be the case in Rorty's actual reasoning. For Rorty, final vocabularies are unavoidable; everyone has them, and he does not think that this fact is a problem. Rather, the problem rests in what one does with and expects of one's final vocabularies. One should neither use nor expect one's final vocabulary to overcome doubts that arise as a result of encounters with other final vocabularies. After reading and reflecting on the present essay, Sarah Rose Dorton captures the practicality of this point concerning "final vocabularies"—especially in relation to the practice of scriptural reasoning—when she writes, "Scriptural reasoning helps facilitate multi-faith discussion and debate by providing the opportunity to hear out people of other faiths and learn their vocabulary. It also lets one reflect on their own vocabulary and realize strengths and weaknesses in it" (Personal correspondence, April 29, 2011).

strict criteria. Those who go the direction of inquiry with strict criteria are seeking to overcome their doubt in some absolute, permanent way. Rorty's ironist learns to live with the doubt that she cannot overcome and finds other final vocabularies attractive, not because they offer more accurate depictions of reality, but because she seeks "diversification and novelty" in her life. We might say that an ironist does not seek accurate depictions of reality but only more descriptions of the world and oneself. Rorty's word for this tendency is "redescription."

How does redescription work, according to Rorty? The practice of reading serves as Rorty's primary example. For Rorty, what matters for interpretation are the images and words the books themselves provide:

> We [ironists] do not care whether ... writers manage ... to live up to their own self-images. What we want to know is whether to adopt those images—to re-create ourselves, in whole or in part, in these people's image. We go about answering this question by experimenting with the vocabularies which these people concocted. We describe ourselves, our situation, our past, in those terms and compare the results with alternative redescriptions which use the vocabularies of alternative figures. We ironists hope, by this continual redescription, to make the best selves for ourselves that we can.[47]

The interesting part of this passage is Rorty's claim of recreating ourselves "in these people's image,"[48] which is a claim that invites us to return to the practice of scriptural reasoning. In a sense, this is SR's hope as well: to provide a concrete practice for re-creation in the "image" found in a text. For SR, though, it is not any text but the scriptural text. The readers do not re-create themselves but instead are re-created by the images and words of the scriptural text. Agency is found in the words and images of the text. Therefore, we might say that SR is a practice of redescription.[49] It provides a time and place for creating more descriptions of the reader.[50]

---

47. Rorty, *Contingency, Irony, and Solidarity*, 79–80.

48. For an interesting theological parallel of Rorty's hermeneutics on this particular point, see Robert Jenson's *Systematic Theology*, 39.

49. For the role of "diversification and novelty" within the logic and practice of scriptural reasoning, see Goodson, "Repressing Novelty?"

50. Stanley Hauerwas describes this aspect of scriptural reasoning well when he says:
   I think there is a danger in interpreting the work of SR in ... terms ... that ... celebrate what wonderful people we are because we respect one another

How does this work within SR? Some of Rorty's terms provide an apt description. Within SR, everyone who comes together to read the Abrahamic scriptures confesses a final vocabulary—what they call their religious traditions. They confess their final vocabulary as vocabularies—that is, as interpretations or language games. To participate in SR is to empty oneself of (what has been called) a God's-eye view of the meaning of the text and to recognize that all interpretations are exactly that: interpretations.

Within the practice of SR, the text becomes the only authority in the room and thus fashions a kind of "contingency" and "fragility" among its readers—that is, the SR practitioners. The "contingency" and "fragility" comes about by making oneself completely vulnerable both to the text as well as to others reading the text. In order for redescription to be a real possibility, this vulnerability is necessary.[51]

Scriptural Reasoning as Public Theology

This vulnerability helps us begin to think about how and why SR can be described as a practice of public theology. Rorty would find the assumption and use of scriptural texts within this practice necessarily makes it a private activity. Reading Scripture is fine with Rorty as long as it is done in solitude and not brought into public discourse.[52] SR challenges Rorty

---

sufficiently to be reading scripture together in the same room. Such a perception is to give a humanistic and cosmopolitan narrative to the activity that I think betrays anyone who has been shaped by Peter [Ochs'] understanding of scriptural reasoning. Those insights . . . draw profoundly on the depth of [Ochs'] Jewishness and his ability to see that depth in Christians and Muslims. The depth about which I speak is his understanding that we are people dependent on a narrative that can only be known through a people's memory across time. So scriptural reasoning does not begin with abstractions but rather with the actual practice of texts shaping the possibilities before us.

(Hauerwas, "Postscript").

51. I discuss the necessity of vulnerability within the practice of scriptural reasoning in *An Introduction to Scriptural Reasoning* (forthcoming).

52. In *Contingency, Irony, and Solidarity*, Rorty thinks that the Christians and Jews who read their Scriptures do so in a way that he describes as a "private allusion." However, in one of the places where Rorty admits his shift from "atheism" to "anticlericalism," he addresses the role of Scripture "in the public square." On the one hand, Rorty claims: "religious believers should not justify their support of or opposition to legislation simply by saying 'Scripture says'" (Rorty, "Religion in the Public Square," 147). On the other hand, Rorty suggests that Christians need to be better readers of Scripture if they are going to reason from Scripture: "I am not sure it counts as having

on this point because it functions in Rortyean terms, but only because it remains centered around the sacred texts of Judaism, Christianity, and Islam. In fact, the practice of SR helps us rethink Rorty's public-private distinction introduced at the beginning of this essay. The best way to display this point is through Rorty's contrast of Habermas and Foucault.

Rorty summarizes the difference between Habermas and Foucault in the following way: "Michel Foucault is an ironist who is unwilling to be a liberal, whereas Jürgen Habermas is a liberal who is unwilling to be an ironist."[53] Of course, Rorty calls himself a "liberal ironist" and therefore wants to describe himself as being somewhere between the two. Foucault strongly resists any kind of God's-eye perspective, even to the point that he refuses to make any kind of judgment concerning the progress of "liberal" politics. Habermas' liberal politics is right, but his inclusion of religion and his rationalism/universalism does not allow for any kind of private irony. Within these terms, Rorty wants Foucault's resistance to any kind of God's-eye view of the world without Foucault's refusal of liberalism. Furthermore, he wants Habermas' liberal politics, but he also wants both a poetic (rather than rationalist/universalist) and privatized (rather than inclusive of the religious) understanding of what is included in that politics.[54]

The practice of SR speaks to Rorty's arguments concerning a poetic politics, which allows for private allusions and religious beliefs, not by asserting that religion ought to be part of public debate, but by

---

such reasons if the person who finds [same-sex] marriage inconceivable is unwilling or unable . . . to discuss the seeming tension between Leviticus 22:18 and 1 Corinthians 13" (Rorty, "Religion in the Public Square," 147). This kind of comment suggests, to me at least, that the kind of practice scriptural reasoning is—and the debates that it fosters—is along the lines of what Rorty thinks is needed here.

53. Rorty, *Contingency, Irony, and Solidarity*, 61.

54. Note that Habermas thus takes it from both sides: for Adams' standards, Habermas does not allow for the deep reasonings of the religious traditions; for Rorty's standards, Habermas remains too inclusive of the religious. I imagine that if understood in post-metaphysical terms, Habermas might agree with Novak's language concerning the wisdom of God. If so, then Adams' suggestions concerning Habermas and scriptural reasoning might gain more momentum in the sense that Habermas might agree that the deeper reasonings of the religious traditions can be a part of public debate if those reasonings are from the wisdom of God rather than the will of God. In this sense, Habermas' comments about the importance of Thomas Aquinas' natural law theory and the role of "scripture" within practical reasoning might offer a way forward for this question. I hope to write on these questions in regards to Habermas' work and relate them to questions raised in n. 36: the moral and political significance of prioritizing divine wisdom over divine volition.

experimenting with a poetic and public practice of reading together in "solidarity," to use Rorty's word, where no God's-eye point of view is allowed or assumed. Employing Rorty's own words, SR can be described as going "about answering this question [of the politics of redescription] by experimenting with the vocabularies which these people concocted."[55] SR works as a controlled experiment for learning how to be an ironist. It encourages and nurtures Rorty's three descriptions of what being an ironist looks like: it serves as a time and place for the encounter and knowledge of other final vocabularies; it nurtures the recognition that one's final vocabulary contains no kind of absolute certainty about itself; and it encourages a concrete way for the ironist to reflect on her own final vocabulary in such a way that the more she reflects on it, the more she recognizes that it is not closer to describing reality any better (or worse) than other final vocabularies.[56] This last point is understood within SR through the recognition that interpretations of Scripture are interpretations and thus not necessarily what biblical or Qur'anic passages mean for all time in all places. The sum result of these three descriptions, once again, is that an ironist remains aware "that the terms in which they describe themselves are subject to change, always aware of the contingency and fragility of their final vocabularies, and thus of their selves."[57]

No part of Rorty's ways of reasoning needs to exclude those who read Scripture and who take the activity of reading Scripture as the way forward for repairing suffering in the world.[58] In my estimation, SR attempts to be a practice for ironists who seek such repairs.[59] In seeking

55. Rorty, *Contingency, Irony, and Solidarity*, 79–80. Of course, religious traditionalists do not think that biblical language is "concocted" by humans—or, more precisely, only by humans. This is an aspect of Rorty's anti-realism, which I neglected to address in my discussion of this quotation earlier in this essay. However, I have argued elsewhere that Rorty's anti-realism makes a theological appropriation of his work most challenging and difficult; see Goodson, "Theology after Epistemology: Milbank between Rorty and Taylor on Truth," 155–69.

56. As one critic of Rorty reminds us, however: "In reality, liberal ironists [like Rorty] ... do not create soup kitchens, tutorial programs, AIDS hospices, health clinics, or hunger coalitions" (Marsh, *The Beloved Community*, 135).

57. Rorty, *Contingency, Irony, and Solidarity*, 74.

58. For more on the possibility concerning the connections between practices of reading Scripture and repairing suffering in the world, see the work of Peter Ochs: *Peirce, Pragmatism, and the Logic of Scripture*, and "Philosophic Warrants for Scriptural Reasoning," 121–38.

59. We might label SR practitioners as "post-liberal" or scriptural ironists in contrast to Rorty's own self-description as a "liberal ironist."

such repairs as ironists, SR practitioners need to learn to distinguish between reasoning based on God's will and reasoning based on God's wisdom. In the terms developed here, we might say that reasoning from God's will assumes a God's-eye view, whereas reasoning from God's wisdom remains possible without making such a philosophical assumption.[60] Reasoning from God's wisdom displays the habit of vulnerability that the practice of SR forms.[61]

Developing a Habit of Reasoning from God's Wisdom

While not in relation to the practice of scriptural reasoning, David Novak suggests a description of reasoning from God's wisdom that might actually work in "secular space."[62] First, the "various traditions must initially postpone discussion of the ontological foundations of [the] respective traditions."[63] This is what Novak calls the "cosmic dimension" of the traditions. Second, "just as adherents of self-consciously religious traditions must now postpone discussion of their own ontological . . . concerns when dealing with the moral issues that arise in secular space, so must adherents of traditions thought to be nonreligious postpone discussion of their non-ontological [or] atheistic concerns here too."[64] The result of these first two entails that both the religious and the secularists abstain from "triumphalism."[65]

---

60. Once again, I need to clarify that reasoning from God's will should be practiced within one's tradition. Following Jonathan Malesic, I understand this aspect of one's religious faith as needing to be kept "secret" in "the public square." See his *Secret Faith in the Public Square*, in which he details the political and theological reasons for keeping one's religious faith "secret." Unlike Malesic, however, I think that some aspects of one's religious faith do not need to remain "secret"—namely, those aspects that involve divine wisdom. In this sense, Malesic's argument would benefit from the same distinction that Novak recommends: reasoning from divine wisdom or from the divine will.

61. In this sense, I am suggesting that the practice of scriptural reasoning assumes a disposition of vulnerability, and then the practice itself *intensifies* that disposition and forms it as a habit.

62. In relation to my use of the phrase "public theology," Novak might say that he prefers the phrase "public philosophy" because reasoning from divine wisdom speaks philosophically while reasoning from divine volition speaks theologically. See Novak, "Public Philosophy in Secular Society," in *The Sanctity of Human Life*, 141–43.

63. Novak, *Natural Law in Judaism*, 24.

64. Ibid.

65. Ibid.

In terms of actual political discussion, Novak recommends that "adherents of human rights in the modern world . . . admit the possibility at least that these cosmic concerns of those who are usually thought to be conservatives . . . could intend an external reality and not just be hypothetical."[66] For religious traditionalists, this requires that political discussions never be used for the purpose of "conversion of any kind."[67] Moreover, members of religious traditions "will also have to admit the possibility that their [own] ontological assumptions *could* be false."[68]

After working through Rorty's thought, we can understand Novak's recommendations in terms of calling for both the religious and the non-religious to treat the "cosmic dimensions" of their traditions in a way that an ironist would. As practical as Novak's advice is, he never describes "an already-existing practice" for how to develop such habits of reasoning that would then nurture "good-quality argument in the public sphere."[69] Such a practice is what SR offers for questions concerning both public theology and the repair of suffering in the world. SR enables its practitioners to develop the habits of an ironist: reasoning from the wisdom of God in public debate or the "secular space."

Scriptural Reasoning and Stout's Typologies

We might say, in returning to Stout's typologies, that SR practitioners are "new traditionalists" without "resentment" toward the secular. SR practitioners enter into secular debates as ironists exhibiting vulnerability.[70] They do not resent secularism as secular but want to repair suffering in the world—suffering that results from religious faction and violence as well as the secular prevention of deep, religious reasonings.[71] For the

---

66. Ibid., 24–25.
67. Ibid., 25.
68. Ibid.
69. Adams, *Habermas and Theology*, 239, 238.

70. It should be noted that Stanley Hauerwas displays this kind of vulnerability in his own way, thereby complicating Stout's typology on his own; see Hauerwas and Romand Coles, *Christianity, Democracy, and the Radical Ordinary*. For the role of vulnerability in these "conversations," see my review in *Contemporary Pragmatism*, 168–72.

71. Though not in these terms, Basit Koshul offers an example of scriptural reasoning as a "new traditionalism" without "resentment," in his "The Qur'anic Self, the Biblical Other, and the Contemporary Islam-West Encounter," 9–38.

sake of Stout's typologies, we might call SR practitioners non-resentful new traditionalists.[72]

In Rorty's terms, we might call SR practitioners post-liberal ironists.[73] Scriptural reasoning's requirement of vulnerability, within its own post-liberal ironist characteristics, calls for more commitment than Rorty's use of contingency and fragility does in his description of the liberal ironist. Again, according to Adams: "Scriptural reasoning models the discovery that making deep reasonings public is . . . risky—because one makes oneself vulnerable when revealing what one loves."[74] The post-liberal ironist requires what the new traditionalists enjoy and protect: a love for their particular tradition.[75] Within the practice of scriptural reasoning, this love manifests itself through a love of the sacred texts of the particular tradition of the practitioner as well as a love for studying those texts.[76] In this sense, post-liberal ironists pull off what Rorty thinks impossible: an awareness "of the contingency and fragility of their final vocabularies"[77] and a love for that tradition as if it were more than a vocabulary.[78]

In conclusion, this (re)description of SR in Rortyean terms both complicates and complements Stout's typologies. It complicates Stout's typologies because Stout himself makes such a strong contrast between new traditionalism and secular liberalism, whereas the practice of SR displays characteristics of the tendencies of both of these types.[79]

72. Being non-resentful, in practice, means being reparative.

73. See n. 59: "post-liberal" here stands in relation to Rorty's self-description as a "liberal ironist."

74. Adams, *Habermas and Theology*, 242.

75. They do so, however, without "resentment" (in Stout's sense of the term).

76. See Pecknold, *Transforming Postliberal Theology*: "The love of God must be embodied in communal practices of scriptural reading which bear effective sociopolitical witness to the religious and secular neighbour, that is, a programme of scriptural reasoning which follows a rule of love, a love that is known by its fruits" (59).

77. Rorty, *Contingency, Irony, and Solidarity*, 74.

78. The "as if" here names the way that religious traditionalists, we might say, live in the first-order reasoning of their own religious lives without questioning or reflection (in Habermas' technical sense).

79. Martin Kavka navigates Stout's work in relation to scriptural reasoning; see Kavka, "Response to Pecknold." While I agree with most of his criticisms of Pecknold's "Augustine's Readable City," I think that his argument that the "choice is rather [instead of Pecknold's puzzling "belief that both Stout and Hauerwas are correct on the issue of the relationship between religion and public life"] between Stout, scriptural reasoning, and a reading of Philippians 2 on one side . . . and Hauerwas on the other" (Kavka, "Response to Pecknold," par. 8) is problematic.

Conversely, it complements them because Stout's own recommendation of democratic traditionalism shares its philosophical roots with the descriptions of scriptural reasoning developed by Nicholas Adams and Peter Ochs:[80] American philosophy (broadly speaking) and pragmatism (more particularly).

I have two qualms with Kavka's claim here. First, Stout and scriptural reasoning should not be so easily equated. At the least, as I suggest in the present essay, I think that scriptural reasoning complicates Stout's typologies.

Second, I think that Hauerwas' work is much more complex than Kavka suggests here; Kavka backs Hauerwas into a corner of not allowing his ecclesiology to be formed by a reading of Philippians 2—that is, in Kavka's terms, to be shaped by "the logic of Philippians" where "the ecclesia has no fixed boundaries" (Kavka, "Response to Pecknold," par. 8). However, Kavka does not account for Hauerwas' actual reading of Philippians 2 where Hauerwas remarks in explicit relation to Philippians 2: "Far from being condensable, this story [the story Christians learn from the Jews about the love of God] expands as we learn and tell it" and, on the same terms employed by Kavka, "[t]he humility and 'emptying,' which stand out in this passage [Phil 2:1–8], offer stark contrast to the pride of the magnanimous man. . . . [T]he excellence of pagan virtue assumed by Aristotle served to elevate its possessor. Likewise, the friendship of virtue, by creating equality and similarity among its participants, cannot but at the same time place distance between them and others who do not share it, or do not share their virtue." Hauerwas continues, "Christians need not deny that a certain kind of friendship elevates its participants to a level of high equality. Indeed the Philippians passage suggests this, for the humility predicated of Christ is offered as an alternative to an isolated equality and similarity" (Hauerwas, "Companions on the Way," 45–46). Kavka makes the point that the church, based on his reading of Philippians 2, "is not necessarily any different, in content or in forms of reasoning, than the 'secular' culture in which it finds itself" (Kavka, "Response to Pecknold," par. 8). From the quotation offered here, Hauerwas might both agree and disagree with Kavka's portrait of the church in the terms of his (Kavka's) reading of Philippians 2. Hauerwas might agree that the church shares "content and forms of reasoning" with some aspects of pagan moral reasoning and "secular culture," but he might ask how the particularity of Christ's "emptying" plays a part of Kavka's own reading of this passage.

80. For the American philosophical "roots" of scriptural reasoning, see the following: Ochs' works cited in n. 54; Adams, "Reparative Reasoning," 447–51; and the special issue of *The Journal of Scriptural Reasoning* titled "The Roots of Scriptural Reasoning." It should be noted that Stout's heroes, from American philosophy, are John Dewey and Ralph Waldo Emerson, while Adams and Ochs emphasize Charles Peirce's work within their reflections on the logic of scriptural reasoning. The suggestion of this conclusion is that both democratic traditionalism and scriptural reasoning build up the virtues of religious reasoning without resentment.

Acknowledgments

I am grateful to David O'Hara, as well as his colleagues and students at Augustana College (in Sioux Falls, South Dakota), for comments and questions on an earlier yet quite different version of this essay. The present essay benefited from the conversation surrounding the essay with the group "Empiricism and Pragmatism in American Religious Thought" at the American Academy of Religion in 2009 (in Montreal); Eddie Glaude deserves mentioning here for moderating such a wonderful conversation. Bill Elkins read a draft at a crucial stage of writing, and he offered the exact suggestions needed to strengthen the essay. Martin Kavka's perspective on scriptural reasoning presents a challenge to the descriptions of SR provided here; Kavka remains a necessary conversation partner for me, and his work inspires and motivates my own.

Part III

The Philosophy and Theology of Social Hope

CHAPTER EIGHT

Rorty's Religion

DAVID L. O'HARA

According to Richard Rorty, the pragmatist is concerned chiefly with things like freedom, justice, and social hope. While the early pragmatists were right to connect thinking, feeling, and acting, and to oppose the dualistic essentialisms characteristic of Enlightenment philosophies, nevertheless pragmatisms like those of Peirce, Royce, and James are irrelevant to the degree that they concern themselves with telic notions like final truth, the absolute, and the divine. I argue that Rorty was inconsistent in this belief, a fact that he came close to acknowledging in his latest writings. In fact, Rorty's philosophy shares many of the hallmarks of religion, including a transcendent hope and belief in the finality of love. In this chapter, I offer a critique of the ways in which Rorty's philosophy functions as both a secular argument for social hope and as something strongly resembling religion.

Introduction

In the tenth chapter of his *Future of an Illusion*, Freud makes a curious admission. Having spent nine chapters undermining religious experience, he admits that all he has to offer in its place must necessarily amount to another religion. As David Foster Wallace once said, there is really no such thing as atheism.[1] No one gets to choose whether to worship or

---

1. Wallace, "David Foster Wallace on Life and Work."

not, only what to worship. Richard Rorty seems to have acknowledged this, in part, in his late-in-life conversation with Gianni Vattimo—where Rorty divulges that what he once described as atheism he should have described as anticlericalism.[2] Rorty acknowledged that his choice of language should have reflected his concern with the political consequences of particular beliefs rather than with the metaphysical question of God's existence. Rorty considered the question of God's existence to be undecidable, and that evidence proffered on either side of the question must be held to be implausible.[3] Still, Rorty did not go far enough to answer Wallace's objection. Rorty was opposed to a particular kind of God, but that does not mean that he was without a God. The God he opposed was one whose existence is knowable only through unwarranted reliance on abstract metaphysics or through similarly unwarranted religious faith, and belief in whom apparently causes people to behave in violent and antisocial ways. Speaking of Rorty's postmodern, pragmatist stance toward truth, Pascal Engel noted that despite such postmodern dismissals of truth, our hunger for it remains. He asked, "Is it one of those familiar paradoxes, by which, having abandoned religion, we continue to search for a substitute or by which, when we no longer accept authority, we still shrink from getting rid of it entirely?"[4] Although he was speaking about truth, Engel could just as well have been speaking of Rorty's view of God. In the same volume, Rorty himself suggested that his stance on truth and his stance on God were of the same kind.[5] Consequently, Edward Grippe argues that Rorty's anticlericalism winds up looking like fundamentalist religion. Grippe writes, "It seems to me that Rorty is asking for the reader to have faith in his, Rorty's, idiosyncratic repackaging of 'pragmatist,' and if one does then one will understand, among other things, 'an important element in the construction of narratives.' Yet this is the pattern of request all religious faiths make . . . 'believe and you will understand.'"[6] In this chapter, I pursue Wallace's claim and argue along similar lines to those drawn by Grippe. My contention is that Rorty was unsuccessful in evicting God from his thinking, and that, at best, Rorty offered a substitute for religion that parallels religion's worst elements with few of its benefits. Ironically, Rorty's religion is a liberal, intolerant

2. Rorty and Vattimo, *Future of Religion*.
3. Ibid., 33.
4. Rorty and Engel, *What's the Use of Truth?*, 1–2.
5. Ibid., 40.
6. Grippe, *Richard Rorty's New Pragmatism*, 148.

one. Nevertheless, his religion represents a step in the right direction and holds a sort of prophetic promise for the advancement of toleration in our time. Rorty's vision of social hope advances on faith that contains a version of the holy, situated in the ideal future. It depends on and grows in a community that is motivated by a shared set of ideals grounded in that faith. This faith is advanced at least as much by poetics and aesthetics as by argument. His proselytizing, like Anselm's *credo ut intelligam*, asks for belief first and then offers understanding. In effect, Rorty's criticism of religious narratives is replaced by another religious narrative in which Rorty offers, not a replacement for God and religion, but a competitor. The upshot of this examination of Rorty's God is not a dismissal of his claims, but first, the assertion that his pragmatism should be understood for what it is, namely, a competing religious claim; and second, the assertion that this competing claim, while too thin a narrative to be an attractive replacement for other cultural forms of religious belief and practice, nevertheless has several valuable features that merit attention. Chief among these are Rorty's emphasis on toleration, the valuation of both the individual and the community, and, in the end, love.

Rorty's Social Hope

One of the prominent features of most of Rorty's later writing is *social hope*. When Giovanna Borradori commented to Rorty that he was "a sort of reincarnation of John Dewey," Rorty gave the following response:

> Dewey was the dominant intellectual figure in America in my youth. He was often called the philosopher of democracy, of the New Deal, of the American democratic intellectuals. If one attended an American university any time before 1950, it would have been impossible not to be aware of him. I think he was a remarkable man. He started out as an Evangelical Christian, then he became a Hegelian, then he read Darwin and he sort of dropped Christianity to try to put together Darwin and Hegel. His philosophy is a kind of naturalization of Hegel—Hegel without the split between nature and spirit. Just as Hegel's philosophy was a kind of secularized Christianity, so Dewey's was a sort of *Christian social hope* combined with a Darwinian way of looking at human beings.[7]

---

7. Rorty, in Borradori, *American Philosopher*, 106 (emphasis mine).

Rorty did not reject Borradori's characterization of him as a Dewey *redivivus*; rather, he affirmed Dewey's philosophy as one whose chief feature is a kind of social hope. It is worth noticing that Rorty identifies that social hope as one that is rooted in the Christian religion.

Rorty articulated social hope, in large part, through storytelling. He advocated retelling the history of thought in a way that redirected our attention from metaphysics to politics and to fallible, achievable social goals. As Rorty put it, ". . . the pragmatist does not try to justify his metaphors by philosophical argument . . . Instead, like Dewey, he tells stories about how the course of Western thought has been stultified by the metaphors he dislikes."[8]

It is significant that Rorty describes these metaphors as unlikeable rather than as untrue. The culture that Rorty hopes for is one in which the idea of some ahistorical truth or transcendent ideal against which all other values could be measured has "dried up and blown away." This includes the end of the idea of "the nature of reality" and of any God to whom people could be responsible. Rorty has described such a culture as both "postmetaphysical" and "poeticized."[9]

Another interesting feature of Rorty's philosophy is the sense of cult or community that his language engenders, a community bound together not so much by a dogmatic creed as by several ideas that are held onto as important doctrines: irony, charity, liberty, contingency, and social hope. Those who adhere to these doctrines find themselves aggregating in solidarity with one another, and Rorty's hope is that theirs will become the dominant political voice. This voice will not destroy other doctrines by prohibiting them, but rather it will replace other doctrines by choosing not to attend to them. He writes, "Pragmatists don't use that sort of language," and he uses the first person plural almost as a call to faith: "We pragmatists" is a frequent locution of his.[10] Much of his writing reads as the autobiography of ideas trying to gain recognition. Pascal Engel complains that Rorty "does not see much difference between philosophical writing and literature."[11] Rorty would agree, since

---

8. Rorty, *Objectivity, Relativism, and Truth*, 81–82.

9. Rorty, *Take Care of Freedom*, 46.

10. See, for instance, his dialogue with Pascal Engel in Rorty and Engel, *What's the Use of Truth?*, 32.

11. Ibid., 49–50.

he thinks that pragmatists like James and Dewey were, at their best, writing chiefly works of literary persuasion.[12]

Rorty's turn away from the language of religion and his turn away from the kind of philosophy that Engel wishes he would practice are similar and related turns. Rorty appears to many theologically minded critics to be rejecting religion and turning instead to politics, just as he appears to many philosophically minded critics to be rejecting philosophy in favor of a more poetic and persuasive literature. In fact, Rorty is rejecting neither religion nor philosophy. Rather, he is trying to rethink both religion and philosophy. What he rejects, in both religion and philosophy, is the claim that we somehow have access to a final version of truth or justice. At the same time, he seems to be embracing and reaffirming those tendencies, in both religion and philosophy, towards making the world a better place for love to flourish. Rorty said of the American poet Walt Whitman that he "thought that we Americans have the most poetical nature because we are the first thoroughgoing experiment in national self-creation: the first nation-state with nobody to please—not even God. We are the greatest poem because we put ourselves in the place of God: our essence is our existence, and our existence is in the future. Other nations thought of themselves as hymns to the glory of God. We define God as our future selves."[13] In Rorty's view, Whitman gets both religion and philosophy right by substituting the hope of a forward-looking community for "knowledge of the will of God."[14] As Rorty put it elsewhere, if we are engaged in an important cultural contest, it is one "between two visionary poems."[15]

Rorty's Criticism of Religion as an Impediment to Social Progress

Those works of philosophy that have attempted to speak on behalf of truth are, Rorty thinks, full of hot air. The idea of truth is simply a substitute for some God, and these kinds of substitutes are frequently clericalisms trying to persuade us to swear fealty to some nonhuman entity that will ultimately distract us from political action in the realm of things we can really hope to affect. Rorty holds that we have given

---

12. See, for instance, his essay "Philosophy as a Kind of Writing," in *Consequences of Pragmatism*, 90–109.
13. Rorty, *Achieving our Country*, 22.
14. Ibid.,18.
15. Rorty, cited in Jeffrey Robbins' foreword to *An Ethics for Today*, xiv.

the God-substitutes a chance, and they have failed to produce for us any positive results. "So I propose that from now on we focus on other distinctions," he says.[16]

> If we do things the Pragmatist way, we will no longer think of ourselves as having responsibilities toward nonhuman entities such as *truth* or *reality*. I have often suggested that we regard pragmatism as an attempt to complete the project common to the Renaissance humanists and the Enlightenment. The pragmatists think that it is time to stop believing that we have obligations either to God or to some God surrogate. The pragmatism of James, like the existentialism of Sartre, is an attempt to convince us to stop inventing such surrogates.[17]

Rorty's criticism of religion focuses on three ways in which religion serves as a distraction from, or a hindrance to, the advancement of social hope. First, religion demands conversion and allegiance to nonhuman entities, and does so in a way that defers understanding, promising that if we believe then we will understand. Rorty bluntly states that "fundamentalists" are "just not trustworthy citizens of the country."[18] It is important to note that he says this without offering a definition of "fundamentalist." Merold Westphal observes succinctly that "[Rorty] explicitly rejects 'the idea that there are nonlinguistic things called "meanings" which it is the task of language to express, as well as the idea that there are nonlinguistic things called "facts" which it is the task of language to represent.' Rorty thinks it is necessary to 'de-divinize' the world in order to shake free from this realism."[19] For Rorty, fundamentalism seems to include anything that asks for this kind of allegiance, but that is a very broad definition.

Second, and along the same lines, religion directs our attention to these nonhuman entities and uses much of our intellectual power in trying to demonstrate them. It is not rational but mythical or poetic, and,

---

16. Rorty and Engel, *What's the Use of Truth?*, 59.
17. Ibid., 40.
18. Rorty, *Take Care of Freedom*, 61.
19. Westphal, "Coping and Conversing," 79. Westphal continues: "No doubt theism is committed to something like the notion that God has a nonhuman 'language of his own.' But Kant and Kierkegaard, to say nothing of Aquinas, should be sufficient to remind us that theism is not necessarily committed to the claim that we have direct access to that language and encode it in natural languages that 'express' the propositions that are, so to speak, God's sentences. One need not be an atheist, like Rorty, to be an anti-realist. It is sufficient for the theist to acknowledge that we are not God epistemically any more than ontologically, that is, we cannot know as God knows any more than we can be God."

therefore, not deserving of our allegiance. Inasmuch as it is aesthetic religion is tolerable, but only if it does not distract us from achieving important social goals.

Third, religion fosters clericalism and so directs our attention away from the political, thus hindering the advancement of social hope. Our allegiance to God is ultimately political, since allegiance to God is finally expressed as allegiance to God's agents. (Late in his life, Rorty suggested that it was this clericalism that was, in fact, religion's most pernicious feature, and that his avowed "atheism" should have been more properly termed "anticlericalism."[20])

Although many proponents of religion would say that religion has been a positive force for social change overall, Rorty holds that, in general, religion as a social force tends to enervate, rather than energize, real progress. As Rorty put it, "I know that there are religions of love as well as religions of fear. But . . . I think that the religion of love has gradually moved out of the churches and into the political arena. That religion is in the process of being transformed into democratic politics. What is left behind in the churches is the fear that human beings may not be able to save themselves without help—that social cooperation is not enough."[21] Rorty's criticism of religion might boil down to this, then: religion has largely traded fear for love, and that fear has translated into the political view that social progress is unachievable.

Rorty's Social Hope as a Substitute for Religion

With this in mind, let us turn to examine Rorty's social hope. It will become clear, in what follows, that Rorty's Deweyan "Christian social hope," in fact, functions as a religion. While this should not trouble us in itself, nevertheless, Rorty's new religion is not immune to his own criticisms of religion.

First, Rorty's social hope depends on a vision of the Holy, one rooted in a kind of faith, and one that aims at an ideal future. Rorty acknowledges this in his dialogue with Vattimo, where he says that he thinks that the holy can be thought of, not in the past, but "only in an ideal future . . . My sense of the holy . . . is bound up with the hope that someday, any millennium now, my remote descendants will live in a

---

20. Rorty and Vattimo, *Future of Religion*, 33.
21. Rorty, in Brandom, *Rorty and His Critics*, 218 n. 5.

global civilization in which love is pretty much the only law."[22] It would be unfair to say that Rorty was arguing for a real holiness, but the fact is that he found himself moved to use the language of religion as one of his "poeticized" metaphors and to offer what begins to look like a competing ideal realism.

His social hope depends on and grows in a community that is motivated by a shared set of ideals that are grounded in that faith. Perhaps because these ideals are "poeticized," Rorty is rarely explicit about this. Occasionally, Rorty speaks as though there would be no shared values, just space in which all values would coexist, though this always seems to imply the negation of those values that negate other values.[23] As I said a moment ago, Rorty seems to have given up trying to advance social hope through argumentation towards truth, but this means that his argumentation is towards something other than truth. Inasmuch as his criticism of religion depends on the claim that religions aim at something that is not demonstrably the case, here he is hoist by his own petard. Of course, Rorty is no fool in these matters, and his criticism of religion is not strongly dependent on the claim that religions are false. Nevertheless, his religion finds itself on no firmer footing in this regard than other religions.

Rorty proselytizes for this faith in hopes of converting others to it, and that proselytizing asks for belief before it offers understanding. In fact, it may be that understanding, if by that word we mean a grasp of the truth, is permanently deferred in Rorty's social hope, since truth is not something to which we have access. Here critics like Edward Grippe have strong words for Rorty. Grippe says Rorty acts like a priest;[24] Rorty is intolerant and prefers his own opinions with the same sort of reason-eschewing faith that characterizes fundamentalist religion; Rorty's aim appears to be proselytizing and conversion, and Rorty "wishes to share his insights" but does so with the same "paternalism" as the "street-corner preacher."[25] In short, Grippe says, "Rorty's liberal agenda is at base intolerant."[26] Grippe charges Rorty with having

---

22. Rorty and Vattimo, *Future of Religion*, 39–40.

23. See chapter 5 of *Take Care of Freedom*, for instance, especially the opening paragraph: "It would be a culture in which people thought of human beings as creating their own life-world, rather than as being responsible to God . . ." (46).

24. Grippe, *Richard Rorty's New Pragmatism*, 153.

25. Ibid., 149.

26. Ibid., 18.

"[taken] back into his pragmatism elements which he has thought he had discarded, [including] the dogmatism associated with religion."[27] Grippe is one of Rorty's more strident critics, but even his friends notice this about him. Jeffrey Robbins puts it like this: "Rorty is actually guilty of the very thing of which he accuses religion—namely cutting the conversation short."[28] This may advance some version of social hope for the future, but it does so at the expense of valuable and present religious experiences, including the enriching experience of conversing about religious questions.

In short, what emerges from Rorty's own description of his social hope is a kind of idealism that is not an alternative to religion but something that closely parallels religion. It would seem that Rorty, despite his best efforts, has imitated Freud and proved Wallace's maxim to be true. Rorty has, it seems, offered a substitute religion, a competing religious claim that is trying to fly under the radar and not be noticed as a religion, but it has all the hallmarks of one and should be acknowledged as such. Granted, it does not have a strict creed or liturgy, but then many new religions have not developed those as well.

This competing claim is too thin a narrative to be an attractive replacement for religion. David McLean points out that the indirect upshot of Rorty's new religion is that it excludes all other religions, a strongly supersessionist religious faith.

> Vattimo and I would like to differ [with Rorty's sense of the "holy," one that seems to preclude others being able to live a public religious life], and what is left out—we shall say, "ironically" —is a vast domain of human experience—the religious domain. Without that domain, life, for billions, is impoverished and would be even if the Rortian Utopia became a reality. The larger, vexing questions of life Rorty assumes would cease in such a Utopia. I boldly assert that they would not. They *could* not. They could not because there is no imaginable future in which the question of our and the "world's" ultimate origins, our explorations, descriptions, and redescriptions about human experience, and our suspicions about various possible "destinies" are likely to cease.[29]

In the end, Rorty's nearly lifelong avowal of atheism looks not unlike Freud's attempt to overcome religion. The result in both cases is a poor

27. Ibid., 162.
28. In his foreword to Rorty, *An Ethics for Today*, xviii.
29. McClean, "Theological Uses of Rortian Ironism," 38.

substitute for the aesthetic of traditional religions, and while both claim to offer a more salutary and sanitary approach to the same kinds of concerns that religions usually address, it is hard to imagine finding either one succeeding as an appealing substitute for traditional religions.

Ubi Caritas: *The Good News according to Rorty*

Perhaps at this point it will seem that my conclusion ought to be that Rorty has nothing to offer religion or its adherents. Grippe appears to be right, at least inasmuch as he indicates that the late Rorty's philosophy looks increasingly like a religion. Furthermore, it is likely that many adherents of religions—perhaps even a majority of them—will find Rorty to be too antagonistic to their religion to be willing to take him seriously. Liberals find Rorty appealing, but conservatives—who may be in the majority of religious practitioners—find Rorty dismissive of some of what they consider to be most important in religion, and especially of the public expressions of religion.

Despite all this, I do not wish to conclude with a dismissal of Rorty. Rather, I would like to keep in mind a helpfully irenic word from Leibniz: "The majority of the philosophical sects are right in the greater part of what they affirm, but not so much in what they deny."[30] Even if conservatives wish to argue that Rorty is wrong in what he denies, there are a number of attractive affirmations in the Rortian faith. Chief among these features are Rorty's emphases on toleration, the valuation of both the individual and the community, and love.

Rorty's religion may not be an adequate substitute for other religions with richer spiritual, liturgical, and communal lives, but does it need to be a substitute, after all? Rorty's religion stands as a prophetic reminder to religions of some things that we do and ought to value. A prophet, after all, is someone who calls out religious hypocrites and who challenges us when we neglect what we claim to cherish. Like all prophets, Rorty does not speak in a vacuum. Rather, he speaks into a particular environment and out of a particular tradition. That tradition has all too often been keen to offer its conclusions as infallible in order to close down inquiry. Rorty's pragmatic progenitor Charles Peirce argued against this tendency in metaphysics. Peirce said that what we need is a "great catholic church,"[31] one that is not choked with creeds, because

---

30. Leibniz, "Letter to Remond," 607.
31. Peirce, *Collected Papers*, 6.443.

creeds, in Peirce's view, tend to close down avenues of inquiry and to divide people from one another.[32] Like Rorty, Peirce objected to the way religion is used to seize hold of political life. Still, Peirce argued, the *agape* love that Christianity affirms is precisely what every community needs.[33] *Agape* is, after all, concerned with the flourishing of the community rather than with the establishment of one's own political position over others. Elsewhere, in one of his journals, Peirce wrote, "There are three essentials to every possible religion. Miracle. Myth. Mystery. *Miracle* is the extraordinary circumstances evidencing something mighty and specially connected with a given religion. *Myth* is the story of the god made imaginable. *Mystery* is the great symbol awaking emotion."[34] It seems to me that the late Rorty's view grew ever closer to that of the late Peirce. Rorty is certainly a mythmaker, one whose vision of social hope is not based on a scientistic view of progress but a poetic one. He would have objected to using the word "miracle" because of its metaphysical baggage, but it seems plain that his faith is one freighted with hope in the possibilities that arise from the extraordinary circumstances of flourishing democracy. The fact that Rorty wrote about religion so often towards the end of his life, frequently in connection with his social hope, shows Rorty's cognizance of the need for "symbol awaking emotions." Social hope is necessarily connected to our affective life, just as any serious religion is. Just as Peirce argued that societies need agapic foundations, so Rorty seemed to echo the words of St. Paul, that if we have not charity, then we have nothing. In a recent dialogue with René Girard, Gianni Vattimo points to Rorty's emphases on toleration, the valuation of both the individual and the community, and love. Vattimo says that Rorty and others like him see (and apparently applaud) the shift in philosophy from an emphasis on *veritas* to an emphasis on *caritas*, that is, from an emphasis on truth to an emphasis on love.[35]

---

32. Ibid., 5.380 n. 1.
33. Cf. Peirce, *Collected Papers*, 6.287, for example.
34. Peirce, *The Charles S. Peirce Papers*, MS 891.22.
35. "Anche l'itinerario della filosofia contemporanea—dai giochi di linguaggio in Wittgenstein, all'idea dell'essere come evento di Heidegger, alla particolare versione di pragmatismo di Richard Rorty—io lo vedo come un passaggio dalla *veritas* all *caritas*. Ovvero a me della verità non importa nulla se non in vista di qualche scopo. Perché studio la chimica? Perché posso costruire delle cose che servono a me e al prossimo." Vattimo, in Girard and Vattimo, *Verità o fede debole?*, 19.

Conclusion: Rorty as a Prophet of Love

Although Rorty is often thought of as antireligious, he recognized some value in certain religious expressions, for instance, in the religious impetus behind the civil rights movement.[36] Unlike some current critics of religion, Rorty was not so single-mindedly opposed to it that he could not see that some good can come from it, especially from "religions of love." Similarly, though he has often been called a relativist, Rorty was not averse to trying to tell a sort of truth. On the one hand, Rorty advocates telling stories that will shape our sense of who we are and of who we can become. On the other hand, he is frank about offering those stories as stories, and not as Platonic "noble lies" that only the noble know to be lies.[37] His objection to religion sometimes (though not always) is not that religion is untrue but that religious stories often present themselves as simply true. Rorty thinks it would be closer to the truth to admit how little we really know about our stories, and to acknowledge that our stories are often poems with which we enchant ourselves. Rorty paraphrases Santayana as saying that poetry "is called religion when it intervenes in life, and religion when it merely supervenes upon life is seen to be nothing but poetry."[38] His point is not that religion is a lie, but that the kind of truth it is telling is one that matters for life.

Rorty was, no doubt, often a strident critic of religion. Nevertheless, his insistence that his own language of social hope was poeticized allows at least some room for religious language to be understood poetically as well. Rorty would probably reply that of course it is, but it is poeticized with metaphors he does not like. In any event, neither traditional religion nor Rorty's religion cancels the other out; each has room for the other. The challenge before us is to find out just where that room is. People value religions in no small part because of the way they shape the life of a community. This shaping of communal life was the source of Rorty's greatest criticisms of religion. But his criticisms do not ultimately boil down to dismissals of religion. If anything, they demonstrate the fact that Rorty took very seriously those things that, like religion, shape our life together, and that love probably matters more than creeds. In this way, Rorty the critic of religion finds himself in what he might have considered strange company indeed: in the end, Rorty is a prophet.

---

36. Rorty, *Take Care of Freedom*, 81.
37. Cf. Duncan, "Question for Richard Rorty."
38. Rorty, *Ethics for Today*, 9.

CHAPTER NINE

Can There Be Hope without Prophecy?
Richard Rorty as Prophetic Pragmatist

BRAD ELLIOTT STONE

Can there be hope without prophecy? Richard Rorty wants to affirm this question. His critique of the prophetic found in *Philosophy and Social Hope* suggests that any appeal to a greater sense of history leaves him quite nervous, especially in light of the horrors made possible by two particular prophetic traditions: Christianity and Marxism. Yet, in his own way, Rorty is a prophet; indeed, he stands as a prophetic pragmatist. This essay seeks to present Rorty's concerns about the prophetic while asserting, nonetheless, that his own blindness to those whose lives constitute what Cornel West would call "the night side of America" keeps him from seeing the exact meaning of prophecy. While Rorty equates prophecy with prediction and worries about "pie-in-the-sky" wishful thinking, West gives us a notion of the prophetic that is very much in the present and this-worldly, allowing a particular group of people (although not limited to that group) to forge ahead in a hostile and absurd scenario. Using West's understanding of the prophetic and his views of Christian and Marxist hope, I show that there is nothing about Rorty's work (other than his own desire not to be associated with it) that prevents it from being understood as prophetic pragmatism. To do this, I turn to his fictional essay "Looking Backwards from the Year 2096," ironically published in *Philosophy and Social Hope* along with his critique of prophecy.

The present essay proceeds in three parts. In the first part, I present Rorty's critique of the prophetic. At the center of his critique is a weariness of those who deem themselves prophets or consider themselves to be the anointed one to bring about other people's prophecies. His critique of the prophetic dimension of Marxism and Christianity is, when charitably read, a power indictment to those who use prophetic traditions in violent ways. Nonetheless, such blanket dismissal of the prophetic remains unsettling. Rorty's critique of the prophetic is interesting to me given the fact that such a critique cannot but be a critique of Cornel West's prophetic pragmatism; it is as if Rorty is returning a paper, written by his graduate student West, covered in red ink. Although the relationship between professor Rorty and student West was always amicable, the student can respond to his teacher's objections. In the second part, I present prophetic pragmatism's likely response to Rorty's criticisms in a way that illuminates the prophetic pragmatist project as a pragmatism that finally (as West expresses in the beginning of *Prophecy Deliverance!*) takes the African-American experience seriously. Since African- Americans for West are prophets of hope, and since pragmatism is best defined as a philosophy of hope,[1] the fusion of the two traditions—prophetic pragmatism—seeks to give voice and intelligibility to the prophetic practices that directly seek social change. Since West is not allergic to the prophetic, he is also able to enter into dialogue with both Christianity and Marxism as movements that seek social change by tapping into their respective prophetic roots.

In the third part of this essay, I return to Rorty's work. I pose a non-contradictory scenario in which he is a prophetic pragmatist—albeit a non-Marxist, anticlerical one. It is important to notice exactly how prophetic Rorty's work is. True, he does not make any predictions about the future. Since the prophetic need not be so conceived, however, West's notion of the prophetic shines throughout Rorty's work. Insofar as the prophetic is present and Rorty is a pragmatist, he can be considered a prophetic pragmatist.

Rorty's Critique of the Prophetic

Rorty's essay "Failed Prophecies, Glorious Hopes," republished in his 1999 *Philosophy and Social Hope*, directly argues against the role of the

---

1. Colin Koopman's work on pragmatism drives this point home very well.

prophetic in the quest for social hope. The essay describes two failed (or at least failing) efforts to produce social hope: Christianity and Marxism. Rorty argues that their lack of success is due to their prophetic dimensions. When added to his critique of *The American Evasion of Philosophy*, we have a strong critique of West's overall philosophical project.

For Rorty, Marxism and Christianity "are expressions of the same hope: that some day we shall be willing and able to treat the needs of all human beings with the respect and consideration with which we treat the needs of those closest to us, those whom we love."[2] Everyone needs to read *The Communist Manifesto* and the New Testament since these two texts are, according to Rorty, the best inspirational texts out there. The lesson they teach, Rorty writes, is essential for the future of liberal democracy:

> We should raise our children to find it intolerable that we who sit behind desks and punch keyboards are paid ten times as much as people who get their hands dirty cleaning our toilets . . . Our children need to learn, early on, to see the inequalities between their own fortunes and those of other children as neither the Will of God nor the necessary price for economic efficiency, but as an evitable tragedy . . . The children need to read Christ's message of human fraternity alongside Marx and Engel's account of how industrial capitalism and free markets—indispensable as they have turned out to be—make it very difficult to institute that fraternity. They need to see their lives as given meaning by efforts towards the realization of the moral potential inherent in our ability to communicate our needs and our hopes to one another.[3]

We have seen Christianity and Marxism do good things in the word: the abolition of slavery and the creation of organized labor, for example. When Marxism and Christianity are truly applied, efforts are made to make the world and its inhabitants better.

If only Christianity and Marxism were truly applied! Rorty laments the violence and outright damage produced in their names. Rorty names Abiel Guzman and Pat Robertson as kinds of "false prophets" who greatly perverted Marxist principles and the Gospel of Jesus Christ. As a result of misuse of the texts over history, "[M]any millions of people were enslaved, tortured or starved to death by sincere, morally

---

2. Rorty, *Philosophy and Social Hope*, 202–3.
3. Ibid., 203–4.

earnest people who recited passages from one or the other text in order to justify their deeds. Memories of the dungeons of the Inquisition and the interrogation rooms of the KGB... should indeed make us reluctant to hand over power to people who claim to know what God, or History, wants."[4] For expressions of social hope, both Marxism and Christianity have caused a great deal of suffering in the world, marring the very principles they were supposed to propagate.

This leads to Rorty's mistrust of prophecy. For Rorty, prophecy requires prediction—which leads people to "interpret" prophecy and see themselves as the agents who will "fulfill" the prophecy. This leads to "false prophets" and murderous regimes. To make it worse, the predictions—at least for now—have failed: Jesus has not come back, and capitalism has not yet met its demise. If these predictions never come to pass, all of the pain caused by the movements will have been *completely* gratuitous, incapable of being written off by those who were trying to live in accordance to the prophecy.

Rorty's lament is amplified by the fact that the predictions were not necessary for the hope that they expressed. The Christian message of fraternity, for example, does not *require* the return of Jesus, nor does improvement of workers' conditions *require* the collapse of the capitalist system. To this end, Rorty recommends that "[w]hen reading the texts themselves, we should skip lightly past the predictions, and concentrate on the expressions of hope."[5] This replaces "hope by false prediction" with hope for social justice or the hope of American democracy.

Troubled as their reception and application have been, Rorty nonetheless considers the New Testament and *The Communist Manifesto* inspiring texts. However, if one needs to pick between Marxism and Christianity as the best expression of social hope, Rorty endorses the *Manifesto*. He writes, "The *Manifesto* is a better book to give to the young than the New Testament. For the latter document is morally flawed by its otherworldliness, by its suggestion that we can separate the question of our individual relation to God—our individual chance for salvation—from our participation in cooperative efforts to end needless suffering."[6] Rorty holds this view in light of Christianity's opposition to Marxism, although Marxism shares Christianity's commitment to the dignity of

---

4. Ibid., 204.
5. Ibid., 205.
6. Ibid., 207–8.

all people. Christianity has simply done a worse job—and with more time to have been successful—than Marxism. Rorty refers to workers' conditions improved by Marxism, noting that "[h]ad they waited for the Christian kindness and charity of their superiors, their children would still be illiterate and badly fed."[7] For an expression of social hope, Christianity has been too abstract, too aloof, and thus too weak to actually change society. Marxism, in its concreteness and solidarity, has, in spite of its many failures, done the most for peoples' conditions. In fact, efforts by Christians to align themselves with socialism are now problematic at best and redundant at worse. Rorty writes: "'Christian Socialism' is pleonastic: nowadays you cannot hope for the fraternity which the Gospels preach without hoping that democratic governments will redistribute money and opportunity in a way that the market never will. There is no way to take the New Testament seriously as a moral imperative, rather than as a prophecy, without taking the need for such redistribution seriously."[8] In the post-*Manifesto* age, Christianity must become sufficiently Marxist if it is going to be effective. Unfortunately, if Marxism works, the Christian message might no longer be needed. In fact, Rorty concludes, the New Testament writers just were not concerned enough about *this* world; they "turn[ed] their attention from the possibility of a better human future to the hope of pie in the sky when we die. The only utopia these writers can imagine is in another world altogether."[9] In contrast, Marxism holds that "the human future can be made different from the human past, unaided by non-human powers."[10] Like Nietzsche, Rorty believes that Christianity's distinction between heaven and earth leads to a nihilism that devalues life "down here"—which allows the furtherance of oppression and victimization in the name of some other place where peace and joy will reign.

Rorty concludes the essay by hoping that someday a new document would emerge that expresses social hope without prophecy, one that "spelled out the details of a this-worldly utopia without assuring us that this utopia will emerge full-blown, and quickly . . . as soon as private property is abolished, or as soon as we have all taken Jesus into

---

7. Ibid., 207.
8. Ibid., 205.
9. Ibid., 208.
10. Ibid.

our hearts."[11] This new text will make no predictions that can then be interpreted by false prophets who consider themselves to be, to use Hegel's phrase to describe Napoleon Bonaparte, "world spirit on horseback."

Given prophetic pragmatism's connections to both Christianity and Marxism, Rorty's objection to the prophetic extends to prophetic pragmatism more broadly. There is one example of Rorty directly critiquing West's project: Rorty's review of West's *The American Evasion of Philosophy*. Here, Rorty wonders whether West can be successful as both a professional philosopher and a pioneer for social justice. The essay is more anti-professionalism than anti-prophetic. I return to Rorty's review in the last part of the present essay.

Prophetic Pragmatism: This-Worldly Prophecy without Prediction

Social hope needs a this-worldly, non-predictive, articulation. West provides such an articulation of social hope. West shares Rorty's distrust of "prophecies" that are pronounced "from on high" and make predictions about the future. Thus, West's view of prophecy must be something different than what Rorty critiques. African-Americans, the basis of West's prophetic pragmatism, are far from utopian and stronger agents than Rorty grants. West describes "hope on a tightrope" as a substitution for what Rorty described as other-worldly wishful thinking. With all this in mind, I examine what West says about Christianity and Marxism in his *Prophecy Deliverance!*.

West on the Prophetic

West is very clear about the meaning of "prophetic" so as to avoid claims that he is referring to prediction or authoritative violence. In an interview with Eva Corredor, for instance, West says that his notion of prophesy

> is not one in which one speaks from on top, which is continuous with the great and grand Jewish and Christian traditions of the prophetic that I know of, in which "Thus says the Lord," or "Eternal truth speaks from on top." My notion of the prophetic is a democratic one in which, in the midst of the quotidian, the commonplace, in the midst of the messy struggle in which one's hands are dirty, that one is holding on to moral convictions and

11. Ibid.

tries to convince others that they ought to be accepted even though these moral convictions themselves can still be subject to criticism and change in vision and what-have-you.[12]

Rorty's concern about prophecy's claim to authority is immediately refuted by this definition. In this definition, West defines for us a pragmatist notion of prophecy: democratic in its core, dealing with the ordinary practices of decent human beings, and totally fallible. This is the "pragmatist prophecy" of prophetic pragmatism. The prophetic for West is a moral concept, not an epistemological one. It is about having the right sense of conviction, one that tries to overcome "messy struggles" and convince others to join the struggle; yet, it is completely open to critique and changes of agenda. In this regard, West shares Rorty's concern about absolutist application of prophecy. Prophecy must be alive, flexible, and honest to the struggles of people. Prophecies that oppress people are neither pragmatist nor prophetic, according to West's definition.

West continues his moral use of the prophetic in other places. In an interview with Peter Osborne, West reasserts that prophecy is not about authoritative prediction but "keeping a certain tradition of resistance and critique alive, in which the issues of the existential and the spiritual, as well as the political, the social, and the economic, are in movement together."[13] Here, we see what West is thinking of by "dirty hands" in the passage above. Prophetic work is the work of resistance and critique. It is hard work fighting the powers of oppression, especially since oppression plays out in multiple areas of society. This is why the prophetic pragmatist must bring the political, religious, social, and economic issues together. Prophecy also requires the courage to get one's hands dirty and fight oppressive powers. West refers to this in the documentary film *Examined Life* when he describes the prophetic as "mustering the courage to love, to empathize, to exercise compassion, and to be committed to justice . . . to courageously live and speak on behalf of the dejected, on behalf of those whose humanity has been rendered invisible, those whose humanity is hidden and concealed."[14]

In sum, the prophetic is a dimension through which one can present "an indictment of those who worship the idol of human power" as well as give oneself over to "*divine* compassion and justice in order

12. West, *Prophetic Reflections*, 66.
13. Osborne, "Cornel West," 36.
14. See Taylor, *Examined Life*.

to awaken *human* compassion and justice... The prophetic goal is to stir up in us the courage to care and empower us to change our lives and our historical circumstances."[15] Our historical circumstances are affairs of *this* world, not some other world to come. The prophetic is here described as a kind of compassion required to be an agent in *this* struggle—the one happening *right now*. Rorty seems unfamiliar with this sense of the prophetic.

Some of this has to do, of course, with the difference between African-American appropriation of the Christian tradition and the tradition as it is known by Rorty. In his essay "Subversive Joy and Revolutionary Patience in Black Christianity," West highlights the existential dimension of the African-American Christian tradition, a dimension that is truly this-worldly given the struggles black people faced (and still face) in the United States. West says it best when he writes: "Black people do not attend churches, for the most part, to find God, but rather to share and expand together the rich heritage they have inherited... The common black argument for belief in God is not that it is logical or reasonable to do so, but rather that such belief is requisite for one's sanity and for entrée to the most uplifting sociality available in the black community."[16] African-American Christianity is not a *theoretical* enterprise but a *practical, on-this-earth* way of being-in-the-nonsensical-racist-world. This is not about a world to come: it is about how to stay sane in *this* world as members of "the wretched of the earth." In *The American Evasion of Philosophy*, West employs personal terms: "My kind of prophetic pragmatism is located in the Christian tradition... the self-understanding and self-identity that flow from this tradition's insights into the crises and traumas of life are indispensable *for me* to remain sane."[17] At the heart of black Christianity, West argues, is a tragic sense of life that instantly shatters any illusions of white supremacy and indicts the alleged multiracial harmony of "the great American melting pot." Black Christianity is subversive: it allows African-Americans to overcome overwhelming odds and have a sense of self-dignity that white supremacy denies them. *This is not "pie in the sky"; it is how to handle "hell on earth."*[18] Yes, black Christianity does allude to "going up

---

15. West, *Democracy Matters*, 114–15.
16. West, *Prophetic Fragments*, 163.
17. West, *American Evasion of Philosophy*, 233.
18. Consider the words of the Negro spiritual "By and By": "I know my suit's going

yonder," but this reference for West "is utopian in that it breeds a defiant dissatisfaction with the present and encourages action,"[19] not because it seeks to avoid the world down here.

West's analysis of black Christianity allows for a new way to think of Christianity's role in American culture overall. Black Christianity is perhaps one of the best formulations of Christian hope in Western history (alongside Latin American liberation theology). West objects to any notion that black Christianity is "pie in the sky," even if mainstream Christianity is:

> The eschatological aspect of freedom in black Christianity is the most difficult to grasp. It is neither a glib hope for a pie-in-the-sky heaven nor an apocalyptic aspiration which awaits world destruction. Rather, it is a hope-laden articulation of the tragic quality of everyday life of a culturally degraded, politically oppressed, and racially coerced labor force. Black Christian eschatology is anchored in the tragic realism of the Old Testament wisdom literature and the proclamation of a coming kingdom by Jesus Christ. Anthropologists have observed that there is a relative absence of tragic themes in the ancient oral narratives of West Africa. Is it no accident that the black understanding of the gospel stresses this novel motif, the utterly tragic character of life and history?[20]

The tragic hope that African-Americans derive from the Judeo-Christian story is indeed a good example of Christianity at its best: as a prophetic promoter of social hope. Rorty fails to address the tragic sense of black Christianity; he is unable, therefore, to see the central role that it can play in liberation from oppression and humiliation.

But West is quite clear that there is no certainty in black Christian hope. It requires struggle every moment of the way. Prophetic black practices are grounded in the hope that is careful not to fall for utopian traps and programs. West says that the hope he describes is "a hope that is grounded in a particularly messy struggle, and it is tarnished by any kind of naïve projections of a better future, *so that it is hope on the*

---

to fit me well (I'm going to lay down my heavy load) / I tried it on at the gates of hell (I'm going to lay down my heavy load)." Hell here is no metaphor, nor is it some other place, state, or dimension; it is the very experience of being black in America.

19. West, *Prophetic Fragments*, 165.

20. Ibid., 163–64.

tightrope rather than a Utopian projection that looks over and beyond the present and oftentimes loses sight of the present."[21]

Christianity and Marxism

Prophetic pragmatism, West tells us, "calls for reinvigoration of a sane, sober, and sophisticated intellectual life in America and for regeneration of social forces empowering the disadvantaged, degraded, and dejected."[22] It is pragmatist insofar as it is "a political form of cultural criticism and locates politics in the everyday experience of ordinary people."[23] It is prophetic due to its "persuasive picture of what one is as a person, what one should hope for, and how one ought to act."[24] In his book *Prophecy Deliverance!*, West seeks to unify two prophetic traditions that often do not intersect: (Black) Christianity and Marxism.

Both Rorty and West refuse to pretend that the history of these traditions is clean. For West, however, the social hope expressed by each offers "a last humane hope for humankind."[25] The Christian message is that "every individual regardless of class, country, caste, race, or sex should have the opportunity to fulfill his or her potentialities," while Marxism strives for "the self-fulfillment, self-development, and self-realization of harmonious personalities."[26] The two goals are not contradictory, and West wants to synchronize the two efforts in order to make intelligible the practices that will lead to liberation primarily for African-Americans. West thinks, moreover, that the results can be generalized for everyone.

According to West, black theologians often fail to be attentive to the market forces that are responsible for so many of the ills that beset African-Americans. Similarly, Marxists tend to reject religion and therefore alienate African-Americans for whom religion is an integral element. In chapter 4 of *Prophecy Deliverance!*, West presents a forum in which the Marxist critique of Christianity and the Christian critique of Marxism can be expressed. In spite of these critiques, West proposes an

---

21. West, *Prophetic Reflections*, 67.
22. West, *American Evasion of Philosophy*, 239.
23. Ibid., 213.
24. West, *Prophesy Deliverance!*, 16.
25. Ibid., 95.
26. Ibid., 16.

"Afro-American Revolutionary Christianity" (the subtitle of the book) that blends—successfully or not—the two traditions.

West begins with Marxism's critique of Christianity, which he summarizes in the following way:

> The Marxist critique of the Christian dialectic of human nature and human history is that the Christian negation of what is and the transformation of prevailing realities are impotent, incorrect, and ill-informed. They are [M1] impotent because they locate ultimate power in a transcendent God who seems to work most effectively beyond history rather than in history, given the historical evidence so far. They are [M2] incorrect in that the very positing of such power and such an almighty Being is intellectually unjustifiable and theoretically indefensible. They are [M3] ill-informed because they possess highly limited analytical tools and scientific understanding of power and wealth in the prevailing social realities to be negated and transformed. The Christian reply to these criticisms is to acknowledge the dimension of impotency of its this-worldly liberation project (and all historical projects), accent the absence of (and lack of need for) intellectual "grounds" to justify its leap of faith in God, and admit the extent to which its project is ill-informed.[27]

In response to M1, West claims that the ultrahistorical position keeps Christians from falling for "utopian aspirations" that often lead to godless violence. God's solution, however, when it comes, will have a finality and perfection that will embarrass any mortal efforts. In response to M2, Christians replace the "Truth"—primarily understood scientifically or philosophically—with the very person of Jesus Christ. As West writes, "If there is any test for the 'truth' of particular Christian descriptions, it is their capacity to facilitate the existential appropriation of Jesus Christ."[28] In response to M3, West proposes a Christian revisionism in which all viewpoints are up for revision as understood, of course, through the person of Christ. One recalls West's fallibilist notion of the prophetic here.

The Christian critique of Marxism focuses on Marxism's concreteness in a way similar to Marxism's focus on Christianity's transcendentalism. West writes that

27. Ibid., 95–96.
28. Ibid., 98.

> The Christian critique of the Marxist dialectic of human praxis and human history is that the Marxist negation of what is and the transformation of prevailing realities are naïve, narrow, and nearsighted. They are [C1] naïve in that they exaggerate the Promethean possibilities of persons and valorize in an uncritical manner the scientific method. They are [C2] narrow in that they deal almost exclusively with the socioeconomic and political realities of persons, and virtually ignore the existential and cultural dimensions of human life. They are [C3] nearsighted in that they provide profound insights and penetrating illuminations of existing capitalist societies, but are blind to the novel social configurations which may usher forth from such societies. The Marxist reply to these criticisms is to acknowledge the naïve elements in its liberation project, accent the narrowness of its concerns, and admit the nearsightedness of its viewpoint.[29]

In response to C1, Marxists are Promethean in order to activate the oppressed to fight for their liberation. In response to C2, West asserts that one must keep in account the power of socioeconomic arrangements. If one ignores the economic and political state of affairs, no true liberation will be possible since a key factor—economic power—is ignored. In response to C3, West defends Marxist nearsightedness by pointing out Marxism's Hegelian inheritance. At the moment, it is the proletariat versus the bourgeoisie, but one does not know what the next dialectical battle will be until we get past this current dialectic. Hegelians are nearsighted because they cannot guess what will be the next antithesis to the synthesis to come.

With these ideological concerns aired, West argues: "regardless of the basic differences and subtle disagreements between the Christian viewpoint and the Marxist viewpoint, their prophetic and progressive wings share one fundamental similarity: *commitment to the negation of what is and the transformation of prevailing realities in the light of the norms of individuality and democracy*."[30] This commitment characterizes prophetic pragmatism. West's task is to outline a Marxist-Christian "political prescription for . . . the specific praxis in the present historical moment of the struggle for liberation."[31] In short, West proposes a radical, revolutionary Christianity grounded in the practices of African-

---

29. West, *Prophesy Deliverance!*, 99.
30. Ibid., 101; West's emphasis.
31. West, *Prophesy Deliverance!*, 23.

Americans that will empower blacks and others who seek freedom from white supremacist, *capitalist* culture. Once African-Americans connect white supremacy and capitalism, West argues, blacks can spend their energies fighting those forces that attack both their blackness and their religious beliefs.

Of course, one cannot blindly follow any alleged Marxist or Christian. This is why there must be a pragmatic philosophy of liberation that will be able to correctly analyze both progressive political policies and religious beliefs and prejudices. Prophetic pragmatism's goals are "to weaken the hegemony of liberalism over the Afro-American community (especially its leadership) and to break the stronghold of Leninism over Afro-American Marxists."[32] Prophetic pragmatists struggle to improve workers' conditions, but they are well aware that these are, at best, efforts without ultimate solution until the kingdom comes. It is an active Christianity that does not substitute human effort for divine activity; it is an active Marxism that believes that God is on the side of liberation for working-class people against the power of capital. As West puts it, "Revolutionary Christian perspective and praxis must remain anchored in the prophetic Christian tradition in the Afro-American experience which provides the norms of individuality and democracy; guided by the cultural outlook of the Afro-American humanist tradition which promotes the vitality and vigor of black life; and informed by the social theory and political praxis of progressive Marxism which proposes to approximate as close as is humanly possible the precious values of individuality and democracy as soon as God's will be done."[33] In other words, Black Christian Marxism will be an active way to approximate the kingdom of God on Earth while never being deceived into believing that such a kingdom has ever been humanly fulfilled. In response to Rorty, this view of Christianity and Marxism cannot be collapsed into Marxism itself, nor can it be expressed with sufficient conviction without the Christian view of tragedy and struggle. Likewise, this view cannot simply collapse into Christianity traditionally understood; West is proposing something active, something critical in response to capitalist forces that oppress working-class people, especially people of color. To use King's phrase, prophetic pragmatism "cannot wait."

32. Ibid., 140.
33. Ibid., 146.

Rorty as Prophetic Pragmatist

"Rorty leaves us very hungry indeed ... His affirmation excites some readers—and for good reason—but it is thin, I am afraid."[34] Bruce Wilshire's lament about Rorty is echoed throughout the literature. Rorty indeed inspires us to "take care of freedom" and let "truth take care of itself,"[35] but it is frustrating for anyone who desires to also be religious, or a little more exact in his arguments about why we should have hope. In other words, in keeping with Wilshire's metaphor, we wish Rorty's work came with more *meat*, that his views gave us food for the long journey and hard battle for freedom. Robert Talisse takes this claim further, pointing out that although "it is difficult to not find Rorty's recent writings inspirational in their own right," Rorty's anti-foundationalism gets in the way of his social vision, leaving us "quite literally *hopeless*."[36] How can one have hope when there is no argument for it or any tradition upon which to found it? The tension in Rorty's work is that he seeks to inspire while undercutting what most people find *inspiring*. Talisse notes:

> The inspired fascination with democracy that Rorty seeks to cultivate *is* important; however, an essential component of hope is the confidence that what is hoped for is in some relevant way *worth* achieving and *better* than the other things that might develop. Yet Rorty's antifoundationalism does not allow one to maintain that democracy is in any relevant way *better* than, say, tyranny. Hence Rorty's "social hope" must be, as he says, "ironic"—we must hope to achieve that which we no longer can think is *worth* achieving, we must draw inspiration from that which we contend is essentially not inspiring.[37]

Honi Haber argues that Rorty's ironism is itself not ironic. Rorty is a fundamentalist—dare we say, a *metaphysican*—about there being no foundations for knowledge or what we are to hope for. Prefering Foucault over Rorty, Haber accuses Rorty of operating from an ethnocentric, hegemonic discourse that is, in its elitism, cruel. This cruelty violates Rorty's own principles.[38]

---

34. Wilshire, *Primal Roots of American Philosophy*, 188–89.

35. Cf. Rorty, *Take Care of Freedom*.

36. Talisse, "Pragmatist Critique of Richard Rorty's Hopeless Politics," 611–12; Talisse's emphasis.

37. Ibid., 624.

38. See Haber, "Richard Rorty's Failed Politics."

What does West say about Rorty's view of social hope? In his essay "The Politics of American Neo-Pragmatism," West writes that Rorty's ethnocentrism and lack of social engagement beyond the academy leave us wanting—especially those who are "on the underside of history."[39] West directly criticizes Rorty's failure to critique, politically, the forces that create the very cruelty that Rorty wants to overcome through solidarity. Rorty's solidarity comes on the sidelines of academia (just as Rorty thinks professors ought), whereas West wishes that Rorty would be more interested in the creation of a new understanding of our country—one that did not ostensibly require the subjection of black and poor people: "Does Rorty's neo-pragmatism only kick the philosophical props from under bourgeois capitalist societies and require no change in our cultural and political practices? What are the ethical and political consequences of adopting his neo-pragmatism? On the macrosocietal level, there simply are none."[40] One must note the subtle use of Charles Peirce's pragmatic maxim here. West claims that being a Rortyan neo-pragmatist does not have a practical effect on the issue Rorty himself discusses. This is a major criticism of Rorty's pragmatism given how impractical it is—worse, that this impracticality is *by design* within Rorty's own reasoning. For a thinker that "leads philosophy to the complex world of politics and culture," Rorty deliberately "confines his engagement to transformation in the academy and apologetics for the modern West."[41] In other words, Rorty's neo-pragmatism is not pragmatist enough since it refuses to actually involve itself in the very overcoming of cruelty it lauds.

So, contrary to Rorty's claim early on that West is not pragmatist enough because he is too involved in politics to do the boring task of pragmatism, West argues that Rorty is not pragmatist enough because he is not involved enough in politics. One could argue that we are in a "Rorty said/West said" scenario, but there is a satisfying test to resolve this quibble. It is quite clear that West cannot fit into Rorty's pragmatist model. But can Rorty fit into West's prophetic pragmatism? I believe so, although Rorty's prophesying will naturally look different than West's since they are fighting for different things and coming from different communities. Since Rorty's system—perhaps even in spite of Rorty—

39. Rajchman and West, *Post-Analytic Philosophy*, 270.
40. Ibid., 267.
41. Ibid., 268.

can be classified as prophetic pragmatism, I am inclined to side with West on the role of prophecy in social hope, *a fortiori* the role of prophecy in pragmatism itself.

Rorty is not *against* social change, and he definitely believes in social hope and moral progress. His main concern is that there is no need for *professional philosophers* to get involved with such an enterprise. Political advancements require neither philosophical underpinnings nor blessings. In his review of West's *The American Evasion of Philosophy*, Rorty, we see, desires more prophets in America; he simply does not believe that any professional academic has the ability to truly be one, nor does the American populace have the resolve to create a better country. He accuses West of a "basic tension . . . between a wish to evade philosophy and a hope that something rather like philosophy will be a powerful instrument of social change. This tension can also be thought of as that between the pragmatist as professor and as prophet."[42]

The pragmatist as professor gets rid of dead philosophical bodies that continue to haunt our understandings of the true, the good, and the beautiful. The task, as Peirce points out, is to make ideas clear—that is, to eliminate vague and practically meaningless notions from the philosophical vocabulary and toolbox. According to Rorty, if West chooses to be this kind of pragmatist, then "the term 'prophetic pragmatism' will sound as odd as 'charismatic trash disposal.'"[43] The pragmatist as prophet does not exist for Rorty. The pragmatist as professor, if there is a prophet who is being attacked by terrible arguments, can be of use. Of his own life, for instance, Rorty writes:

> I can go on for hours about how to be antirepresentationalist in philosophy of language, antiessentialist in metaphysics, anti-Cartesian in philosophy of mind, antifoundationalist in epistemology, and so on. But it is hard to find occasions to do so which serve some political purpose, hard to feel that my professional services are just what victims of injustice need . . . I do not think that professorial pragmatism is a good place to look for prophecy, or for the sorts of rich possibilities which the prophetic imagination makes visible.[44]

---

42. Rorty, "Professor and the Prophet," 75.
43. Ibid.
44. Ibid.

There are several things in Rorty's statement worth highlighting. Of course, Rorty is in a position to claim that his "professional services" might not be needed by victims of injustice: he is not considered, under any definition, to be a victim of injustice. West might have more impetus to put himself out there given that, as West points out in the beginning of *Race Matters*, to the nonacademic world he is just another black man to be feared and mistreated. Rorty does not even nod to West's racial reasons for seeking to wed his philosophical program to a prophetic agenda.

Rorty believes that there was a time in which the pragmatist helped the prophets. He refers to William James and John Dewey as pragmatists who cleared out the problematic underbrush to help particular social changes come about. This was possible, Rorty claims, because at the time there were arguments on both sides of issues such as racial prejudice and labor rights. Rorty is gleeful that nowadays "[w]e have nobody worthy of the name 'rightist intellectual' who needs to be confuted. Nowadays nobody even bothers to back up opposition to liberal reforms with argument."[45] This large assumption of Rorty's explains a lot. The professional philosopher is not needed in society because there is really no intellectual problem out there, just one of power and wills. Rorty laments that "the problem is not a failure of imagination—a failure of the sort which philosophers might help with. It is more like a failure of nerve, a fairly sudden loss of generous instincts and of patriotic fellow-feeling."[46] No philosopher, especially given the professionalization of philosophy in the United States, can help with failure of nerve.

While I agree with Rorty's sentiments in "The Professor and the Prophet," I cannot accept the fact that pragmatism has to be confined to professional philosophy. West, if we are to consider him a pragmatist, already refutes Rorty's narrow definition. Even at the time *The American Evasion of Philosophy* was written, West had not—and still has not—worked in a philosophy department. In more recent years, his status as a public figure has grown exponentially—entering even into the music scene. West would not have it any other way: he keeps one leg in the academy (mostly in Religion and African-American Studies Departments) and one leg on the street, with and among the black community, whom he sees as worthy of having their practices made intelligible.[47]

45. Rorty, "Professor and the Prophet," 76.
46. Ibid.
47. See my "Making Religious Practices Intelligible."

The only thing holding Rorty back is his own definition of what philosophers can and cannot do. However, there are occasions in which Rorty throws his hat into the ring of the world. Two examples come to mind, both of which can be classified as *prophetic*. The first, *Achieving Our Country*,[48] is a mini-manifesto on the need to reinvigorate the American Left from being strictly an academic exercise to a return to active labor politics and civic engagement. This text is prophetic for several reasons. First, like Old Testament prophets, Rorty calls an errant, wayward Left to repentance and renewed focus on the goal. It is also prophetic insofar as it reminds its reader what is at stake with the American Left, why those on the Left think that being Leftist matters. Rorty cannot give a reason why people should be Leftist, but given that those on the Left claim to be Leftist, Rorty critiques them ethnocentrically since they are all allegedly in the same vocabulary. Finally, Rorty is prophetic in *Achieving Our Country* because, having evoked Baldwin's phrase "achieving our country," he has envisioned an America that instantly puts the current system into question and indicts the guilty party. In this case, it is an "inside" affair: he criticizes those on the Left for not being willing to sacrifice enough for Leftist causes and staying too comfortable inside the walls of academe (although he had no problem with that when responding to West!).

More interesting is Rorty's fictional essay "Looking Backwards from the Year 2096." This text, perhaps ironically, is published in the same volume that contains "Failed Prophecies, Glorious Hopes." Rorty wanted a text that could inspire social hope without prediction. Insofar as it imagines a better America without at all hinting that the "historical" events in the story are going to come to pass, this text achieves his goal. Even though it makes no predictions, one has to see it as a kind of prophetic text, akin to the ending of the book of Revelation. Its "abstract" is itself prophetic given its reference to one of the editors being a female Jesuit priest.[49] In the text, the author describes America in 2096. It eerily shows us what America could look like if everyone had become Rortyan:

> Here, in the late twenty-first century, as talk of fraternity and unselfishness has replaced talk of rights, American political discourse has come to be dominated by quotations from Scripture and literature, rather than from political theorists or social

---

48. See Rorty, *Achieving Our Country*.
49. See *Philosophy and Social Hope*, 244.

scientists. Fraternity, like friendship, was not a concept that either philosophers or lawyers knew how to handle. They could formulate principles of justice, equality and liberty, and invoke these principles when weighing hard moral or legal issues. But how to formulate a "princple of fraternity"? Fraternity is an inclination of the heart, one that produces a sense of shame at having much when others have little. It is not the sort of thing that anybody can have a theory about or that people can be argued into having.[50]

This passage echoes themes in *Contingency, Irony, and Solidarity*[51] as well as what he believes was right in Marxism and Christianity. It prophesies a world in which philosophers, lawyers, and other academics are "in their place"—without their ideas overtaking the good and liberal democratic will of the citizens. Although Rorty is not making a prediction, he expresses his hope for the future.

Of interest at the end of the "article" is his vision of solidarity around particular early twentieth-century slogans, songs, and texts:

In the first two centuries of American history Jefferson's use of rights had set the tone for political discourse, but now political argument is not about who has the right to what but about what can best prevent the re-emergence of hereditary castes—either racial or economic. The old union slogan "An injury to one is an injury to all" is now the catch phrase of American politics. "Solidarity Forever" and "This Land Is Your Land" are sung at least as often as "The Star-Spangled Banner" . . . In the churches, the "social gospel" theology of the early 20th century has been rediscovered. Walter Rauschenbusch's "Prayer against the servants of Mammon" . . . is familiar to most churchgoers.[52]

Besides the gentle nod Rorty gives his grandfather Walter Rauschenbusch, there are other prophetic elements here. Rorty's decision to make songs like "Solidarity Forever" and "This Land Is Your Land" sung as often as "The Star-Spangled Banner" is a critique of a present-day ultrapatriotic culture. The social gospel of Rauschenbusch criticizes the current religious right. Rorty, through this futuristic writer, imagines a day in which religion is private and not oppressive; but that too is prophecy!

---

50. Ibid., 248.
51. See Rorty, *Contingency, Irony, and Solidarity*, especially chs. 3, 4, and 9.
52. Rorty, *Philosophy and Social Hope*, 249.

In short, Rorty's prophecy is a prophecy about the end of "prophecy" as he understands it—oppressive, predictive foundationalism that appeals to a higher power of either God or History—and the promotion of human solidarity. For Rorty, the imperative might be "Prophesy solidarity!"—and this was precisely what Rorty did. The prophetic pragmatist is able to make Rorty's task intelligible, even against those who disagree with his antifoundationalism and antirepresentationalism. In spite of himself, Rorty is, indeed, a prophetic pragmatist.

I conclude by returning to my original question: can there be hope without prophecy? I respond in the negative: prophecy is a necessary condition for hope. In order to hope, one must have a prize upon which one should keep her eyes. One must have a sufficient amount of imagination to be able to proclaim that things ought to be different than they currently are. One must also have a sufficient amount of courage to critique the powers that be. Rorty would be a prophet in this sense, if only he were to allow himself to be free of old notions and philosophical deadwood that the pragmatist is supposed to clear. West claims that prophetic pragmatism is "pragmatism at its best."[53] This is the case, I argue, because pragmatism is at its best when it makes practices intelligible in order to maximize hope. The maximization of hope requires prophetic imagination, courage, and action. In this sense, all pragmatism worthy of its name is prophetic pragmatism—even they prophesy who are critical of the prophetic.

---

53. See West, *Keeping Faith*, 139.

CHAPTER TEN

The Difficulty of Imagining Other Persons, Reimagined

Rorty on Moral Imagination and the Transformation of Conflict

JASON A. SPRINGS

When you visualized a man or woman carefully, you could always begin to feel pity—that was a quality God's image carried with it. When you saw the lines at the corners of the eyes, the shape of the mouth, how the hair grew, it was impossible to hate. Hate was just a failure of imagination.[1]

[T]he thought that membership in our biological species carries with it certain "rights," [is] a notion that does not seem to make sense unless the biological similarities entail the possession of something nonbiological, something which links our species to a nonhuman reality and thus gives the species moral dignity. This picture of rights as biologically transmitted is so basic to the political discourse of Western democracies that we are troubled by any suggestion that "human nature" is not a useful moral concept. . . . The pragmatist . . . thinks that to say that certain people have certain rights is merely to say that we should treat them in certain ways. It is not to give a reason for treating them in certain ways.[2]

---

1. Greene, *Power and the Glory*, xii.
2. Rorty, *Objectivity, Relativity, and Truth*, 32.

> To the Serbs, the Muslims are no longer human. . . . Muslim prisoners, lying on the ground in rows, awaiting interrogation, were driven over by a Serb guard in a small delivery van. . . . A Muslim man in Bosansi Petrovac . . . [was] forced to bite off the penis of a fellow-Muslim. . . . If you say that a man is not human, but the man looks like you and the only way to identify this devil is to make him drop his trousers—Muslim men are circumcised and Serb men are not—then it is probably only a short step, psychologically, to cutting off his prick. . . . There has never been a campaign of ethnic cleansing from which sexual sadism has gone missing.[3]

This report from the ethno-nationalist conflict in the former Yugoslavia is thought by many to illustrate the limits of conceptions of "personhood" or "humanity" as abstract moral categories. In and of themselves, such terms suffer from potentially debilitating relativity. In the case above, Muslims lacked the salient features of humanity from the perspective of the Serb soldiers. Moreover, any impression of similarity only inspired greater cruelty. The Serb soldier, who might act quite honorably in other circumstances—who might be quite humanitarian to those whom he recognizes as fellow members of "humanity"—instead acts savagely. In this context and circumstance, to confront the Serb soldier for his in*humanity*—accusing him of violating the basic human rights of his victims—is to introduce a non sequitur. It was not "fellow humans" upon whom he perpetrated violence; these were Muslims.

Richard Rorty identified the refusal to recognize others as "persons like us" as a recurring feature of nationalist, tribal, ethnic, and religious conflicts. Time and again, such conflicts have been based upon distinctions between who is and is not a candidate for recognition, and thus, who does and does not count as fully human. "For most white people, until very recently, most black people did not so count," he wrote. "For most Christians, until the seventeenth century or so, most heathen did not so count. For the Nazis, Jews did not count." The examples multiply. "For most males in countries in which the average annual income is less than two thousand pounds, most females still do not so count. Whenever tribal and national rivalries become important, members of rival tribes and nations will not so count."[4] In such instances, the identities of the people or groups in question are determined and oriented

3. Rieff, "Letter from Bosnia."
4. Rorty, *Truth and Progress*, 177.

largely by who (or what) they are not. A nonnegotiable element of the Nazi's identity was that, down to the last drop of blood, he was not a Jew, the white that he was not black, and the Christian that he was not heathen.

Rorty devoted much of his social criticism to inveighing against the perils of too narrowly circumscribed conceptions of humanity. At the same time, however, he argued against shortcuts to universal inclusion—appeals to epistemically self-evident principles, or moral categories that purported to apply themselves. In this Rorty stood at odds with much of modern moral philosophy, a tradition that sought to cure the inabilities and refusals to recognize others as "of one's own kind" by appealing to self-evident and self-justifying bases for the universal inclusion. On one hand, Rorty agreed that the best hope for expanding the category of "people like us" was to render the bases for those divisions and exclusions increasingly irrelevant. But he was convinced that this would have to be cultivated first on the ground and in practice, rather than dictated in principle from above.

A principle, after all, will always have to be applied in particular times and places. As Wittgenstein had demonstrated, a rule never comes with its own self-interpreting instructions for use. Application will include, somewhat unavoidably, the applier's understanding of what it looks like to apply accurately or adequately the rule. Applications, thus, reflect the embodied and practical understandings that fill out—often tacitly—the social and cultural context in question (what Wittgenstein referred to as the user's "form of life"). So understood, applying a moral principle is a social practice that is itself embedded in broader networks of social practices and extended over time. So much depends upon the ethical life of the people in question, and in particular, their conception of what it means to count as a person in the first place (whether, for instance, one can or must be a man, a white, a landowner, a citizen, or a corporation).

Rorty saw the cultivation of moral imagination as indispensable to developing the capacity for mutual recognition. The challenge was for each to put him or herself in others' shoes, and especially in the shoes of the despised and oppressed.[5] Any attempt to address "all human beings" would have to begin at home, on the ground, and in one's immediate vicinity. Such appeals to the cultivation of sentimentality

5. Ibid., 179–81.

and moral imagination have met with sustained and searching criticism from thinkers who hold fast to the necessity of moral and epistemic foundations. Moreover, Rorty's penchant for rhetorical excess—even when motivated by his own well-meaning effort to josh his readers out of entrenched ways of thinking—has little aided the clarity of these conversations. In fact, his rhetoric has often provoked critics to characterize their differences as fundamental and irreconcilable, to the detriment of potentially constructive investigation of points of compatibility.

At the same time, the capacity to imagine others charitably and empathetically has become an increasingly central point of inquiry in recent years for many who work in efforts to transform conflict and in restorative justice. Theorists and practitioners have come to identify empathetic imagining as an indispensable practice for any who would hope to soften conceptions of justice as "blind," and thereby, impartial and retributive.[6] Furthermore, this strand of thinking sees moral imagination and fellow feeling as central to the tasks of transforming conflict, and indispensable for purposes of building conditions of peace that cannot be conceived apart from a simultaneous pursuit of justice. How conflict is framed, and how the actors involved therein understand and imagine one another, influences deeply which options for transforming that conflict are understood to be available and viable.

In the interest of administering criticism where it is warranted, yet cultivating compatibilities and points of overlap where possible, in the pages that follow I explore as charitably as possible Rorty's claims about the indispensability of moral imagination for reframing and transforming conflict. In particular, I sift through recent debates among philosophers and literary theorists about the pedagogical effectiveness of appealing to sentimental and literary forms of moral imagination. My purpose is to glean insights from these conversations that might further enrich, illuminate, and expand a grounded and concretely engaged account of moral imagination. I hope to show that Rorty's work in this area has made available resources with which I propose to develop an understanding of "moral imagination" as a practice—an embodied set of skills requiring cultivation, discipline, and practical wisdom.

Rorty saw modern philosophy's quest for universal inclusivity as littered with all-too-narrow applications of principles that are admiringly

---

6. Sullivan and Tifft, "What Are the Implications of Restorative Justice for Society and Our Lives?," 391–404; Lederach, *Moral Imagination*.

encompassing in articulation. Thus could Thomas Jefferson declare the self-evidence of the claim that "all men are created equal" without an inkling of self-contradiction about the multitude of black men and women that he owned. The shared understanding informing that context was that slaves, at best, approximated the humanity to which the principles of equality and liberty applied.[7] Likewise, Immanuel Kant could forward the respect for universal law predicated upon the distinctively human rational application of the categorical imperative, though not available to women, children, and non-European races. Such examples quickly multiply.

With the advantage of hindsight, we twenty-first-century cosmopolitans know better now. Moreover, to hold our colossal-but-blinkered forbears accountable to what "universal inclusion" has come to mean today would be uncharitably anachronistic. We must forgive the context-specific parochialism that skewed the applicability of Kant's categorical imperative. We look past the far too narrow reference class indexed to Jefferson's phrase "all men" in the opening lines of the Declaration of Independence.

For Rorty, however, the context-specific parochialism that contemporary cosmopolitans congratulate themselves for having overcome is precisely the point. Self-congratulation for having discovered the truly universal application of such principles risks blindness to all the practical complexities of application inscribed in the inescapability of cultural location and historical circumstance. For these reasons, Rorty thought it imperative to understand how something like "human rights culture"—recognized as a fully contingent and fragile achievement—had progressed to expand the scope and fill in the content of a formally universal principle such as that set forth by Jefferson, and gradually to inform the intuitions of persons that such cultures produced.

To speak of this culture as fragile indicated that the idea of human rights was not an inevitable discovery that had been waiting to happen. It was, rather, an achievement that emerged and evolved from a range of contingent historical developments. Its fragility meant that, without sufficient vigilance, these accomplishments could be subject to misdirec-

---

7. As Jefferson himself explained, the slaves' existence reflected much more "sensation than reflection," as their bodies were prone toward sleep when not occupied with labor or some other diversion. Jefferson, "Notes on Virginia," in *Writings*, Andrew A. Lipscomb and Albert Ellery Bergh, eds., 1:194, cited by Rorty in *Truth and Progress*, 167 n. 2.

tion, or lost altogether. Their contingency made it all the more pressing to understand what would be needed to minimize analogous exclusions in the present and future, and to remain attuned to blind spots to which human rights frameworks are predisposed.

Rorty endorsed the aim and scope of Jefferson's principle. He viewed the fact that this principle was born of, and embedded in, a self-correcting and flexible democratic enterprise of discursive exchange based upon mutual recognition and reciprocal accountability as further evidence of democracy's experimental success.[8] But successes in gradually filling in the content, and expanding the boundaries of the principle to include those it excluded for so long, would have to be tempered by the reality that this gradual (at times, excruciatingly so) historical emergence had—in the case of the United States—required a civil war, political and religious movements such as abolitionism and women's suffrage, the Civil Rights movement, and countless other social movements to concretely fill in the content of the abstract universal. Progress up the moral promontory from which contemporaries look back and identify the deficiencies of the abstract universals set forth by Jefferson, Kant, and others had been painful and, and times, treacherous. More importantly, we who benefit from the past vicissitudes of moral progress are not exempt from similar vicissitudes today. The problem was that foundationalism invoked by many philosophers and rights theorists invited a dangerous form of forgetting. Moral foundationalism, while in fact a socially embodied, historically extended and contingent range of arguments, was either unable or unwilling to recognize itself as such. From Rorty's perspective, the best hope for such foundationalists was to reconceive themselves as situated within a historical and contingent tradition of inquiry.[9]

---

8. Rorty understood democracy in contrast to state theory. Perhaps more aptly put, he saw democracy as a set of social practices and associational forms to which democratic state theory is secondary and upon which it is dependent. In this, he followed John Dewey's account in "The Ethics of Democracy." For Dewey, democracy can be a form of government only because it is more basically a mode of spiritual and moral association. (Menand, *Pragmatism*, 196). Rorty devoted the opening chapter of his book *Achieving Our Country* to explicating how Walt Whitman and Dewey provide key articulations of democracy as a collaborative endeavor of self-creation that takes the form of a tradition of deliberation and discursive exchange.

9. Rorty attributes the concept of "tradition" that he has in mind to Alasdair MacIntyre. He endorsed MacIntyre's pivotal claim in *After Virtue* that all reasoning is "tradition-bound." See Brandom, *Rorty and His Critics*, 20 and MacIntyre, *After Virtue*, 207.

Unlike the epigraph by Garrett Greene above, empathetic recognition can be no matter of simply doing what comes naturally if one will only take the time to look at others carefully enough. Neither the moral law within, invocations of history- and culture-transcending reason or intuition, nor the self-evident image of God in each of us can serve as a de facto guarantor for the mutual recognition of shared humanity—not, at least, for Rorty. Looking, rather, must be accompanied by seeing. "Seeing" in the relevant sense is a capacity that takes practice. Such perception might become immediate—intuitive, second nature. It might even come to be understood as something that ought to be practiced universally. Nonetheless, it must be acquired. Moreover, it is subject both to adjustment and to better and worse execution. Rorty's hope for the moral imagination as a vista for overcoming the divisions that motivate conflict hung upon the cultivation of both empathetic perception, and the types of normative attitudes and intuitions that make such perception possible.[10]

As Rorty has it, expanding the capacities for moral imagination and cultivation of moral sentiments calls on the parties involved in conflict to maximize the sense in which others are "like us," or "someone like myself," that is, someone whom I can feel for and care about as I do my own friends and family members. That these changes occur in the direction of a more broadly encompassing account of who ought to qualify for respect and protection from arbitrary treatment—creatures to whom some things ought never be done, and for whom some things ought always be done—is what Rorty called "moral progress." The possibility of such progress is intimately bound up with the social hope that it is possible to cultivate and sustain sentimental antipathy—even revulsion—toward certain actions, attitudes, and dispositions. The challenge then becomes how to cultivate the conditions, capacities, and sensibilities that would make, for instance, misogyny, gay bashing, and exploitation of the poor obviously shameful and intolerable, even unthinkable—much the way that the repugnance of interning Jews for extermination, or branding and whipping one's slave, have become prevailing moral intuitions in North Atlantic societies. Rorty wondered what it would take to make those of us who spend most days at work in

10. This was a pivotal insight that Rorty spent much of his career unpacking. For an especially early articulation of it, see Rorty's entry on "Intuition," 204–12; for an account of the moral and social-critical implications of perceptual acquisition and cultivation of normative attitudes, see Stout, *Democracy and Tradition*, ch. 9.

front of keyboards and computer screens, come to feel similar repugnance for the typical treatment of those who empty our garbage cans, vacuum our offices, and clean our toilets.

Broadening the compass of the word *humanity* is a task that falls to the moral educators and artists rather than philosophers or social theorists. The education of the moral imagination and the expansion of empathy required sidestepping rationalism's general and abstract questions, "Why should I be moral?" and "Do moral absolutes exist?" and if so, "How can we access them?" Rorty was equally doubtful about the usefulness of critical social theory for the purposes of social transformation. He argued, for instance, that unmasking social-system pervading dynamics of sadism illuminated by Freudian analytical lenses in fact permitted more banal (though no less insidious) forms of inhumanity to flourish in the form of realistic and thoughtful, yet simple, selfishness. For instance, in laissez-faire capitalist societies in which the phrase "greed is good" has morphed into a mantra of common sense, what are in fact other-destroying forms of selfishness are characterized benignly as "enlightened self-interest." Rorty put it this way:

> You would not guess from listening to the cultural politicians of the academic left that the power of the rich over the poor remains the most obvious, and potentially explosive, example of injustice in contemporary America. For these academics offer ten brilliant unmaskings of unconscious sadism for every unmasking of the selfishness intrinsic to American political and economic institutions. Enormous ingenuity and learning are deployed in demonstrating the complicity of this or that institution, or of some rival cultural politician, with patriarchy or heterosexism or racism. But little gets said about how we might persuade Americans who make more than $50,000 a year to take more notice of the desperate situation of their fellow citizens who make less than $20,000.[11]

Rorty was similarly skeptical about the prospects of rights talk to do the fine-grained, detailed work of remedying the most banal and everyday injustices. In societies enchanted by laissez-faire capitalism, for instance, "'the right to a job' (or 'to a decent wage') had none of the

---

11. Rorty, "What's Wrong with 'Rights,'" 17–18. I have examined the strengths and weaknesses of Rorty's suspicion of social-theoretical critique in contrast to the work of his former student, friend, and fellow pragmatist, Cornel West, in my article "The Priority of Democracy to Social Theory," 47–71.

resonance of 'the right to sit in the front of the bus' or 'the right to vote' or even 'the right to equal pay for equal work.' Rights in the liberal tradition were, after all, powers and privileges to be wrested from the state, not from the economy."[12] How else to account for the millions of fellow citizens excluded from regular access to a doctor and a living wage in a society both as fabulously wealthy and saturated with rights talk as the early twenty-first-century United States? Similarly, in that context, gays and lesbians who invoke the notion of "marriage equality," or African-Americans who speak of reparations for slavery in affirmative action policies, are pilloried for seeking "special rights," and thereby promoting a species of the inequality they claim to deplore. At the same time, free market fundamentalists passionately forward the banner of rights, invoking Jefferson's right to liberty and John Locke's right to property with the same frequency and passion with which they invoke Adam Smith's account of the providence of the unconstrained market's "invisible hand." "Rights" to a job and living wage, they argue, entail redistribution of wealth that violates more fundamental rights of property ownership, self-possession, and self-determination. Such redistribution allegedly is equivalent to forced labor.[13] A context so saturated by rapacious, possessive individualism, consumption, and distraction has conveniently assimilated claims on behalf of inviolable rights to the point of conceiving of corporations as persons bearing inalienable rights to free speech.[14]

For Rorty, the hope of transforming unjust social conditions lay in the kind of self-cultivation that enlarges imagination individually and collectively, rather than one first concerned to ascertain principles and standards dictated from outside the human abode generally, or much beyond one's own neighborhood or family more specifically. Such transformation attends to a specific context and situation in question, and works with the ad hoc and daily detail to cultivate the capacity for mutual recognition and empathetic understanding. He explained: "[Pragmatists] hope to minimize one difference at a time—the difference between Christians and Muslims in a particular village in Bosnia, the difference between blacks and whites in a particular town in Alabama,

12. Rorty, "Fraternity Reigns."

13. See, for instance, Friedman, *Capitalism and Freedom*, chs. 1 and 12; Friedman and Friedman, *Free to Choose*, introduction and ch. 5; Nozick, *Anarchy, State, Utopia*, 164–73.

14. For helpful discussion, see Fish, "What Is the First Amendment For?" and "How the First Amendment Works."

the difference between gays and straights in a particular Catholic congregation in Quebec. The hope is to sew such groups together with a thousand little stitches—to invoke a thousand little commonalities between their members, rather than specify one great big one, their common humanity."[15] The task of the moral educator becomes the task of dealing with concrete social and historical contexts and stories. Moral formation of this kind searches for answers to the question, "Why should I care about the stranger, a foreigner, someone I find disgusting?"[16] Answers to such questions best take the form of stories, Rorty says: "[T]he sort of long, sad, sentimental story that begins, 'Because this is what it is like to be in her situation—to be far from home among strangers,' or "Because she might become your daughter-in-law,' or 'Because her mother would grieve for her.' Such stories, repeated and varied over the centuries, have induced . . . the rich, safe, powerful people to tolerate and even to cherish powerless people—people whose appearance or habits or beliefs at first seemed an insult to our own moral identity, our sense of the limits of permissible human variation."[17] The motivating insight in both cases is that how one acts toward others is informed powerfully by how one imagines them, whether or not one recognizes them at all, and whether one is so disposed that they inspire one to respond. Seeing and being moved by "the human face of others" is a necessary (if not altogether sufficient) condition for motivating humane intervention, assistance, and protection, and for gradually cultivating the unthinkability of certain actions and attitudes.

The Difficulty of Imagining Other Persons

Appeals to sentimentality, empathetic understanding, and moral imagination of the kind that Rorty championed have come under intense scrutiny in recent years. To many, they seem hopelessly facile—a particularly glib outgrowth of moral nihilism. Earlier in his career, Rorty had infamously enunciated the antimetaphysical implications of his pragmatism: "[W]hen the secret police come, when the torturers violate the innocent, there is nothing to be said to them of the form, 'There is something within you which you are betraying. Though you embody

---

15. Rorty, *Philosophy and Social Hope*, 86–87.
16. Rorty, *Truth and Progress*, 184–85.
17. Ibid.

the practices of a totalitarian society which will endure forever, there is something beyond those practices which condemns you."[18] Was Rorty now suggesting that when the secret police come knocking, and torturers violate the innocent, we regale them with sad, sentimental stories?

Moral imagination, as Rorty construed it, is not a tool for argument or justification. It is a means for assembling the kind of audience "to whom they would have a sporting chance of justifying their view." It hopes to find a pathway around or through the cognitive defenses and visceral prejudices that make communication—and perhaps discursive exchange—intractable. Such discursive exchange might make "bringing the bastards over to our way of doing things" conceivable, but only by, first, opening the possibility of a kind of conversion. Perhaps this conversion occurs in the immediacy of a moment of sudden awakening or recognition, as when Nathan opened the eyes of David ("You are that man!"[19]), or the blind seer Tireseus provoked Creon's recognition of the catastrophe that his pride had wrought upon Thebes in the final moments of Sophocles' *Antigone*.

More likely, the cultivation of moral imagination occurs as a gradual progression—an education of sentiments. Rorty described the kind of changes necessary to effect a cultural transformation. This is to cultivate a shift of orientation in individual and culturally articulated intuitions and background understandings from which action and change can ensue—in the shaping of deeply reaching dispositions and sensibilities that would not simply find abstract articulation in the forms of moral principles and laws, but would specify their content and orient their application.

Literary theorist Elaine Scarry makes the case that the primary deficiencies of appeals to moral sentiment and imagination do not exist in their refusal of metaphysical foundations or a common human essence. Their deficiencies are far more mundane. Even in the most practiced imaginings, the stranger remains a stranger as such; he or she remains the stranger as imagined by me. The imaginer understands the needs, desires, and identities of this imagined other inevitably in reference to

---

18. Rorty, *Consequences of Pragmatism*, xlii.

19. In 2 Samuel 11–12 (esp. 12:1–7), Nathan deploys a parable to awaken David to God's anger at his committing adultery with Bathsheba and having her husband sent to his death in order to cover it up.

the imaginer's own. Scarry calls the result a "perceptual disability."[20] Imagining other people easily becomes gratuitous. It risks making the "imagined other" a reflection of our own image, desires, wants, needs, and hopes, even in our most sincere intention to act altruistically toward them. "The human capacity to injure other people has always been much greater than its ability to imagine other people," Scarry continues. "Or perhaps we should say, the human capacity to injure other people is very great precisely because our capacity to imagine other people is very small. . . . Our injuring of others results from our failure to know them; and conversely, our injuring of persons, even persons within arm's reach, itself demonstrates their unknowability. For if they stood visible to us, the infliction of that injury would be impossible."[21]

If the feebleness of our imaginings inhibits our "truly knowing" the others in our immediate environment, then it compounds the difficulties of imagining those removed from us several times over. Here we have in mind vast numbers of a distant population or group. The sheer size of the numbers becomes mind-numbing and imagination-stifling: the twelve million illegal immigrants estimated to reside currently in the United States; as many as 110,000 documented Iraqi civilian deaths from violence since the US-led invasion in 2003;[22] or the seventy million people estimated to die and suffer should the United States launch one of its nuclear missiles.[23] Numbers so vast quickly lose any sense of realistic proportion and meaning, and with that vanishes what Scarry calls "the density of personhood."[24] The result is an invitation to become, in effect, "empty of ethical worry."[25]

Even if Scarry is correct in her forgoing criticisms, are there not examples where literary inspiration in novel reading and theatregoing have broadly altered people's ability to recognize others? Scarry acknowledges, for example, that Harriet Beecher Stowe's *Uncle Tom's Cabin* profoundly touched the popular imagination in mid-nineteenth century America, and gradually altered the normative attitudes of that time. That novel "made blacks—the weight, solidity, injurability of

20. Scarry, "Difficulty of Imagining Other Persons," 43.
21. Ibid., 45, 43–44.
22. Online: http://www.iraqbodycount.org/.
23. Scarry, "Difficulty of Imagining Other Persons," 45.
24. Ibid., 47.
25. Ibid., 44.

their personhood—imaginable to the white population in the pre-Civil War United States."[26] At this juncture, Scarry and Rorty find fleeting agreement. For purposes of educating moral sentiments and cultivating moral imagination—that is, for learning to imagine and perceive other persons and communities in ways that make building relationships with them an authentic possibility despite entrenched predispositions to find them disgusting—the impact of a work like Stowe's *Uncle Tom's Cabin* cannot be overestimated.[27]

Can we count on this to be sufficient to make a difference in mollifying perceptions of others as beasts, as inhuman, as polluted and disgusting, when these perceptions are rooted in ethnic, nationalist, and religious identities? Reliance upon moral imagination to reframe oppositional relations—to imaginatively reconceive the "others" in question—ultimately cannot hope to be binding unless grounded in legal and constitutional stipulations, Scarry cautions. "[I]f the U.S. Constitution lacked the Reconstruction Amendments (prohibiting servitude; ensuring due process across race and religion; prohibiting racial restrictions on voting) no daily rereading of *Uncle Tom's Cabin* by the United States population ... could in [itself] have the smallest healing power."[28] In other words, appeals to the cultivation of sentiment and imagination must be backed up by enforceable legal provisions to be effective. Moreover, to ground the derivation of laws in moral sentiment and imagination is surely to inscribe them in partiality.

What, then, does Scarry propose? "Dis-imagining" is the term she uses. Rather than imagining others, *dis-imagining oneself* might facilitate what Scarry calls "statistical compassion"—compassion for the masses of distant, nameless, faceless, others. This is something for which literary imagination and sentimental education are inadequate.

26. Ibid., 49.

27. Literary theorist Jane Tompkins writes that Stowe's novel stands as an exemplary instance of what she calls the "sentimental novel." A novel of this sort aims to execute a "political enterprise, halfway between sermon and social theory," in that it "both codifies and attempts to mold the values of its time." Tompkins refers to *Uncle Tom's Cabin*, the first American novel to sell more than a million copies, as "the *Summa Theologica* of nineteenth-century America's religion of domesticity, a brilliant redaction of the culture's favorite story about itself—the story of salvation through motherly love. Out of the ideological materials at their disposal, the sentimental novelists elaborated a myth that gave women the central position of power and authority in the culture; and of these efforts *Uncle Tom's Cabin* is the most dazzling exemplar." Tompkins, *Sensational Designs*, 126.

28. Scarry, "Difficulty of Imagining Other Persons," 50.

Such dis-imagining of oneself can be effected by placing oneself behind a veil. Rather than trying to make one's knowledge of others as weighty and robust as one's knowledge of oneself, the point is to "make one ignorant about oneself, and therefore as weightless as all the others." Here Scarry aims to overcome the limitations of moral sentiments and imagination by applying John Rawls' "veil of ignorance" articulated in *A Theory of Justice*.[29]

Rawls famously argued that by taking up "the original position" —temporarily making oneself ignorant of one's "physical, genetic, psychological, and even moral attributes"[30]—one can make decisions about matters of basic justice impartially, without consideration for the particular role, status, history, relationships, or conception of the good that one has in the projected social framework.[31] Inspired by Rawls, Scarry writes:

> [T]he act of making oneself featureless. . . . Is a way of bringing about equality not by giving the millions of other people an imaginative weight equal to one's own—a staggering mental labor—but by the much more efficient opposite strategy, the strategy of simply erasing for a moment one's own dense array of attributes. By becoming featureless, by having a weightlessness, a two-dimensonality, a dryness every bit as "impoverished" as the imagined other, the condition of equality is achieved. One subtraction therefore has the same effect as a hundred thousand additions. Through it we create what Rawls describes as "the symmetry of everyone's relations to each other" . . . The only trait encouraged is psychological and moral "tolerance" of high levels of difference.[32]

---

29. Rawls, *Theory of Justice*, 136–41.

30. Scarry, "Difficulty of Imagining Other Persons," 51.

31. "[N]o one knows his place in society, his class position or social status; nor does he know his fortune in the distribution of natural assets and abilities, his intelligence and strength, and the like. Nor, again, does anyone know his conception of the good, the particulars of his rational plan of life, or even the special features of his psychology such as his aversion to risk or liability to optimism or pessimism. More than this, I assume that the parties do not know the particular circumstances of their own society. That is, they do not know its economic or political situation, or the level of civilization and culture it has been able to achieve. The persons in the original position have no information as to which generation they belong" (Rawls, *Theory of Justice*, 137).

32. Scarry, "Difficulty of Imagining Other Persons," 52.

The veil of ignorance has come under severe scrutiny since the writing of *A Theory of Justice*, by friendly and unfriendly critics alike. On these accounts, any effort to dis-imagine oneself and one's situation—in which the parties are rational and mutually disinterested—in fact, presupposes a fairly philosophically specific conception of the self. It is the kind of self that is able stand back at some distance from its prejudices and biases and impartially bracket or filter them out. It is the rational, choosing self, the Kantian self. Such a self is, in fact, historically specific, even though it purports to disencumber itself from all historical specificity, taking up a view from nowhere.

Michael Sandel describes this "self behind the veil" as wholly *unencumbered*. It is a self whose deepest beliefs, commitments, relationships, memories, and history are finally optional, no more indispensable to it than the clothes that it can put on and take off as need or desire dictate.[33] Such a position excludes the intrinsic moral relevance of desire, passion, sympathy, and compassion and categorizes them as nonrational—to be filtered out by the self-deliberating dryly behind the veil. It brackets from the start the very possibility—indeed, the necessity—of distinguishing good desires, passions, and needs from bad, as well as cultivating the skills of critical self- and other-awareness required to make such distinctions.[34]

Still, must the cultivation of moral imagination and the legal enforcement stand in opposition? Rorty came to a point in his thinking that illuminated the usefulness of moral principles such as those characteristic of human rights discourse. It was not the case that he saw no value in thin and broad categories to be applied across contexts. He was persuaded, in particular, by Michael Walzer's argument that moral concepts and principles applied trans-contextually get their normative content only because they have been derived from the "thick" accounts and histories, which emerge on the ground and in particular contexts and circumstances. "[W]e have to drop the Kantian idea that the moral law starts off pure but is always in danger of being contaminated by irrational feelings that introduce arbitrary discriminations among persons," he wrote. "We have to substitute the Hegelian-Marxist idea that the so-called moral law is, at best, a handy abbreviation for a concrete

---

33. Sandel, *Liberalism and the Limits of Justice*, 149.
34. Young, "Impartiality and the Civic Public," 62–63.

web of social practices."³⁵ Rorty agreed with Walzer that the difference between "thick" and "fully resonant" conceptions of justice and peace are the "detailed and concrete stories you can tell about yourself as a member of a smaller group and the relatively abstract and sketchy story you can tell about yourself as a citizen of the world." He also agreed that thin articulations, when properly ordered and understood, are crucial for the purposes of criticism of on-the-ground conditions and for generating cross-cultural solidarity.³⁶

Of course, if Rorty's account of moral sentiments does not founder upon Scarry's concerns, it may founder for far more banal reasons. As we saw, Rorty's objective in appealing to moral imagination is to rearticulate a conception of justice that is oriented by "the expansion of the circle of beings who count as 'us.'"³⁷ His primary means to achieve this end lay in cultivating students who are "nice," "tolerant," and "unconcerned" about what other people do in private, in order to expand what he deems best about modern, liberal democratic culture. He explains:

> [I]f, like many of us, you teach students who have been brought up in the shadow of the Holocaust, brought up believing that prejudice against racial or religious groups is a terrible thing, it is not very hard to convert them to standard liberal views about abortion, gay rights, and the like. You may even get them to stop eating animals. All you have to do is to convince them that all the arguments on the other side appeal to "morally irrelevant" considerations. You do this by manipulating their sentiments in such a way that they imagine themselves in the shoes of the despised and oppressed. Such students are already so nice that they are eager to define their identity in nonexclusionary terms. The only people such students find any trouble being nice to are the ones they consider irrational—the religious fundamentalists, the

---

35. Rorty, *Philosophy as Cultural Politics*, 46–47.

36. While Rorty's thinking about human rights shows signs of considerable development over the last two decades of his life, nowhere did he discuss rights as justification for coercive intervention in situations of mass atrocity in international contexts. If he had written explicitly of it at the end of his life, in my judgment, his position would have looked something like a mix between Walzer's account of rights in *Thick and Thin* (which Rorty endorsed in his late writings) and Michael Ignatieff's antimetaphysical characterization of rights as a cultural and political discourse which could, if necessary, justify armed intervention in the midst of genocide or atrocity. See Ignatieff's *Human Rights as Politics and Idolatry*. For an example of what such an integration of Ignatieff and Walzer might look like, see Omer, "'It's Nothing Personal,'" 497–518.

37. Rorty, *Philosophy as Cultural Politics*, 45 n. 3.

smirking rapist, or the swaggering skinhead. Producing generations of nice, tolerant, well-off, secure, other-respecting students of this sort in all parts of the world is just what is needed—indeed all that is needed—to achieve the Enlightenment utopia. The more youngsters like these we can raise, the stronger and more global our human rights culture will become.[38]

"Being nice" is not a virtue. When it comes to the task of actually cultivating the kind of relationships that might enable the reframing and redirection of conflict in constructive directions, I wonder if Rorty's recommendation here will be as effective as he seems to think. I have my doubts. Moreover, in my judgment, his vision of an "Enlightenment utopia" as the motivation and objective for pursuing peace and seeking justice has proven woefully deficient. The ideal inhabitant of such a society is innocuous and uncontroversial for the sake of being tolerable and tolerant in public, civil, or political matters.[39]

Rorty was never hesitant to admit that his advocacy for "justice as a larger loyalty" was a product of his own ethnocentrism. He would ask, in response, for an example of some prognosis and proposed remedy that is not, itself, similarly ethnocentric. At this point, an objector is up against Rorty's own brand of democratic faith and social hope, a range of preferences that are unapologetically contingent; however, this did not stop him from asserting their superiority. Democratic arrangements have, after all, met with a great deal of experimental success.[40] Rorty would ask to be shown some mode of political and social associations that have been more effective at diminishing human suffering and opening up possible avenues for self-cultivation than modern, democratic ones. Nonetheless, when it comes to the difficult cases of engaging in the processes of conflict analysis and reframing, which are indispensable to conflict transformation, Rorty's self-ascribed postmodern bourgeois liberalism and its predilection to let a thousand flowers bloom may themselves prove lacking in imagination.

Unqualified, Rorty's proposal lacks the gravity—the seriousness—to be effective in situations where the intractability of conflict makes tolerance and simple coexistence unlikely. His approach overlooks how deeply running are the commitments that can spark and fuel violent

---

38. Rorty, *Truth and Progress*, 179.
39. Fish, *Trouble with Principle*, 243–78.
40. Rorty, *Philosophy and Social Hope*, 273.

conflict. Rorty does not address how agonistic even political conflict can be, nor does he broach the possibility that the very commitments that motivate conflict—if reframed or reimagined—might themselves become resources for constructively redirecting that conflict, reframing its circumstances, or transforming its elements. In turn, he does not recognize that just as the virtues of moral imagination, if properly cultivated and sustained, open a world of possibilities for transforming conflict, so ill-formed habits of imagination perpetuate viciousness, rendering the tendencies to dehumanize and demonize all the more likely. Donald Shriver captures the depth of the challenge, writing:

> Our century is littered with the outrages of dehumanization. Those whom we would kill, we first make subhuman. It is a war strategy of vast destructive power. From Auschwitz to Coventry to Dresden to Hiroshima to Phnom Penh to Sarajevo to Soweto to Kigali to Pristina, we have accumulated precedents of mass murder, usually preceded by some synonym for "subhuman" pasted over the image of enemies. We can call this phenomenon "beastly," but that is an unjustified insult to the beasts. To be sure, it takes training to peer through a dark lens long enough to begin to see one's neighbors as essentially inferior to oneself. Harder for most of us, perhaps, is training in the habit of seeing the worst of neighbors as still human like ourselves. To adopt the latter habit is to acquire empathy for the "repulsive," a habit quite different from either sympathy or excuse . . . to empathize is to discover the common humanity that links victims to their perpetrators.[41]

Here Shriver broaches the heart of the issue. Tendencies to dehumanize others are so often habituated and thus deeply inscribed in cultural understandings, even the personalities and practices through which we engage the world around us. Is there a way of conceiving moral imagination as an ethical practice aimed at the formation—or perhaps the reformation—of good habits and skills of imagination, what we might call virtues of the imagination? What would be required in order to take the rigors of moral imagination with sufficient gravity? What would it look like?

Ivory-Tower Aestheticism and Conflict Transformation

"Transcending violence is forged by the capacity to generate, mobilize, and build the moral imagination," writes Mennonite peacebuilder John

---

41. Shriver, "Is Justice Served by Forgiveness?," 38.

Paul Lederach in his book *The Moral Imagination*. Lederach unpacks this claim: "Stated simply, the moral imagination requires the capacity to imagine ourselves in a web of relationships that includes our enemies; the ability to sustain a paradoxical curiosity that embraces complexity without reliance on dualistic polarity; the fundamental belief in and pursuit of the creative act; and the acceptance of the inherent risk of stepping into the mystery of the unknown that lies beyond the far too familiar landscape of violence."[42] Of course, it is no easy task to recognize the inescapability of the "webs of relationships" in which we are always and already caught up, reframing what appear to be unavoidably oppositional structures, and learning how to cultivate and utilize these networks of relationships in order to transform the elements of conflict. In many cases, simply recognizing the existence of a relationship presupposes the arduous challenge of learning to recognize some group of people as "fellow humans" that, otherwise, one finds it quite natural to despise and respond to with disgust.

Acknowledging the power of such prejudices illuminates two pressing challenges. On one hand is the challenge of identifying the frequently entrenched and tacit forms of understanding and behaviors that elude even intentional introspection, and either fuel the causes of conflict or impede the path of recognizing of others as fellow humans (or both). On the other hand is the challenge of recognizing the indispensability of cultivating transformative relationships with others—the very others with whom we are caught up in "patterns of violence that are still present."[43]

The kind of practice Lederach proposes here entails learning how to recognize others in their full weight and solidity, even when, upon closer inspection, the ways that these other people look or live—their features, habits, manners, and mores—may inspire visceral revulsion owing to one's own cultural prejudices. Learning the skill of recognition through the cultivation of moral imagination entails the critical task of *self*-recognition, for it is through such encounters that one's own prejudices, limitations, and violence come to light. Such encounters confront one with questions like, "Why is it that I respond this way when I encounter these people and practices?" and "How is it that people of this

---

42. Lederach, *Moral Imagination*, 5.
43. Ibid., 61–62.

sort appear to me as exotic, or disgusting, or puerile, or fascinating, and what insight do such perceptions offer into who I am?"

Reframed as a virtue, the moral practice of imagining others for the purposes of reframing conflict and transforming its elements must pursue a balance between two vices that lie on either hand. On one hand is the temptation to what the Jewish philosopher Gillian Rose has called "the sentimentality of the ultimate predator."[44] This is the kind of affective engagement that degenerates into voyeurism. It results in insulating oneself from the conflict and atrocity one encounters. The encounter is portrayed so consumably as to permit the viewer's or reader's self-absolution from any collusion or complicity in—or even potential identification with—the evils portrayed. It conscripts the reader or viewer as a "predator" by enlisting his or her sentiments for any possible cause or condition. The difference between the affective responses inspired by Jacob Riis's *How the Other Half Lives* or John Steinbeck's *The Grapes of Wrath*, on one hand, and Ayn Rand's *Atlas Shrugged* on the other, are understood to be purely a matter of consumer shopping-mall preference. On the other hand, critics see introspection and self-interrogation—"turning the searchlight inward"—as playing into the hands of culture in which the kind of self-cultivation associated with the virtues has been absorbed by a gratuitous therapeutic culture of self-help. Any society saturated with shallow and distracted emotionalism risks heralding as empathetic understanding what is, in fact, titillating self-absorption.

Along precisely these lines, Elaine Scarry gestures toward William James' castigation of what he called "the nerveless sentimentalist and dreamer," someone "who spends his life in a weltering sea of sensibility and emotion, but who never does a . . . concrete deed." Scarry specifically has in mind James' claim that "the habit of excessive novel-reading

---

44. Rose addresses grave risks of moral imagination and sentimentality in her philosophical examination of Stephen Spielberg's film *Schindler's List* as a particularly influential representation of Holocaust atrocities. Characteristic of a latter twentieth-century cultural industry that both capitalizes upon and perpetuates what she calls "holocaust piety"—a disposition to posit this atrocity as so extreme as to be, in effect, non-representable, and thus, something that is not possible to engage in a discursive way. "To argue for . . . non-representability is to mystify something we dare not understand, because we fear that it may be all too understandable, all too continuous with what we are—human, all too human" (Rose, *Mourning Becomes the Law*, 43). For more recent work in Christian ethics that explores in depth each of these forms of affective and imaginative viciousness and what is required by a virtuous dispositional understanding of self-critical affectivity, see Cates, "Experiential Narratives of Rape and Torture," 43–66.

and theatre-going will produce true monsters.... [The audience member at the theatre weeps] over the fictitious personages in the play, while her coachman is freezing to death on his seat outside, is the sort of thing that everywhere happens on a less glaring scale." James continues, "But every one of us in his measure, whenever, after glowing for an abstractly formulated Good, he practically ignores some actual case, among the squalid 'other particulars' of which that same Good lurks disguised, treads straight on [this path]."[45]

Taken on its own, this characterization appears to substantiate Scarry's claims about the deficiencies of moral imagination. The full context of the passage, however, actually provides resources by which we might incorporate the key insights from Shriver and Lederach in a way that is enriched by Rorty's pragmatist sensibilities. Quite specifically, James is concerned about what he calls "the relaxing effect" that such empty sentimentalism has on one's character. The "relaxing effect" takes root in mistaking an affective experience as an end in itself, rather than as a moment in a complex reflexive process of experience and embodied action.

What is the cause of this "relaxing effect," according to James? It is caused by failing to act after one's sentiment or imagination has been evoked. It is perpetuated by the sedentary, disengaged, and unresponsive habits and character that are produced, over time, through sentiment followed by inaction. "One becomes filled with emotions which habitually pass without prompting to any deed, and so the inertly sentimental condition is kept up," James writes. The remedy he proposes at this point is action: "The remedy would be, never to suffer one's self to have an emotion at a concert [at the theatre, or in engagement with some literary imagining], without expressing [that emotion] afterwards in some active way."[46] In other words, James' cure for an empty sentimentalism is not an appeal to abstraction, but concrete, particular action. In fact, he goes so far as to say, "Let the expression [action] be the least thing in the world—speaking genially to one's grandmother, or giving up one's seat in a horse-car, if nothing more heroic offers—but let it not fail to take place."[47]

---

45. James, *Writings*, 1878–1899, 149.
46. Ibid.
47. Ibid.

Action as the reflex response of sentiment and imaginative inspiration is so crucial for James because this combination is central to shaping character, identity, and personhood. To respond actively to some sentimental appeal is to participate actively in shaping one's identity. As such, it is a way to keep one's character and identity flexible, to some degree negotiable, and capable of appropriate and proportionate response in a situation where some such response is called for. On James' view, "the cultivation of sentiments and sympathies" and "development of skills of imagination and empathy" as tools when it comes to reframing and transforming the elements of conflict bear upon the shape that such education and formation must take. James would say that such cultivation of sentiments for the purposes of moral education must be followed by concrete action and sustained practice. With this point, James provides a way of circumventing the gratuitous sentimentalism or vulgar emotivism to which appeals to imagining others and empathetic understanding are prone. For James, acting in response to affective experience aids in disciplining those experiences. It enmeshes a person in the cultivation of habits.

At this point, however, a second concern arises for moral imagination: Will any old action do, just so long as it follows concretely upon the moral imagining? While James may sound like he suggests as much in certain passages, it is crucial to note that for James, the aim here is not to cultivate bourgeois proclivities to refrain tolerantly from judgment and to be non-exclusionary. James is concerned with cultivating habits that encompass the intellect *and* the moral sensibilities. These habits are crucial precisely because moral sentiments and imaginations are manipulable in any number of directions. The education of sentiments, for which James argues, aims to develop skills of critical self-reflection and action that are part and parcel to cultivating and expanding one's ability to empathize. This is because the imaginer is implicated as a participant in the outcome of the engagement just as much as those she encounters within the horizon of this imaginative and empathetic encounter. The question, "How should I respond?" is really the immediate face of a much deeper and abiding question: each time one asks, "What should I do?" one simultaneously asks "Who and what am I becoming?" Each encounter bears impact upon the character, disposition, and identity of the imaginer. As James sees it, there is no moral imagining and responsive effort that can be unaccompanied by the question, Where do I stand in the imaginative act in relation to the people and situations I imagine and encounter? The practice of moral imagination is essentially and inescapably relational. It is not epistemically neutral; it is self-involving. The action chosen must be accompanied by further reflection upon, and interrogation of, the affective and visceral responses that first inspired that action. This makes the task of critical interrogation of one's affective experiences indispensable for the purposes of moral imagining, and for the possibilities of transforming the elements of conflict. Moreover, it is this inescapable relationality that ethically orients the imaginative enterprise. There is no "doing unto others"—or *not* doing unto others— that does not simultaneously implicate one in doing unto oneself.

Conclusion

The question remains as to how all the above might relate to Christian theological ethics. This issue is pressing if only because Rorty himself succumbed to the temptation to highlight and stiffen the differences between Christian theological ethicists, among others. Arguably, this reflected his own lack of imagination and failure at reflective self-inventory. If Rorty warmed to some forms of Christian thought toward the end of his life, this was because he came to recognize, for instance, that Paul Tillich's God of "ultimate concern" stood at a hair's breadth from Alfred Whitehead's God—"the fellow-sufferer who understands." Likewise, he came to affirm Gianni Vattimo's understanding of Christianity as "self-emptying" because he found it consistent with his own faith in the inexorable disenchantment of the world. In spite of prodding from close friends and fellow pragmatists, Rorty was largely unable to empathetically imagine himself in the shoes of his Christian interlocutors, a facet of his thinking that itself became a conversation-stopping roadblock along the path of difference-making inquiry.[48]

What would it take for those who approach concerns raised about the machinations of corporate despotism and a religion of perpetual consumption and distraction to find common cause with Rorty on those issues we find ourselves similarly compelled to speak against and resist? Christians would, of necessity, identify as a compulsion of the Holy Spirit their own peculiar motivations for assuaging the suffering of the least of

---

48. See, in particular, Jeffrey Stout's contribution to Hauerwas, Rorty, Stout, and West, "Pragmatism and Democracy."

these and resisting the satanic mills and incessantly novel varieties of soul- and body-crushing corporation-driven slaveries and addictions. So understood, moral imagination entails reflective and embodied practices to which Christians are called by the witness of One who replied to the religious lawyer's cross-examination of the principled heart of the Mosaic law ("But *who* is my neighbor?") with a story: "A Jewish man was traveling from Jerusalem to Jericho . . ."[49] Of course, Christians will have to identify the capacity to see the plight of those around them, and imagine themselves in the shoes of the despised and oppressed, as a gift of the Holy Spirit and a response to a Love who loved them first. But despite Rorty's intransigence, is there no common cause to be found here? When she was in jail in Occoquan, Dorothy Day wrote,

> Solitude and hunger and weariness of spirit—these sharpened my perceptions so that I suffered not only my own sorrow but the sorrows of those about me. I was no longer myself. I was mankind. I was no longer a young girl, part of a radical movement seeding justice for those oppressed. I was the oppressed. I was the drug addict screaming and yelling in her cell, beating her head against the walls. I was that shoplifter who for rebellion, was sentenced to solitary. I was that woman who had killed her children, who had murdered her lover.[50]

---

49. Luke 10:25–37.
50. Day, *Meditations*, 9.

Afterword

Charles Marsh[1]

You know, when I was a graduate student at the University of Virginia in the 1980s, the intellectual scene there was very much sub-clustered around these exciting conversations in literary theory and philosophical hermeneutics, and I want to tell you a story about that and segue into my thoughts about King.

Postmodernism ruled in the discourse of the human sciences, and one of my involvements was this theory group, a monthly seminar that discussed all the new literature. Not only graduate students in English but also in religious studies, in German and French Lit, in history and philosophy, met in the Colonnade Club and other places on grounds where lunches sometimes dragged late into the afternoon.

This is how I first came to know a philosopher named Richard Rorty, the former university professor at UVA whom *The New York Times* called "one of the world's most influential contemporary thinkers" when he died last June in Palo Alto, California. Professor Rorty was in the midst of all of this intellectual ferment, and indeed a catalyst of it, and from what I could see, he was having the time of his life. Rorty was not at all your usual sort of pomo [postmodernist] wannabe with the black jeans and the gravity-defying haircut. In fact, he preferred khakis, and a wrinkled dress shirt, and a navy blue blazer which he would just kind of toss on a chair when he entered the classroom. More importantly, he wanted us to know that reading books and talking about theory must do more than make us interesting scholars. Indeed, reading and debate and conversation must make us more compassionate citizens.

---

1. Transcribed and edited by Connie Goodson and Rebecca Dzida.

Standing in the traditions of such critical patriots as John Dewey and Herbert Croly, Rorty advanced a pragmatic standard of truth and told us that progress in knowledge and society should be about attending to and solving the specific problems that obstruct ever more novel, ever richer forms of human happiness.

Rorty's words, and his arguments, his cautionary words, were well aimed at a generation of graduate students living in Reagan's America concerned more about their sexual-psycho adventures than the staggering numbers of homeless and unemployed pouring onto our nation's city streets.

Rorty criticized the French philosophers like Michel Foucault and many other philosophers and theorists for a dryness produced by a lack of identification with any social context, any communication. This is a criticism Rorty brilliantly recasts in his 1997 Massey lectures at Harvard, published in that splendid volume *Achieving Our Country: Leftist Thought in Twentieth-Century America*, a short little book that I use in my undergraduate course on religion and social movements in the United States. Rorty spared no punch in his attack on the political evasions of the contemporary academy, which he accused of siding too often with the sort of etherealized politics of academic radicalism and forgetting the reformist, you know, "get your hands dirty" disciplines of the old left he so loved.

Mr. Rorty also weighed in on contemporary debates about postmodernism and religion that were currently in vogue at the time. One trendy movement in theological studies was what was called "deconstructionist theology." Now, if you were a deconstructionist theologian, you believed that the disappearance of God and the disappearance of the self as advanced in the discourse of modern atheism and in postmodern philosophy and theory, did not signal the end of religion, but in fact created exciting new possibilities for religious self-expression.

For my money, one memorable afternoon in old Jefferson Hall marked the end of the deconstructionist theology movement and, at least in my own mind, further exemplified the exhaustion of a certain theological habit of trying to make the idea of God palatable by hooking it up with some trendy philosophical or theoretical notion.

It was not quite the momentous black day in August 1914, which the Swiss theologian Karl Barth described in his book *The Humanity of God*, when ninety-three German philosophers, professors, and writers proclaimed their support of the war policies of Kaiser Wilhelm II, but it was close.

The deconstructionist theologian—and bear with me a minute, this is going somewhere—who liked to call himself an a/theologian, began with a quote from a then fashionable book called *The Parasite*, which included a scene of rats chewing on a Persian rug in a sewer. The a/theologian proceeded to talk about the demonized Other of the West and to accuse Rorty of promoting a dialogue that concluded in a monologue spoken/written to colonize the Other. Rorty was called a cultural imperialist, a privileged white male wielding his "machete of irony" against the otherness of the Other, hacking away at the difference of the different and Other that is forever other, and so on and so forth. The book called *The Parasite* included such chapters as "Rats' Meals," "Satyrs' Meals," "Rats' Dinners," "More Rats' Meals," "Lunar Meals," "Meals of the Lord in Paradise," "The Cows Come Out of the River," "Cows Eat Cows," and it was praised for its capacity to unsettle the logocentrism of the Western tradition. I refer you to a forlorn 1989 University Press of America volume titled *On the Other: Dialogue and/or Dialectics*, "for more on rodents and the cows eating the cows."

As for Rorty's own response to these charges that fine spring afternoon in 1989 in Jefferson Hall, let me share with you two gems, okay? First, "Pascal earned himself a footnote in the theology books by distinguishing between the God of Abraham, Isaac, and Jacob, and the God of the philosophers. Since Pascal's time the former God has remained about the same but the latter God has gotten weirder and weirder." Second, "As the old-fashioned kind of atheist, the kind without the slash, the kind who believes that when you die, you rot, I keep wishing we didn't have any theologians. The world would be a better place," he said, "if theologians all went away."

Well, as much as I enjoyed this performance, I think deconstructionist theology was too easy a target. Ridiculing the flaws of an intellectual franchise doomed from the start by its overwrought management was like intellectual overkill, pure and simple. Rorty's thrashing of the postmodern "slashers," as he called them, got out of hand, and I don't mean in the sense in which he confided in me the next day in his office in new Campbell Hall that he was feeling a little ashamed of himself, sort of regretting his performance. I reassured him he had no reason to second-guess his response. His was the most brilliant piece of stand-up comedy I have seen to this day. I mean, I wish I could have helped dear Mr. Rorty understand that the kind of theologian he had publicly, and deservedly, mocked had long been exposed for fraud by a different theologian, by a theologian of a very different stripe.

Over the past several years, as our nation has been at war, and the world in global community has grown ever more troubled, my thoughts have turned time and again to sermons preached by Dr. Martin Luther King Jr. in the final years of his civil rights ministry: "A Christmas Sermon on Peace," "I See the Promised Land," and in the searing, heartbroken "A Time to Break Silence," delivered at Riverside Church in New York one year to the date of his murder in Memphis, that grim date whose fortieth anniversary we remember this afternoon.

These are sermons in which one hears an unmistakably heightened, prophetic urgency, and one might say an eschatological intensification. In those late years of 1967 and 1968, with chaos and disillusionment all around and with so many of his early supporters long gone, let's not forget that Dr. King railed against the prophecies of smooth patriotism and against those who would exchange their devotion to the teachings of Jesus with the Southern way of life and with American ambitions. With America unhinged by violence at home and abroad, King's final sermons read, at places, like a lament for the nation. "It is midnight in our world today. We are experiencing a darkness so deep we can hardly see which way to turn. Everywhere paralyzing fear has harrowed people by day and haunted them by night. Our world is sick with war. I fear our nation's soul has been poisoned."

These words are telling. Ten years earlier the same Baptist preacher, while serving a congregation in Montgomery, Alabama, which I'll say more about presently, had summoned together a group of social gospel reformers calling themselves the Southern Christian Leadership Conference, and their mission and their motto was "Redeeming the Soul of America." But now, if there is any redemption to be found in the darkening soulscape of the nation as the war casts its shadows over those glorious, those short-lived experiments in social reform, it will not be found in military might, or in political power, or in the acquisition of material goods. "Our only hope today," Dr. King says, "lies in our ability to recapture the revolutionary spirit and to rededicate ourselves to the long and bitter, but oh-so-beautiful, struggle for a new world. This is the calling of the children of the living God. We stand today," Dr. King said, "in the fierce urgency of now."

Why had my dear Mr. Rorty not for a second imagined that asking the theologians to go away might mean showing Dr. King to the door? Perhaps this demonstrates the utter poverty, utter inability of the secular mind's capacity to understand the real sources of social hope, and social responsibility, and responsible engagement in the world. But I also think we as Christians share a lot of the blame as well, having traded freely on the kind of popular secularization of King and his legacy. He might be a brilliant orator, a poet of democracy, a shrewd organizer, a man who could speak truth to power and, yes, perhaps a predictable, predictably Protestant liberal, social progressive, but a deeply devoted Christian? Um . . . maybe not. Never mind the fact that he once said, "In the inner recesses of my heart, I am a preacher. I am many things to many people but in the inner recesses of my heart, I am a preacher, the son of a preacher, the grandson of a preacher, the great-grandson of a preacher." He was also not to be forgotten: a brilliant young philosophical theologian; a freshman at Morehouse College at the age of fifteen; first in his class at Crozier Theological Seminary; a PhD graduate from the influential Boston University School of Theology. So let's take some time together this afternoon to rethink our public, secular, and, very often, Christian construction of this theologian, pastor, and martyr of the church, who said: "Segregation is first and foremost the blatant denial of the unity we have in Christ Jesus"; who said, "The end of life is not to achieve pleasure and avoid pain. The end of life is to do the will of God, come what may"; who said that "the great event of Calvary signifies more than a meaningless drama that took place on the stage of history. It is the telescope through which we look into the long vista of eternity and see the love of God breaking into time."

My students are often surprised to learn that when Dr. King came to Montgomery in 1954—actually, he wasn't Dr. King at the time, he was "ABD" King, all-but-dissertation King; he would be Dr. King in about a year—civil rights activism was not a priority for him. King came to Montgomery because Dexter Avenue Baptist Church offered a nice salary, offered a comfortable parsonage and a highly educated congregation. Dexter Avenue Baptist Church had no interest in bringing in a racial crusader, either, after just having endured the rather tumultuous tenure of Vernon Johns, a story that we could talk about later. Church members had long prided themselves on access to white elites and their own relative social privilege—a congregation filled with educated professional African-Americans. They certainly shared a common hope for a future without Jim Crowe, but by and large, they were not going to be the folks who ignited the fires of dissent. In fact, Dr. King actually had to be talked into accepting the leadership of the Montgomery Improvement Association by Ralph Abernathy when the organization was formed the day after Rosa Parks refused to move from the front of the bus on the first day of December 1955. And King accepted, only after being reassured, perhaps even tricked by Abernathy into thinking that the protest was going to be over in twenty-four hours. He was busy with other things.

In King's—Dr. King now—first list of demands as president of the Montgomery Improvement Association, he made clear that the protest was not about challenging segregation laws. His list of demands was so moderate that the NAACP refused to endorse them, and a cadre of more progressive African-Americans—primarily women, Joann Robinson and Rosa Parks, E. D. Nixon—were furious with Dr. King. They felt betrayed by his list of demands. King was no fan of nonviolence either. One of my favorite stories about this comes from a white Texas Presbyterian minister working for an organization, a Quaker organization called Fellowship of Reconciliation, who was in Montgomery in early 1956, within the first month of the bus boycott, to help educate the protestors on principles of nonviolent direct action; and in a field report back to his supervisors, Glen Smiley noted his utter surprise to have discovered in the parsonage on South Jackson Street an arsenal of weapons. King said, "When I was in graduate school I thought the only way we could solve our problems was through armed revolt." By the end of the second month of the boycott, King had fallen into despair about his leadership and the direction of the movement. The protest was in disarray and the fragile unity was on the verge of breaking down all together. On a gloomy afternoon in mid-January 1956, King, feeling as a failure, demoralized and exhausted, offered his resignation as president of the Montgomery Improvement Association. It was not accepted, but his doubts about his own ability to provide leadership and to offer a kind of vision remained strong, and one gets a sense of his own kind of demoralization at this point.

The next week, Dr. King returned to his parsonage late one night after a long day of organizing and planning, and he had also just endured his first arrest and incarceration, and he wanted nothing but to climb in bed and surrender to a good night's rest. But then the phone rang, and on the other end of the line rushed a torrent of obscene words, and then the death threat: "Listen, *n*-word, we've taken all we want from you, but before next week you will be sorry you ever came to Montgomery." King hung up the phone without comment, as had become his custom, but hopes of much needed rest were long gone. And though from the perspective of the NAACP, King's involvement was all too gradual, from the perspective of the guardians of the white South, King's leadership was altogether subversive. And so, threatening phone calls had become a daily routine throughout the weeks of the protest and in recent days, though the phone calls had started to take a toll, increasing in number to thirty to forty a day. But there was something about this particular call. Maybe it was the kind of exhaustion from having been up all night in a jail cell, the sense of his own failure, a sense of his own kind of "coming to the end of his own courage and his own capacity to lead." In any case, King felt himself suddenly seized with fear, and in his memoir *Stride Toward Freedom*, King says, "I got out of bed and began to walk the floor. I had heard these phone calls before, but for some reason that night it got to me." So King walked down the hall, made himself a pot of coffee, and sat down at the kitchen table. "I was ready to give up," he said. "I felt myself faltering." Alone now, in this midnight kitchen, you know, with these vast Alabama silences, King grasped, I think for the first time, really, the utter seriousness of his situation, and with it, the inescapable fact that he could be snatched away from it at any moment, or more likely, he from his family. King tells us in his memoir that he felt, like the psalmist, at his wit's end. "I couldn't take it any longer. I felt weak and I felt afraid."

With his head now buried in his hands, King bowed over the kitchen table, and he prayed aloud, "Lord, I'm down here trying to do what's right, but I'm weak. I'm faltering. I'm losing my courage. I'm afraid. I have nothing left. I've come to the point where I cannot face it alone." King tells us then in his memoir that out of those silences he heard a voice speak to him; he heard the voice of Jesus. And King writes, "I heard the voice of Jesus saying, 'Martin Luther, stand up for righteousness. I will be with you. Stand up for the truth.' Jesus promised never to leave me, never to leave me alone." It was almost a kind of sense in which the words of Jesus were spoken as a litany: "No never to leave me alone, no never alone, no never alone. He promised never to leave me, never to leave me alone. Never, never alone." And as the voice of Jesus washed over the vile words of the caller, King reached a shore beyond anxiety and despair. "I experienced the presence of God that night," King said, "as I had never experienced it before. My uncertainty began to disappear and I was ready to face the future."

In the South, there's this distinction that we make between a pastor being "called" and a pastor being "schooled." Dr. King had been schooled in the finest institutions that any seminarian could attend—Morehouse, and Crozier, and Boston University—but that night in Montgomery, Dr. King was called.

A week later, and a few days after his home was bombed by Klan terrorists, King preached a sermon at Dexter Avenue Baptist Church called "It's Hard to Be a Christian." We don't have the sermon in full, but thanks to the wonderful work of Clayborne Carson and his editorial team at the King Papers Project in Stanford, we now have notes of that message, and an amazing volume of King's most theological writings has just been published as volume six of the King Papers Project. King's sermon that night was based on chapter 16, verse 24 of St. Matthew's Gospel: "If any person will come after me, let him deny himself, and take up his cross and follow me."

"Most of us in the American congregations," King wrote in his notes and preached in his sermon, "have substituted a cushion for the cross. We have substituted the soothing lemonade of escape for the bitter cup of reality, but Jesus never left men and women with such illusions. Jesus made it crystal clear that the Gospel was difficult because it demands a dangerous and costly altruism. Authentic faith is hard because it demands that the 'I' be immersed in the deep waters of the 'thou,' that we put our whole being into the struggle against inhumanity and in service to the disenfranchised, and the poor, and the downtrodden."

I think it is also worth emphasizing, in response to popular atheism's charge that religious faith is world-denying and inhibits responsible action in the world, that after King's experience in the midnight kitchen, his engagement in the social order became more rather than less courageous, more rather than less confrontational. He became more rather than less willing to contest the material and legal conditions of injustice as his life became more a living witness to the untapped possibilities of agape love. King authorized, shortly thereafter, attorney Fred Gray to challenge segregation laws. "My uncertainty disappeared," King said, and he made clear that he supported immediate integration of the buses, not just better seating, or more stops in black neighborhoods, or courteous treatment of African-American drivers. "Segregation is evil," King said, "and I cannot, as a minister, condone evil." King told reporters that his decision against calling segregation itself into question had been a mistake and needed to be reversed. And you know what else? King gave up the gun. He wrote, "I realized I could not serve God and the gun."

And King's long, passionate bearing of the nonviolent cross of Jesus was crystallized in that year. And from that year until his death on April 4, 1968, King risked everything, everything on the proposition that the immanence of agape can be concretely conceived in human nature, in human history.

King's experience in Montgomery pressed upon him a sober counting of the cost of his ministerial calling. One of his pastor friends, Marcus Garvey Wood, minister of the Providence Baptist Church in Baltimore and a seminarian of King's years earlier, observed his friend's transformation and said it best in a letter: "Martin, you have thrown aside Crozier, and you have found the real God, and you can tell the world now that He is a God who moves in mysterious ways." King came to realize in the crucible of lived experience that intellectual abstractions cannot, and do not, empower acts of compassion and sacrifice or sustain the courage to speak against the day.

In that 1967 address to Riverside Church I mentioned earlier, King resolved that America's only hope lay in the spirit of repentance, in the willingness to be a servant among the nations by caring creatively and preferentially for the poor and broken and distressed of the earth. Repentance may not be part of the grammar of the secular university where I teach, but for King it was the very condition of the dream.

In the final weeks of the 382-day protest that launched the twentieth century's greatest social movement, King told a jubilant audience of Holt Street Baptist Church gathered in November of 1956—an audience, by the way, that had just received word from the United States Supreme Court that the court was ruling in support of the Montgomery Improvement Association's protests—King told this jubilant crowd that "yeah, we will have to protest, we will have to boycott, and we will have to work collectively and collaboratively and find ways to challenge the unjust conditions of the broken social order, but the end is not the boycott. The protest is not the end." King said, "The end of our struggle is redemption. The end is reconciliation. The end is the creation of the beloved community."

A few days later, Dr. King and Glen Smiley boarded the first integrated bus, and when reporters asked King to comment, he said, "Now we must move from protest to reconciliation." Sometimes when I think about that line, I think we're still, as a nation and as a church, frozen at that very moment.

Beloved community gave the Civil Rights Movement its one sustaining and unifying spiritual vision. Although some of the younger sort of more student-edgy groups like Student Nonviolent Coordinating Committee and CORE [Congress of Racial Equality] and COFO [Council of Federated Organizations] are often described as the secularizing way of the movement. That's nonsense, and in my research I try to explain why it's nonsense, because you look at the founding documents, and you listen to the transcripts, and you go behind the scenes, and the vision is very much saturated with the language of the Gospel.

Charlie Scherrod, for example, one of Dr. King's young foot soldiers who's one of the first organizers in southwest Georgia, a student of Niebuhr from Union Theological Seminary and a Baptist minister from Virginia, said, "What we are doing in southwest Georgia is celebrating the Easter world." Try that on for an organizing strategy. What are we doing? We are affirming the Easter world, and in light of that vision we can then talk about the nuts-and-bolts matters that need to be done in caring for the disenfranchised community.

It's important, I think, to look at King and Montgomery. Montgomery was really King's only pastorate. He went to Ebenezer Baptist after Montgomery, but he went largely to have a position in his father's church and to launch a national kind of ministry.

Montgomery was the year that formed King as a theologian and as a pastor. It's a year in which many of the kinds of intellectual and theological abstractions he had brought with him from the classrooms underwent deep reexamination on the basis of the demands of the social crisis. In a sense, I like to think of King's experience in Montgomery as a way of, sometimes, how I like to think of Karl Barth's years of pastoring in an industrial village in Switzerland, in Safenwil, or Bonhoeffer's one year in New York in 1930 and 1931. It's the year when we really see the emergence of King's consistently and relentlessly Christocentric and Christological focus and self-understanding, and anytime you hear someone wanting to secularize King, go grab volume four of the Martin Luther King Papers Project and hold it up and say, "Read this from start to finish."

Well, over the course of King's lifetime, especially in the last two years of his ministry, the deep wounds wrought by the sinfulness of the human condition—as he began to say once again with a renewed kind of emphasis—in American society intensified theologically the vision and idea of the beloved community. And in time this theme of the beloved community in King's sermons came to express with an even greater sense of crisis the eschatological inbreaking of God in history, although it is certainly true that King's use of the term "beloved community" was always different in tone and in tension than its liberal Protestant antecedents. It is also true that in these final years we discern an astonishing rhetorical and theological shift in his speeches and, I think, a sense that grows and heightens that the structures of creation are fundamentally broken, and that only God can save us from ourselves.

"Life is a continual story of shattered dreams," King told his Ebenezer congregation in March of 1968. "The world is all messed up, the nation is sick, trouble is in the land, confusion all around." The righteousness of God would not transmogrify the human frame from the inside like some inextricable and innate force. The eschatological, even at times, gives way, I think, to the apocalyptic. The righteousness of God divides and sunders. It comes as the crisis of history and culture.

In the last year of his life, King, as you know, turned his attention directly to the economic sources of racism, organizing the Poor People's Campaign, which he hoped would dramatize the sobering fact that the right to vote and to eat in any establishment had failed to affect the systemic conditions of African-Americans or whites, that the poor needed something more. Among the demands of the Poor People's Campaign were full employment, a guaranteed annual income, and construction funds for low-income housing. King had planned to lead a procession of mule carts with thousands of people in tow from Mississippi to Washington where the participants would construct a shantytown near federal buildings. King thought it would be especially powerful to actually bring some of the decrepit shotgun shacks from the Mississippi Delta on flatbed trucks all the way to the D.C. site. The proposed date for the beginning of the Poor People's Campaign was April 22, 1968. On April 3, as we know, Dr. King took some time away from the Poor People's Campaign to visit Memphis, where he spoke on behalf of the striking sanitation workers. Two African-American sanitation workers, who were working a shift on a day of thunderous torrential rains, had been unable to take refuge underneath one of the public shelters because it was "white's only," and had sat inside the back of the trash compactor and accidentally set the lever that crushed them to death. And so King had come to show his support of the striking sanitation workers at the invitation of his old colleague, James Lawson. The city's mayor was refusing to recognize their union, and King thought he could bring a helping hand. On April 3 he delivered his final sermon at the Mason Temple in Memphis, at the headquarters of the Church of God in Christ, the largest African-American denomination in the United States.

It was an early spring day like today, clear. It was also unseasonably hot, and then by the time the service began, the blue skies had been overtaken by these dark thunderstorms we get in the Deep South that time of year. One of King's biographers, Marshall Frady, wrote that when King took the pulpit, the lightning began to flash outside with claps of thunder. King seemed exhausted and agitated. And a few times the ceiling fans in the room would make a banging sound, and King seemed visibly startled by the noise. So the fans were shut off, and this made the sanctuary almost insufferably hot but nonetheless complete in its concentration on King's words. King spoke directly to the church that night, and he urged the preachers of America to be like Amos and say, "Let justice roll down like waters and righteousness like an everflowing stream." Somehow, too, King said, the preacher must say with Jesus, "The spirit of the Lord is upon me because he hath anointed me to deal with the problems of the poor." King told the ministers, too—isn't this interesting—that it's okay to talk about the long white robes over yonder. It's okay to talk about the kingdom of God that will come in splendor and in glory on that last day. It's all right to talk about the streets flowing with milk and honey. He also talked about economic power and the power of collective action and finally spoke in words that registered a profound, haunting sense of his own imminent death. "No, I don't know what will happen now. We have some difficult days ahead, but it doesn't matter with me now because I've been to the mountain, and I don't mind. Like anybody, I would love to live a long life. Longevity has its place, but I'm not concerned about that now. I just want to do God's will. He's allowed me to go up to the mountain, and I've looked over, and I've seen the Promised Land. I may not get there with you, but I want you to know tonight that we, as a people, will get to the Promised Land, and I'm happy tonight, and I'm not afraid of any man. I'm not worried about anything because mine eyes have seen the glory of the coming of the Lord." King saw the Promised Land, and the Promised Land was the blinding light of the coming God.

After King finished, he fell backwards, exhausted, into the arms of his lifelong friend Ralph Abernathy, and the next morning he was murdered in the Lorraine Motel in Memphis.

Well, Richard Rorty's classes at the University of Virginia in the late 1980s, and his intellectual courage, and his writings help teach us, I think, that the intellectual life and the life we live as citizens and our democracy must seek to promote human flourishing, prevent cruelty, and build solidarity among diverse communities. "Disengagement from practice produces theoretical hallucinations," Richard Rorty said famously. And isn't it a wonderful line? You know, for his life and legacy and his many acts of kindness to me as a graduate student and to so many others in religious studies, I will be forever grateful. But it is Dr. King and the theological agitators, and malcontents, and reformers, and dreamers who teach us that disciplined and focused and sustained practice require spiritual nourishment and the hope of the risen Christ.

Friedrich Nietzsche, the great "death of God" philosopher of the nineteenth century, once said that Christians would need to sing better songs before he would believe in their Redeemer. You know what? We have beautiful songs to sing. If you listen closely, you will hear that the men and women who work day in and day out in inauspicious places to bring hope and healing to our broken and blistered world are people who are carried, and strengthened, and nourished by deep spiritual waters, who show that vivid and synoptic realism, if you will, about the nature of social existence is more honest and clearly drawn against horizons of grace.

I mean, think about the great progressive social movements of American history and the movements for human flourishing after we unravel them from their secular narratives: the campaigns to end slavery; the great struggles of the labor movements; for women's suffrage; the social gospel movement; the work of mercy and justice in the historic peace churches; the contemporary flourishing of people of faith dedicated to reconciliation and community building; and, of course, the Civil Rights Movement. Visit a soup kitchen, a hospitality house, a tutorial program for low-income children, an AIDS clinic, a hunger relief agency, a Habitat for Humanity site, and you will find there men and women who are moved to act in response to the world's concrete needs because they have seen a light shining in the darkness, who believe that transcendence empowers, rather than diminishes, the love of life, that hope and miracle and mystery animate the protest against cruelty, focus moral energy, and heighten awareness of those places in the world that cry out for wholeness and healing. The philosopher Søren Kierkegaard, in *Fear and Trembling*, spoke of faith as "the most complex and difficult artwork and yet the most exquisite."

Dr. King spoke of the *spiritual* movement in Montgomery—didn't even call it the Civil Rights Movement, once called it the Christian Movement in Montgomery. Clarence Jordan, one of my heroes, spoke of the God Movement in Georgia. Fannie Lou Hamer spoke of the New Kingdom in Mississippi. John Perkins, one of my dearest friends and heroes, speaks of the quiet revolution of building hope in distressed and excluded communities. Our friend Mark Gorman talks about the "shalom of the city." Victoria Gray Adams, the Civil Rights saint, spoke of the "infleshioned church, of the peacemakers and reconcilers."

These are all ways of talking about the Body of Christ, set free from political and cultural bondage to be the space in the world where the world sees the love it longs for and the hope it desperately needs. The Civil Rights Movement that took place in the 1950s and 1960s not only changed unjust laws but also brought about, I think, a profound spiritual awakening, and one that we still have not fully grasped in the churches and in our public spaces. And this story, unleashed from its bondage to secular historiography, teaches us, even today, important lessons about what Dr. Perkins likes to call a "holistic faith."

Dr. King's dream was not his dream, not the dream of the '60s, but it was the dream of God. It was a gift of the spirit. It was a dream of the beloved community of Christ. It was a dream for the renewal of the church's mission in the world. King shows us, I think, in closing, a generous orthodoxy, an exuberant and costly love of Jesus that, precisely for that reason, remains open to all who come to the work of building the beloved community. King's vision, King's particular Christian vision, might even be called a kind of chastened evangelicalism. In it, Christians are asked to learn to participate in God's created order and thus to use our commitment to Christ, not as some kind of special claim on others, but in order to invite other people into the work of caring for the human condition in the created order. King shows us that our mission as followers of Christ in the social order is, in a profound sense, learning to struggle along with everybody else and collaborate with everybody else in the difficult, frustrating task of seeking a solution to common problems. It is to speak with the humility that is appropriate to our limited vision and, by speaking, to take part in shared human struggle.

"One must not only speak a sermon with his voice," Dr. King said, "he must preach it with his life."

Bibliography

Adams, Nicholas. *Habermas and Theology.* New York: Cambridge University Press, 2006.
———. "Making Deep Reasonings Public." In *The Promise of Scriptural Reasoning,* edited by David F. Ford and C. C. Pecknold, 41–57. Oxford: Blackwell, 2006.
———. "Reparative Reasoning." In *Modern Theology* 24:3 (2008) 447–57.
Anderson, Benedict. *Imagined Communities: Reflections on the Origin and Spread of Nationalism.* Rev. ed. New York: Verso, 1991.
Aquinas, Thomas. *Summa Theologica.* Translated by Fathers of the English Dominican Province. New York: Benziger, 1948.
Aristotle. *Nicomachean Ethics.* Translated by Martin Ostwald. Indianapolis: Bobbs-Merrill, 1962.
———. *Politics.* Translated by Carnes Lord. Chicago: University of Chicago Press, 1984.
Asad, Talal. *Genealogies of Religion: Discipline and Reasons of Power in Christianity and Islam.* Baltimore: John Hopkins University Press, 1993.
Augustine. *The City of God against the Pagans.* Edited and translated by R. W. Dyson. New York: Cambridge University Press, 1998.
———. *Expositions of the Psalms.* Vol. 1. Edited by John Rotelle. Translated by Maria Boulding. Hyde Park, NY: New City, 2000.
Austin, J. L. "Truth." In *Truth,* edited by George Pitcher, 18–31. Englewood Cliffs, NJ: Prentice-Hall, 1964.
Barrett, Justin L. *Why Would Anyone Believe in God?* Walnut Creek, CA: AltaMira, 2004.
Berman, Lila Corwin. *Speaking of Jews: Rabbis, Intellectuals, and the Creation of an American Public Identity.* Berkeley: University of California Press, 2009.
Bloom, Harold. *The Anxiety of Influence: A Theory of Poetry.* New York: Oxford University Press, 1975.
Bonhoeffer, Dietrich. *Ethics.* Translated by Reinhard Krauss et al. Minneapolis: Fortress, 2005.
———. *Letters and Papers from Prison.* Translated by Christian Gremmels et al. Minneapolis: Fortress, 2009.
Borradori, Giovanna. *The American Philosopher: Conversations with Quine, Davidson, Putnam, Nozick, Danto, Rorty, Cavell, MacIntyre, and Kuhn.* Translated by Rosanna Crocitto. Chicago: University of Chicago Press, 1994.
Bragues, George. "Richard Rorty's Postmodern Case for Liberal Democracy: A Critique." *Humanitas (Journal of the National Humanities Institute)* 19:1–2 (2006) 158–81.
Brandom, Robert B. *Rorty and His Critics.* Malden, MA: Blackwell, 2000.
Burrell, David B. *Freedom and Creation in Three Traditions.* Notre Dame: University of Notre Dame Press, 1993.

———. "An Introduction to Theology and Social Theory, Beyond Secular Reason." *Modern Theology* 8:4 (1992) 319–29.

Carter, J. Kameron. *Race: A Theological Account*. New York: Oxford University Press, 2008.

Carter, Stephen L. *The Culture of Disbelief: How American Law and Politics Trivialize Religious Devotion*. New York: Basic, 1993.

Cates, Diana Fritz. "Experiential Narratives of Rape and Torture." *Journal of Religious Ethics* 38:1 (2010) 43–66.

Cavanaugh, William T. *Torture and Eucharist: Theology, Politics, and the Body of Christ*. Malden, MA: Blackwell, 1998.

Cicero. *De re publica; De legibus*. Translated by Clinton Walker Keyes. Cambridge: Harvard University Press, 1951.

Cohen, Patricia. "Richard Rorty, Philosopher, Dies at 75." *New York Times*, June 27, 2007. Online: http://www.nytimes.com/2007/06/11/obituaries/11rorty.html.

Copleston, Frederick C. *A History of Philosophy*. Vol. 2, *Mediaeval Philosophy: Augustine to Scotus*. Westminster, MD: Newman, 1950.

Cunningham, Conor. *Genealogy of Nihilism: Philosophies of Nothing and the Difference of Theology*. Radical Orthodoxy Series. New York: Routledge, 2002.

Davidson, Donald. *Inquiries into Truth and Interpretation*. New York: Oxford University Press, 1984.

———. "Paradoxes of Irrationality." In *Philosophical Essays on Freud*, edited by Richard Wollheim and James Hopkins, 289–305. New York: Cambridge University Press, 1982.

———. "The Structure and Content of Truth." *Journal of Philosophy* 87:6 (1990) 279–328.

Day, Dorothy. *Meditations*. Edited by Stanley Vishnewski. New York: Paulist, 1970.

Derrida, Jacques. *The Gift of Death* [*Donner la mort*]. Translated by David Wills. Religion and Postmodernism. Chicago: University of Chicago Press, 1995.

Duncan, Christopher M. "A Question for Richard Rorty." *The Review of Politics* 66:3 (2004) 385–413.

Fennell, Jon. "Harry Neumann and the Political Piety of Rorty's Postmodernism." *Interpretation: A Journal of Political Philosophy* 26.2 (1998) 257–73.

Fiddes, Paul. *The Promised End: Eschatology in Theology and Literature*. Oxford: Blackwell, 2000.

Fish, Stanley. "Boutique Multiculturalism, or Why Liberals Are Incapable of Thinking about Hate Speech." *Critical Inquiry* 23 (1997) 378–95.

———. "How the First Amendment Works." *New York Times*, February 8, 2010.

———. *The Trouble with Principle*. Cambridge: Harvard University Press, 1999.

———. "What Is the First Amendment For?" *New York Times*, February 1, 2010.

Florovsky, Georges. "Empire and Desert: Antinomies of Christian History." *The Greek Orthodox Theological Review* 3 (1957) 133–59.

Ford, David F. *Christian Wisdom: Desiring God and Learning in Love*. New York: Cambridge University Press, 2007.

———. "An Inter-faith Wisdom: Scriptural Reasoning between Jews, Christians and Muslims." In *Christian Wisdom: Desiring God and Learning in Love*, 273–303. New York: Cambridge University Press, 2007.

Friedman, Milton. *Capitalism and Freedom*. Chicago: University of Chicago Press, 1962.

Friedman, Milton, and Rose Friedman. *Free to Choose: A Personal Statement*. New York: Harcourt Brace Jovanovich, 1980.

Fukuyama, Francis. *The End of History and the Last Man*. New York: Free Press, 1992.
Gettier, Edmund L. "Is Justified True Belief Knowledge?" *Analysis* 23 (1963) 121–23.
Gillespie, Michael. *Nihilism before Nietzsche*. Chicago: University of Chicago Press, 1995.
Girard, René, and Vattimo, Gianni. *Veritào fede debole? Dialogo su cristianesimo e relativismo*. Edited by Pierpaolo Antonello. Massa: Transeuropa, 2006.
Goodson, Jacob. *An Introduction to Scriptural Reasoning*. The Cascade Companion Series. Eugene, OR: Cascade Books, 2013.
———. "Repressing Novelty? William James and the Reasoning of Scriptural Reasoning." In *The Journal of Scriptural Reasoning* 8:2 (2009). http://etext.lib.virginia.edu/journals/ssr/issues/volume8/number2/ssr08_02_e04.htm.
———. "A Review of Jeffrey Stout's *Democracy and Tradition*." In *The American Journal of Theology and Philosophy* 25:2 (2002) 185–90.
———. "A Review of Romand Coles and Stanley Hauerwas, *Christianity, Democracy, and the Radical Ordinary*." In *Contemporary Pragmatism* 5:1 (2008) 168–72.
———. "Theology after Epistemology: Milbank between Rorty and Taylor on Truth." In *Contemporary Pragmatism* 1:2 (2004) 155–69.
———. "What Is Reparative Reasoning? Jürgen Habermas' Philosophy, Practical Reasoning, and Theological Hermeneutics." *The Journal of Scriptural Reasoning* 10:2 (2011). Online: http://etext.lib.virginia.edu/journals/ssr/issues/volume10/number2/ssr10_02_e06.html.
Grant, George Parkin. "Research in the Humanities." In *Technology and Justice*, 97–102. Notre Dame: University of Notre Dame Press, 1986.
———. *Technology and Empire*. Toronto: Anansis, 1969.
Greene, Graham. *The Power and the Glory*. London: Heinemann, 1940.
Grippe, Edward J. *Richard Rorty's New Pragmatism: Neither Liberal Nor Free*. London: Continuum, 2007.
Grover, Dorothy L., Joseph L. Camp, and Nuel D. Belnap. "A Prosentential Theory of Truth." *Philosophical Studies* 27:2 (1975) 73–125.
Gutting, Gary. *What Philosophers Know*. Cambridge: Cambridge University Press, 2008.
Haber, Honi. "Richard Rorty's Failed Politics." *Social Epistemology* 7.1 (1993) 61–74.
Hardy, Daniel W. "Reason, Wisdom, and the Interpretation of Scripture." In *Reading Texts, Seeking Wisdom: Scripture and Theology*, edited by David F. Ford and Graham Stanton, 69–88. Grand Rapids: Eerdmans, 2003.
Hart, David Bentley. *The Beauty of the Infinite*. Grand Rapids: Eerdmanns, 2003.
Harvey, Barry. *Can These Bones Live? A Catholic Baptist Engagements with Ecclesiology, Hermeneutics, and Social Theory*. Grand Rapids: Brazos, 2007.
Hauerwas, Stanley. *Christian Among the Virtues: Theological Conversations with Ancient and Modern Ethics*. Notre Dame: University of Notre Dame Press, 1997.
———. *In Good Company: The Church as Polis*. Notre Dame: University of Notre Dame Press, 1995.
———. "Postscript." *The Journal of Scriptural Reasoning* 8:1 (2007). http://etext.lib.virginia.edu/journals/ssr/issues/volume8/number1/ssr08_01_b01.html.
Hauerwas, Stanley, and Romand Coles. *Christianity, Democracy, and the Radical Ordinary: Conversations between a Radical Democrat and a Christian*. Eugene, OR: Wipf & Stock Publishers, 2007.
Hauerwas, Stanley, Richard Rorty, Jeffrey Stout, and Cornel West. "Pragmatism and Democracy: Assessing Jeffrey Stout's *Democracy and Tradition*." *Journal of the American Academy of Religion* 78:2 (2010) 413–48.

Havel, Václav. "The Power of the Powerless." In *Living in Truth*, edited by Jan Vladislav, 36–122. London: Faber & Faber, 1987.

Heidegger, Martin. *Basic Writings*. Translated by David Farrell Krell. New York: HarperCollins, 1993.

Hobbes, Thomas. *Human Nature and De Corpore Politico*. Oxford: Oxford University Press, 1994.

———. *Leviathan*. Edited by Edwin Curley. Indianapolis, IN: Hackett, 1994.

Hughes, Kevin. "Introduction: The Cry of the Poor." In *Crisis, Call, and Leadership in the Abrahamic Traditions*, edited by Peter Ochs and William Stacy Johnson, 89–91. New York: Palgrave Macmillan, 2009.

Ignatieff, Michael. *Human Rights as Politics and Idolatry*. Princeton: Princeton University Press, 2001.

James, William. *Essays in Radical Empiricism*. Lincoln: University of Nebraska Press, 1996.

———. *The Essential Writings*. Edited by Bruce W. Wilshire. Albany: State University of New York Press, 1984.

———. *Pragmatism*. New York: Longmans, Green, 1943.

———. "Pragmatism's Conception of Truth." In *Pragmatism and the Meaning of Truth*. Cambridge: Harvard University Press, 1978.

———. *Writings, 1878–1899*. Edited by Gerald Eugene Myers. New York: Literary Classics of the United States, 1992.

———. *The Will to Believe*. New York: Dover, 1956.

———. *Writings, 1902–1910*. Edited by Bruce Kuklick. New York: Literary Classics of the United States, 1987.

Jefferson, Thomas. *Notes on the State of Virginia*, Query XVII. In *The Writings of Thomas Jefferson*, edited by William Peden. Chapel Hill: University of North Carolina Press, 1954.

Jenson, Robert. *Systematic Theology: The Triune God*. Vol. 1. New York: Oxford University Press, 1997.

Kant, Immanuel. *Critique of Pure Reason*. Translated by Norman Kemp Smith. New York: St. Martin's, 1965.

Kavka, Martin. "Response to Pecknold: The Unity of Scriptural Reasoning." *The Journal of Scriptural Reasoning* 6:1 (2006). http://etext.lib.virginia.edu/journals/ssr/issues/volume6/number1/ssr06_01_r04.html.

Kerr, Fergus. "Aquinas and Analytic Philosophy: Natural Allies?" *Modern Theology* 20:1 (2004) 123–39.

Knuuttila, Simo. "Time and Modality in Scholasticism." In *Reforging the Great Chain of Being: Studies of the History of Modal Theories*, 163–257. Synthese Historical Library 20. Boston: D. Reidel, 1981.

Koshul, Basit Bilal. "The Qur'anic Self, the Biblical Other, and the Contemporary Islam-West Encounter." In *Scripture, Reason, and the Contemporary Islam-West Encounter: Studying the "Other," Understanding the "Self,"* edited by Basit Koshul and Steven Kepnes, 9–38. New York: Palgrave Macmillan, 2007.

Kreeft, Peter, editor. *A Summa of the Summa: The Essential Philosophical Passages of St. Thomas Aquinas' Summa Theologica*. San Francisco: Ignatius, 1990.

Lash, Nicholas. *Believing Three Ways in One God: A Reading of the Apostles' Creed*. Notre Dame: University of Notre Dame Press, 1993.

Lederach, John Paul. *The Moral Imagination: The Art and Soul of Building Peace*. Oxford: Oxford University Press, 2005.

Leibniz, G. W. F. "Letter to Remond." 10 January 1714. In *Die Philosophischen Schriften von G. W. Leibniz*, edited by C. I. Gerhardt, 3:607. Berlin: Weidman, 1875–1890. Reprinted Hildesheim: Olms, 1965.

Lepore, Ernest, editor. *Truth and Interpretation: Perspectives on the Philosophy of Donald Davidson*. Oxford: Blackwell, 1989.

Lindbeck. George. "The Church." In *Keeping the Faith*, edited by Geoffrey Wainwright, 179–208. Philadelphia: Fortress, 1988.

———. *The Nature of Doctrine: Religion and Theology in a Postliberal Age*. Philadelphia: Westminster, 1984.

Locke, John. *An Essay Concerning Human Understanding*. Oxford: Oxford University Press, 1965.

Long, D. Stephen. *The Goodness of God: Theology, Church, and the Social Order*. Grand Rapids: Brazos, 2001.

———. *Speaking of God: Theology, Language, and Truth*. Grand Rapids: Eerdmanns, 2009.

Louthan, Stephen. "On Religion—A Discussion with Richard Rorty, Alvin Plantinga and Nicholas Wolterstorff." *Christian Scholar's Review* 26:2 (1996) 177–83.

Lowe, Walter. "Prospects for a Postmodern Christian Theology: Apocalyptic Without Reserve." *Modern Theology* 15 (1999) 17–24.

MacIntyre, Alasdair. *After Virtue*. Notre Dame: Notre Dame University Press, 1981.

Malesic, Jonathan. *Secret Faith in the Public Square: An Argument for the Concealment of Christian Identity*. Grand Rapids: Brazos, 2009.

Marsh, Charles. *The Beloved Community: How Faith Shapes Social Justice, from the Civil Rights Movement to Today*. New York: Basic, 2004.

———. *God's Long Summer: Stories of Faith and Civil Rights*. Princeton: Princeton University Press, 1997.

McClean, David E. "The Theological Uses of Rortian Ironism." *Journal of Speculative Philosophy* 22:1 (2008) 33–39.

McDermott, John. *The Drama of Possibility: Experience as Philosophy of Culture*. Edited by Douglas R. Anderson. New York: Fordham University Press, 2007.

McGrane, Bernard. *Beyond Anthropology: Society and the Other*. New York: Columbia University Press, 1989.

Meeks, Wayne A. *The Origins of Christian Morality: The First Two Centuries*. New Haven: Yale University Press, 1993.

Menand, Louis. *Pragmatism: A Reader*. New York: Vintage, 1997.

Mensch, Elizabeth, and Alan Freeman. *The Politics of Virtue: Is Abortion Debatable?* Durham: Duke University Press, 1993.

Milbank, John. *Being Reconciled: Ontology and Pardon*. Radical Orthodoxy Series. New York: Routledge, 2003.

———. "Can a Gift be Given? Prolegomena to a Future Trinitarian Metaphysic." *Modern Theology* 11 (1995) 119–61.

———. "The Second Difference: For a Trinitarianism without Reserve." *Modern Theology* 2:3 (1986) 213–34.

———. *Theology and Social Theory: Beyond Secular Reason*. 2nd ed. Malden, MA: Blackwell, 2006.

Milbank, John, Catherine Pickstock, and Graham Ward. *Radical Orthodoxy: A New Theology*. New York: Routledge, 1999.

Mill, John Stuart. *On Liberty, and Other Essays*. Edited by Emery Neff. The Modern Readers' Series. New York: Macmillan, 1926.

Miner, Robert. *Truth in the Making: Creative Knowledge in Theology and Philosophy.* London: Routledge, 2004.

Murdoch, Iris. *The Sovereignty of Good.* New York: Routledge, 2001.

Novak, David. "Avoiding Charges of Legalism and Antinomianism in Jewish-Christian Dialogue." *Modern Theology* 16:3 (2000) 275–91.

———. *Natural Law in Judaism.* New York: Cambridge University Press, 2008.

———. "Religious Communities, Secular Societies, and Sexuality: One Jewish Opinion." In *Tradition in the Public Square: A David Novak Reader*, edited by Randi Rashkover and Martin Kavka, 283–303. Grand Rapids: Eerdmans, 2008.

———. *The Sanctity of Human Life.* Washington, DC: Georgetown University Press, 2007.

Nozick, Robert. *Anarchy, State, and Utopia.* New York: Basic, 1974.

Ochs, Peter. *Peirce, Pragmatism, and the Logic of Scripture.* Cambridge: Cambridge University Press, 1998.

———. "Philosophic Warrants for Scriptural Reasoning." In *The Promise of Scriptural Reasoning*, edited by David F. Ford and C. C. Pecknold, 121–38. Oxford: Blackwell, 2006.

Ochs, Peter, and William Stacy Johnson. *Crisis, Call, and Leadership in the Abrahamic Traditions.* New York: Palgrave Macmillan, 2009.

Omer, Atalia. "'It's Nothing Personal': The Globalization of Justice, the Transferability of Protest, and the Case of the Palestine Solidarity Movement." *Studies in Ethnicity and Nationalism* 9:3 (2010) 497–518.

Osborne, Peter. "Cornel West: American Radicalism." *Radical Philosophy* 71 (1995) 27–37.

Pecknold, C. C. "Augustine's Readable City: Beyond the Politics of Empire." *The Journal of Scriptural Reasoning* 6:1 (2006). http://etext.lib.virginia.edu/journals/ssr/issues/volume6/number1/ssr06_01_e02.html.

———. *Transforming Postliberal Theology: George Lindbeck, Pragmatism, and Scripture.* New York: T. & T. Clark, 2005.

Peirce, Charles Sanders. *The Charles S. Peirce Papers.* Microfilm edition. Harvard University Library, Photographic Service, 1966.

———. *Collected Papers of Charles Sanders Peirce.* Edited by C. Hartshorne, P. Weiss, and A. Burks. Cambridge: Harvard University Press, 1931–1958.

———. "What Pragmatism Is." In *Pragmatism, the Classic Writings*, edited by H. S. Thayer, 101–20. Indianapolis: Hackett, 1970.

Pickstock, Catherine. *After Writing: On the Liturgical Consummation of Philosophy.* Challenges in Contemporary Theology. Malden, MA: Blackwell, 1998.

Plantinga, Alvin. "Is Belief in God Properly Basic?" *Nous* 15:1 (1981) 41–51.

———. "On Reformed Epistemology." *The Reformed Journal* 32 (1982) 13–19.

———. "Reformed Epistemology Again." *The Reformed Journal* 32 (1982) 7–8.

———. *Warrant and Proper Function.* New York: Oxford University Press, 1993.

———. *Warranted Christian Belief.* New York: Oxford University Press, 2000.

Plato. *Gorgias.* Translated by Donald J. Zeyl. Indianapolis: Hackett, 1987.

Quine, Willard van Orman. *From a Logical Point of View: Nine Logico-Philosophical Essays.* Cambridge: Harvard University Press, 1953.

———. *Philosophy of Logic.* 2nd ed. Cambridge: Harvard University Press, 1986.

———. "Two Dogmas of Empiricism." *Philosophical Review* 60 (1951) 20–43.

Rajchman, John, and Cornel West. *Post-Analytic Philosophy.* New York: Columbia University Press, 1985.

Rawls, John. *A Theory of Justice.* Cambridge: Harvard University Press, 1971.

Rieff, David. "Letter from Bosnia." *The New Yorker*, November 23, 1992, 82–95.

Rorty, Richard. *Achieving Our Country: Leftist Thought in Twentieth-Century America.* Cambridge: Harvard University Press, 1998.
———. *Consequences of Pragmatism: Essays, 1972–1980.* Minneapolis: University of Minnesota Press, 1982.
———. *Contingency, Irony, and Solidarity.* New York: Cambridge University Press, 1989.
———. "The Decline of Redemptive Truth and the Rise of a Literary Culture." No pages. Online: http://www.scribd.com/doc/7167390/Rorty-The-Decline-of-Redemptive-Truth-and-the-Rise-of-a-Literary-Culture.
———. *Essays on Heidegger and Others.* Philosophical Papers 2. New York: Cambridge University Press, 1991.
———. *An Ethics for Today: Finding Common Ground between Philosophy and Religion.* New York: Columbia University Press, 2011.
———. "Fraternity Reigns." *The New York Times Magazine,* September 29, 1996.
———. "Intuition." In *The Encyclopedia of Philosophy,* edited by Paul Edwards, 4:204–12. New York: Macmillan, 1967.
———, editor. *The Linguistic Turn: Recent Essays in Philosophical Method.* Chicago: University of Chicago Press, 1967.
———. *Objectivity, Relativism, and Truth.* Philosophical Papers 1. New York: Cambridge University Press, 1991.
———. *Philosophy and the Mirror of Nature.* Princeton: Princeton University Press, 1979.
———. *Philosophy and Social Hope.* New York: Penguin, 1999.
———. *Philosophy as Cultural Politics.* Philosophical Papers 4. New York: Cambridge University Press, 2007.
———. "The Priority of Democracy to Philosophy." In *The Virginia Statute for Religious Freedom,* edited by Merrill D. Peterson and Robert C. Vaughan, 257–82. New York: Cambridge University Press, 1988.
———. "The Professor and the Prophet." *Transition* 52 (1991) 70–78.
———. "Religion in the Public Square: A Reconsideration." In *Journal of Religious Ethics* 31.1 (2003) 141–49.
———. *Take Care of Freedom and Truth Will Take Care of Itself: Interviews with Richard Rorty.* Edited by Eduardo Mendieta. Stanford: Stanford University Press, 2006.
———. *Truth and Progress.* Philosophical Papers 3. New York: Cambridge University Press, 1998.
———. "What's Wrong with 'Rights.'" *Harper's,* June 1996, 17–18.
Rorty, Richard, and Gianni Vattimo. *The Future of Religion.* Edited by Santiago Zabala. New York: Columbia University Press, 2006.
Rorty, Richard, and Pascal Engel. *What's the Use of Truth?* Edited by Patrick Savidan. Translated by William McCuaig. New York: Columbia University Press, 2007.
Rose, Gillian. *Mourning Becomes the Law.* Cambridge: Cambridge University Press, 1997.
Sandel, Michael. *Liberalism and the Limits of Justice.* Cambridge: Cambridge University Press, 1998.
Scarry, Elaine. "The Difficulty of Imagining Other Persons." In *The Handbook of Interethnic Coexistence,* edited by Eugene Weiner, 40–62. New York: Continuum, 1998.
Shaybani, Muhammad ibn al-Hasan. *The Islamic Law of Nations: Shaybani's Sivar.* Translated by Majid Khadduri. Baltimore: John Hopkins University Press, 1966.
Shriver, Donald. "Is Justice Served by Forgiveness?" In *Burying the Past: Making Peace and Doing Justice after Civil Conflict,* edited by Nigel Biggar, 25–44. Georgetown: Georgetown University Press, 2003.

Skinner, Quentin. *The Foundations of Modern Political Thought*. Vol. 2, *The Age of Reformation*. London: Cambridge University Press, 1978.
Smith, Christian. *Souls in Transition*. Oxford: Oxford University Press, 2009.
Snyder, Gary. *Turtle Island*. New York: New Directions, 1969.
Springs, Jason. "'Dismantling the Master's House': Freedom as Ethical Practice in Robert Brandom and Michel Foucault." *Journal of Religious Ethics* 37:3 (2009) 419–48.
———. "The Priority of Democracy to Social Theory." *Contemporary Pragmatism* 4:1 (2007) 47–71.
Stone, Brad Elliott. "Making Religious Practices Intelligible: A Prophetic Pragmatic Interpretation of Radical Orthodoxy." *Contemporary Pragmatism* 1:2 (2004) 137–53.
Stout, Jeffrey. *Democracy and Tradition*. Princeton: Princeton University Press, 2004.
Sullivan, Dennis, and Larry Tifft. "What Are the Implications of Restorative Justice for Society and Our Lives?" In *Critical Issues in Restorative Justice*, edited by Howard Zehr and Barb Toews, 391–404. Monsey, NY: Criminal Justice, 2004.
Surin, Kenneth. "A Certain 'Politics of Speech': 'Religious Pluralism' in the Age of the McDonald's Hamburger." *Modern Theology* 7 (1990) 67–100.
Talisse, Robert. "A Pragmatist Critique of Richard Rorty's Hopeless Politics." *The Southern Journal of Philosophy* 39:4 (2001) 611–26.
Tarski, Alfred. "The Semantic Conception of Truth." *Philosophy and Phenomenological Research* 4 (1944).
Taylor, Astra. *Examined Life*. Documentary film. Sphinx Productions, 2008.
Taylor, Charles. "After Epistemology." Unpublished manuscript.
———. *The Ethics of Authenticity*. Cambridge: Harvard University Press, 1992.
———. *Modern Social Imaginaries*. Durham: Duke University Press, 2004.
———. *A Secular Age*. Cambridge: Belknap Press of Harvard University Press, 2007.
Tompkins, Jane. *Sensational Designs*. Oxford: Oxford University Press, 1985.
Van Hook, Jay M. "Knowledge, Belief, and Reformed Epistemology." *The Reformed Journal* 31 (1981) 12–15.
Virgil. *The Aeneid*. Translated by Robert Fitzgerald. New York: Vintage, 1990.
Wallace, David Foster. "David Foster Wallace on Life and Work." *Wall Street Journal*, September 19, 2008. Online: http://online.wsj.com/article/SB122178211966454607.html.
Walzer, Michael. *Thick and Thin: Moral Argument at Home and Abroad*. Notre Dame: University of Notre Dame Press, 2006.
Ward, Roger, and David Gushee. *The Scholarly Vocation and the Baptist Life*. Macon: Mercer University Press, 2008.
Ward, Roger, and Philip Thompson. *Tradition and the Baptist Academy*. Carlisle: Paternoster, 2010.
West, Cornel. *The American Evasion of Philosophy: A Genealogy of Pragmatism*. Madison: University of Wisconsin Press, 1989.
———. *Democracy Matters: Winning the Fight against Imperialism*. New York: Penguin, 2004.
———. *Keeping Faith: Philosophy and Race in America*. New York: Routledge, 1994.
———. *Prophesy Deliverance! An Afro-American Revolutionary Christianity*. Louisville: Westminster John Knox, 2002.
———. *Prophetic Fragments: Illuminations of the Crisis in American Religion and Culture*. Grand Rapids: Eerdmans, 1988.

———. *Prophetic Reflections: Notes on Race and Power in America*. Beyond Eurocentrism and Multiculturalism 2. Monroe, ME: Common Courage, 1993.

Westphal, Merold. "Coping and Conversing: The Limits and Promise of Pragmatism." *The Hedgehog Review* 3:3 (2001) 73–92.

Wilken, Robert L. *The Christians as the Romans Saw Them*. New Haven: Yale University Press, 1984.

Williams, Michael. "Introduction to Thirtieth Anniversary Edition." In *Philosophy and the Mirror of Nature*. Princeton: Princeton University Press, 2009.

Williams, Rowan. *On Christian Theology*. Malden, MA: Blackwell, 2000.

Wilshire, Bruce. *The Primal Roots of American Philosophy: Pragmatism, Phenomenology, and Native American Thought*. University Park: Pennsylvania State University Press, 2000.

Wright, N. T. *Christian Origins and the Question of God*. Vol. 1, *The New Testament and the People of God*. Minneapolis: Fortress, 1992.

Wyschogrod, Michael. "A Theology of Jewish Unity." *L'Eylah Journal* 21 (1986) 26–30.

Young, Iris Marion. "Impartiality and the Civic Public." In *Feminism as Critique*, 56–76. Oxford: Blackwell, 1987.

Žižek, Slavoj. *The Puppet and the Dwarf: The Perverse Core of Christianity*. Cambridge: MIT Press, 2003.

Subject Index

Indexes prepared by Allison E. Hicks (College of William & Mary)

Aesthetics, 8, 13, 23–24, 35, 56, 67, 143, 147
Altar of Public Expedience, 50; *empire,* 51; *imperialism,* 46, 51, 199
American Politics, 48, 171, 156, 162
Analytic Philosophy, 5, 24–29, 33, 41
Anticlericalism, 49, 86, 142, 147
Anti-realism, 35, 43, 85, 133, 146
Apocalypse, 15, 17–18, 21–22
Art, 10–11, 38, 64, 66–67, 145, 180

Boutique Multiculturalism, 56

Cartesianism, 5–6, 11, 16, 129, 168
Charity, 32, 83, 91, 101–5, 112–18, 144, 151, 157
Contingency, 3–11, 93–94, 114, 129–33, 136, 144, 178
Courage, 154–72, 197–210
Culture, 4, 12–13, 16, 48, 53–57, 76, 86, 121, 137, 144, 148, 161, 165–71, 177–79, 185–89, 192, 207; *cultural diversity,* 52–53

Democracy, 5, 11, 46–53, 56–58, 92, 155, 166; *American,* 156; *function of:* 110–11, 209; *poetic,* 6; *priority of:* 3–6, 11–12, 87; *"revolutionary,"* 4; *social imaginary of:* 61–63; *virtues of:* 119
Divine Will (Will of God), 125–28, 132, 134

Divine Wisdom, 125–28, 132, 134–35

Ecclesiology, 49, 65, 86, 124, 137
Ecology, 11–12; *environmental ethics,* 109
Eschatology, 15, 21–22, 65, 114–18, 161, 200, 207
Ethnocentrism, 4, 8, 12–13, 54, 166–67, 170, 174, 189

Faith, 19–20, 47–49, 64, 78–79, 88, 101–2, 118, 119–37, 142–51, 189, 195, 204, 209–10
Foundationalism, 3, 5, 26, 48, 72–74, 84, 166–72, 178
Fundamentalism, 56, 142, 146–48, 166, 181, 188

Hermeneutics, 23, 92–95, 104, 109–13, 117, 121, 130, 197
Hope, 22, 41, 101–2, 145, 205, 210; *apocalyptic,* 14; *Christian,* 101–2, 109, 153–56, 161, 209; *hopelessness,* 166; *liberal,* 4, 47; *Marxist,* 153–56; *pragmatism as philosophy of hope,* 154; *self creation as,* 98; *social hope,* 112, 141–44, 146–62, 166–201
Human Nature, 45, 52, 59–61, 95–96, 103–6, 163, 173, 205

Irony, 10–11, 118, 132, 144, 199

Justice, 102, 141, 145, 156, 158–60, 169–71, 176, 180, 186–89, 196, 209

Law, 54, 64–66, 94, 99, 120, 183–86, 210; *divine law*, 20, 126, 196; *moral law*, 23, 179, 187; *natural law*, 123–26; *rights*, 52, 56, 100–103, 170–73, 177–78, 180–81, 187; *universal law*, 177
Liberty, 50–51, 111, 144, 171, 177, 181
Love, 20, 81–83, 101–2, 122, 141–48, 150–52, 155, 159, 185, 196–205; *agape*, 101, 151, 204–5; *beloved community*, 205–7, 210; *of God*: 49, 110, 116–17, 136–37, 201, 210; *of neighbor*: 102

Marxism, 73, 153–58, 162–65, 171, 187
Multiculturalism, 56
Myth-Making, 7–10, 22, 50, 146–47, 151, 185

Narrative, 4, 7–8, 11, 15–17, 21–26, 42, 58, 102, 131, 142–43, 209
Natural Law. *See* law
Nominalism; *methodological*, 8, 25–36, 38–45, 60, 95, 114

Parallel *polis*, 65
Peace, 51–52, 99–104, 111, 128, 157, 176, 188–200; *pax Americana*, 66
Penultimate/Ultimate, 49, 65–67
Pluralism, 12, 56–57, 89
Poetic Metaphors, 148, 151–52
Politics, 4, 7, 47, 48–53, 61–66, 86, 95, 99–103, 108, 112, 117, 121–27, 132–35, 147, 162, 167–71, 198, 210
Possibility, 91–95, 98, 112, 118, 133
Practical Reasoning, 132, 160, 175–76
Pragmatism, 6, 10–11, 15, 17, 21, 34, 37–38, 87, 95, 141–46, 154, 167–69, 182

Prophecy; *prophetic pragmatism*, 153–54, 158–65, 168, 172
Prudence, 67
Public/Private Distinction, 3–4, 9–12, 41, 48–49, 89–92, 96, 117, 121, 127, 131–32

Radical Orthodoxy, 102–18
Realism, 35, 42–44, 90, 108, 148, 161, 209
Religious Belief, 47, 50, 71–73, 78, 85, 89, 103, 132
Resentment, 119, 135–37

Sacrifice, 50, 57–58, 205
Scriptural Reasoning (SR), 119–23, 126–38
Secular, 23, 54, 100–101, 110–11, 119–27, 134–37, 141, 201, 206–10
Social Imaginary, 60–63
Solidarity, 4, 11, 13, 55, 133, 144, 157, 167, 171–72, 188, 209
Storytelling, 8, 144

Trinity, 27, 29, 41–43, 84, 114–16
Truth, 4–10, 23–30, 32–50, 71–77, 83–89, 94–95, 142–51, 163, 166, 198

Violence, 103, 108–14, 117, 135, 158, 163, 174, 190–91, 202
Virtue, 98, 119, 124, 190, 192; *Christian virtues*, 91, 101–2; *Aristotelian virtue*, 137; *see also: faith, hope, love, charity*
Vulnerability, 122, 131, 134–36

Wisdom, 24, 63, 121, 127, 161, 176

Name Index

Adams, Nicholas, 120–23, 127–28, 132, 135–37
Anselm of Canterbury, 116, 143
Aquinas, Thomas, 27, 36, 38, 43, 60, 74, 126, 132, 146
Aristotle, 35–36, 45, 51, 64, 67, 99, 106, 137
Augustine of Hippo, 59, 82–83, 111, 121, 136

Barth, Karl, 198–99, 206
Bonhoeffer, Dietrich, 66–67, 206
Borradori, Giovanna, 143–44

Carter, Stephen, 40, 124

Davidson, Donald, 5–7, 13, 25–26, 32, 40–45
Descartes, Rene, 63
Dewey, John, 16, 48, 71, 137, 143–47, 169, 178, 198

Foucault, Michel, 132, 166, 198
Freud, Sigmund, 6, 11–13, 73, 97, 141, 149, 180

Goya, Francisco, 8–11, 13
Grippe, Edward, 142, 148–50

Habermas, Jürgen, 121, 127, 132, 135–36
Hauerwas, Stanley, 57, 119, 130–31, 135–37, 195

Heidegger, Martin, 7, 16, 25, 44, 92, 98, 151

James, William, 14–17, 19–22, 37–38, 107, 141, 145–46, 169, 192–94
Jefferson, Thomas, 49–50, 124, 171, 177–78, 181

Kant, Immanuel, 5–6, 11–12, 19, 28, 31, 44, 54, 57, 63, 146, 177–78, 187
King, Martin Luther, 165, 197, 200–210

Leibniz, Gottfried, 150
Lindbeck, George, 45, 65

MacIntyre, Alasdair, 178
Marx, Karl, 73, 105, 153–58, 162–65, 171, 187
McLean, David, 149
Milbank, John, 51, 62, 91, 100–110, 112–19, 126, 133

Nietzsche, Friedrich, 6–7, 11–13, 25, 29, 49, 57, 98, 157, 209
Novak, David, 64, 123–28, 132, 134–35

Ochs, Peter, 131, 133, 137

Paul of Tarsus (Saint Paul), 20, 151
Peirce, Charles Sanders, 87, 129, 133, 137, 141, 150–51, 167–68
Pickstock, Catherine, 102–3
Plantinga, Alvin, 71–90

Name Index

Plato, 6–7, 11, 37, 51, 107, 126, 152

Quine, W. V. O., 5, 10, 13, 15, 25–26, 34, 42–45, 77

Rawls, John, 11–13, 119, 186
Rorty, Richard: *Achieving Our Country*, 48, 145, 170, 178, 198; *Consequences of Pragmatism*, 145, 183; *Contingency, Irony, and Solidarity*, 3–4, 6 9, 46, 48, 55, 61, 75, 93–98, 100, 111, 120, 128–33, 136, 171; *Essays on Heidegger*, 92; *An Ethics for Today*, 145, 149; *Fraternity Reigns*, 181; *Intuition*, 179; *The Linguistic Turn*, 4; *Objectivity, Relativism, and Truth*, 4, 52, 99, 110–11, 144; *Philosophy and the Mirror of Nature*, 3, 15–18, 71, 85–86; *Philosophy and Social Hope*, 48, 94–97, 110–12, 124, 153–55, 170–71, 182, 189; *Philosophy as Cultural Politics*, 188; *The Priority of Democracy*, 3–4, 11; *The Professor and the Prophet*, 169; *Religion and the Public Square*, 120, 124, 131–32; *Take Care of Freedom*, 144, 146, 148, 152, 166; *Truth and Progress*, 45, 77, 87, 92, 174, 177, 182, 189; *What's Wrong with 'Rights,'* 180; *The Future of Religion*, 112; *What's the Use of Truth?*, 142, 144, 146

Sandel, Michael, 187
Santayana, George, 152
Scarry, Elaine, 183–88, 192–93
Shaybani, 126
Snyder, Gary, 12–13
Stout, Jeff, 119–20, 124, 135–37, 179, 195

Taylor, Charles, 25–26, 31, 43–45, 60–62, 92–94, 113, 133

Vattimo, Gianni, 49, 57, 86, 112, 142, 147–51, 195

Wallace, David Foster, 141–42, 149
West, Cornel, 153–55, 158–65, 167–72, 180, 195
Westphal, Merold, 146
Whitman, Walt, 48, 145, 178
Wittgenstein, Ludwig, 16, 25–26, 32, 39, 41, 44, 78, 104, 151, 175
Wolterstorff, Nicholas, 76

www.ingramcontent.com/pod-product-compliance
Lightning Source LLC
Chambersburg PA
CBHW020406230426
43664CB00009B/1205